Moral Development Theories—Secular and Religious

Recent Titles in
Contributions to the Study of Education

The Emerging Worldwide Electronic University
Parker Rossman

A New History of Educational Philosophy
James S. Kaminsky

Does College Make a Difference?: Long-Term Changes in Activities and Attitudes
William E. Knox, Paul Lindsay, and Mary N. Kolb

Assessing What Professors Do: An Introduction to Academic Performance Appraisal in
Higher Education
David A. Dilts, Lawrence J. Haber, and Donna Bialik

Encounters with Difference: Student Perceptions of the Role of Out-of-Class Experiences
in Education Abroad
Michael R. Laubscher

Public School Reform in Puerto Rico: Sustaining Colonial Models of Development
José Solís

Diversifying Historically Black Colleges: A New Higher Education Paradigm
Serbrenia J. Sims

Socialization and Education: Essays in Conceptual Criticism
Wolfgang Brezinka

The Importance of Learning Styles: Understanding the Implications for Learning, Course
Design, and Education
Ronald R. Sims and Serbrenia J. Sims

Achieving Racial Balance: Case Studies of Contemporary School
Desegregation
Sondra Astor Stave

The Politics and Processes of Scholarship
Joseph M. Moxley and Lagretta T. Lenker, editors

The History of American Art Education: Learning About Art in American Schools
Peter Smith

Moral Development Theories—Secular and Religious

A Comparative Study

R. MURRAY THOMAS

Contributions to the Study of Education, Number 68
Paul Pedersen, Series Adviser

GREENWOOD PRESS
Westport, Connecticut • London

Library of Congress Cataloging-in-Publication Data

Thomas, R. Murray (Robert Murray), 1921–
    Moral development theories—secular and religious : a comparative
study / R. Murray Thomas.
        p.   cm.—(Contributions to the study of education, ISSN
0196–707X ; no. 68)
    Includes bibliographical references and index.
    ISBN 0–313–30236–7 (alk. paper)
    1. Moral development.   2. Ethics.   3. Conduct of life.   I. Title.
II. Series.
    BF723.M54T48   1997
    155.2′5—dc20   96–33070

British Library Cataloguing in Publication Data is available.

Library of Congress Catalog Card Number: 96–33070
ISBN: 0–313–30236–7
ISSN: 0196– 707X

First published in 1997

Greenwood Press, 88 Post Road West, Westport, CT 06881
An imprint of Greenwood Publishing Group, Inc.

Printed in the United States of America

The paper used in this book complies with the
Permanent Paper Standard issued by the National
Information Standards Organization (Z39.48–1984).

10 9 8 7 6 5 4 3

To Rob Thomas
and
Lissa Thomas

Contents

Tables and Figures

Tables

Figures

Preface

A few books describe a variety of secular theories of moral development. And numerous books compare two or more religious traditions. But I have not found any that furnish both a sampling of secular models of moral development and a sampling of moral development theories deriving from religious doctrine. The purpose of the present book is to provide such an offering. My intention has been to display within the covers of a single volume this pair of perspectives toward moral development—the secular and the religious—that typically are isolated from each other in scholarly discourse.

Obviously there is far too little space in this one book to include descriptions of all available moral development theories. Therefore, the following pages do not pretend to furnish a definitive survey of the field. Rather, the collection represents only the most apparent major types of theories—secular and religious—and several lesser variants of secular models and minor religious faiths.

The principal secular varieties include commonsense attribution theory, cognitive-structural models, social-learning theories, psychoanalysis, Marxist conceptions, and a composite theory. The major religious persuasians are those of the Judaic-Christian-Islamic line, Hinduism and three derivatives (Buddhism, Jainism, Sikhism), and the Confucian and Shinto belief systems.

Part I

A Framework for Comparing Theories

Theories—or models—of human development are intended to account for how and why people grow up as they do. A convenient way to distinguish one type of theory from another is to identify the aspects of life on which different types focus. For example, some concentrate on intellectual development, attempting to explain how people's skills of analyzing and memorizing improve with the passing years. Others center attention on physical development, seeking to clarify how the body as a biochemical organism increases in size, complexity, and coordination. Still other theories concentrate on how people's morally good and morally bad behavior evolves. This third group—the ones intended to explain the development of moral thought and action—is the concern of this book.

Obviously, dividing human development into such categories as intellectual, physical, and moral distorts the reality of life, a reality that finds these aspects intimately interwoven. It is apparent that intellectual growth depends on the biochemical condition of one's body, and moral reasoning is just one kind of intellectual activity. However, the task of comprehending development as a whole is so daunting that we are obliged to approach the task piece by piece. Moral development is one such piece.

A theory of moral development, in essence, is an attempt to explain how individuals acquire moral values and how such values help guide the way those persons treat other people and—in the case of some theories—the way they interact with supernatural spirits.

As the title of this book indicates, the contents include two general classes of theory—the secular and the religious. Secular theories are proposals based on empirical observations that avoid any reference to such notions as invisible supreme beings (gods, spirits of ancestors) that influence people's behavior, continued spiritual life after one's physical death, or unseen places (heaven, hell) in which a person's disembodied spiritual essence (soul) may interminably dwell after death. In other words, secular theories are presented as products of scientific investigation and logical analysis of observed events. Religious theories, in contrast, are offered as products of divine revelation or inspiration in addition to empirical observation and some form of logic. As such, religious theories include such matters as unseen cosmic forces and perhaps a spiritual life that extends beyond the physical life span. Part II of this book inspects representative secular theories, while Part III focuses on representative religious models.

The purpose of Part I is to describe the framework on which the ensuing chapters have been constructed, a framework deriving from two assumptions:

1. A multifaceted, balanced understanding of any moral-development theory is gained from learning the theory's answers to a comprehensive set of questions.
2. The adequacy of each theory should be judged by a specified set of criteria.

Chapter 1, "The Content of Theories," is founded on the first assumption, whereas Chapter 2, entitled "Evaluating Theories," derives from the second.

1

The Content of Theories

Each of the chapters following Part I describes a particular theory or cluster of theories. To cast the chapters in a form that facilitates comparing one theory with another, I have been guided by 12 questions designed to identify the kinds of information I consider most useful for conveying theories' principal features. The purpose of this opening chapter is to explain the 12 questions. They are first listed in an overview fashion, then analyzed in some detail. A thirteenth question addresses the matter of a theory's popularity.

THE GUIDE QUESTIONS SUMMARIZED

The Moral Domain. How does the theory delineate the kinds of thought and action that belong in the realm of morality?

Moral Versus Immoral. What guidelines does the theory offer for deciding whether a thought or act is moral or immoral?

Good and Bad Development. How is good development distinguished from bad development?

Sources of Evidence. From what kinds of evidence and modes of investigation does the theory draw its substance?

Moral-Development Reality. What is the theory's conception of reality?

Moral Human Nature. What is the natural moral condition of human beings?

Length of Development. How is the length of a person's moral development calculated, and is such development more intense at one time of life than at another?

Personality Structure. What components of personality are important for moral development, and how do these components function?

Directions, Processes, and Stages. How is development defined in terms of directions, processes, and/or stages of growth?

Causal Factors. What factors determine people's moral thought and action?

Individual Differences. What sorts of differences between individuals are regarded as significant, and what are the causes of those differences?

Nomenclature. What terminology used in the theory is especially important?
Popularity. Who subscribes to the theory and why?

THE GUIDE QUESTIONS EXAMINED

In the following pages, the significance of each question is described in some detail. The questions then form the foundation for selecting and organizing the content of the chapters that address particular types of moral-development theory (chapters 3 through 13).

The Moral Domain

How does the theory delineate the kinds of thought and action that belong in the realm of morality?

It is apparent that not everyone defines the realm of morality in the same way. Hence, it is important to learn what the term *moral* is intended to mean within a given theory. Two perspectives toward identifying what sorts of thought and action exemplify the moral domain are those of the *objects encompassed* and the *selection focus.*

Objects Encompassed

Moral values typically refer to the quality of relationships among people, thereby reflecting standards of social conduct. In addition, some people extend moral values beyond the realm of human relations to encompass relationships between humans and a supreme being, so that failing to abide by God's laws becomes a moral issue. Moral values may extend even further to include nonhuman aspects of nature—animals and plants and even such inanimate objects as lakes and mountains. For people who hold these extended views, using cats and chimpanzees for medical experiments becomes a moral issue, as do killing whales and infant seals, destroying ancient trees, and polluting waterways. Hence, it is useful to learn what objects are embodied in a given theory's definition of the realm of morality.

Selection Focus

The diversity of perspectives that can direct the selection of what belongs in the moral domain is illustrated by the following six foci—rules, justice, compassion, obedience to authority, social consensus, and eclecticism.

Piaget (Chapter 4) wrote that "All morality consists in a system of rules, and the essence of all morality is to be sought for in the respect which the individual acquires for these rules" (Piaget, 1965, p. 13).

In contrast, Siegel proposed that the moral domain concerns justice, which he equated with a *sense of fairness.* This sense, he suggested, "involves an ability to consider consistently and without contradiction the interests and intentions of others: to act bearing these in mind and without the guidance of a superior authority and to generalize this behavior in all relevant situations. . . . Fairness is a rational attribute not reducible to mechanistic processes. Actions taken without cognition cannot be considered moral" (Siegel, 1982, pp. 2, 5).

Gilligan (Chapter 9) argued that males and females base their conceptions of morality on different motives. Females, she said, are motivated by compassion, by a desire to care for others that "centers around the understanding of responsibility and relationships, just as the [male's] conception of morality as fairness ties moral development to the understanding of rights and rules" (Gilligan, 1982, p. 19).

Morality grounded in obedience to authority is perhaps best exemplified in religious doctrine which holds that humans are obligated to abide by precepts issued by one or more supernatural beings. Such a concept of morality is at the heart of the Judaic-Christian-Islamic tradition (Chapter 10). As the psalmist declared:

> The law of the Lord is perfect, converting the soul . . . . The statutes of the Lord are right . . . . the commandment of the Lord is pure . . . . The judgments of the Lord are true and righteous altogether . . . . Let the words of my mouth, and the meditation of my heart, be acceptable in thy sight, O Lord, my strength, and my redeemer. (*Holy Bible*, 1611, Psalm 19)

And in a general letter to the early Christian community, the apostle John wrote that "the world passeth away . . . but he that doeth the will of God abideth for ever" (*Holy Bible*, 1611, 1 John, chap. 2).

As another perspective, educators operating from a social-relativist position describe values as beliefs "shared in a social group about what is good or right. . . . [Social action is] behavior a group defines as good or right and for which the social group administers social sanctions" (Maccoby, 1968, p. 229). From this point of view, moral values are not universal, applying equally to all societies. Instead, each society establishes for itself the set of values that the young are expected to acquire.

The term *eclecticism* in the present context refers to the practice of selecting moral values without being directed by a consistent philosophical criterion. Eclectic choice often involves a mixture of tradition, convenience, and political pressure. *Tradition* means the sorts of values that have been promoted in the society in the past. *Convenience* means holding expectations or setting rules that facilitate the peaceful, systematic conduct of a society. *Political pressure* refers to efforts of people (parents, a religious order, a business organization, a patriotic group, or the like) to have their own values featured in a society and to have opposing values eliminated.

In summary, our understanding of a model of moral development is enhanced if we learn what focus the theorist adopted for selecting the contents of the moral domain.

Moral Versus Immoral

What guidelines does the theory offer for deciding whether a thought or act is moral or immoral?

In distinguishing between morality and immorality, it is first important to recognize the definitions of *facts* and of *values* intended throughout this book. Facts are descriptions of either (a) discrete observations and measurements of people, objects, or events or (b) summaries of such observations and measurements. Statements of fact are beliefs about what exists, in what amount, and perhaps in what relation to other facts. In contrast, values are opinions about the desirability or propriety or goodness of something. The "something" can be a person, a group of people, an object, a place, an event, an idea, or a kind of behavior. Statements of value tell whether something is good or bad, well done or poorly done, suitable or unsuitable. As related to moral development, statements of value concern whether a thought or action regarding some aspect of the moral domain is good or bad, proper or improper, desirable or undesirable. In brief, facts are beliefs about "what is," whereas values are beliefs about "what should be."

Moral values can be represented as *principles* and *conditions*. Principles are *unqualified statements of belief*, meaning that the application of a principle to an event in life is not influenced by circumstances particular to the people, time, or place involved in the event. Examples of unqualified statements found in the biblical Ten Commandments are: do not have any gods other than Jehovah; do not carve idols of gods; never use God's name lightly, as in cursing; do not work on the Sabbath day; honor your parents; and do not kill, steal, lie about others, commit adultery, or yearn for your neighbors' possessions (*Holy Bible,* 1611, Exodus, chap. 20). Examples of principles from Gert's (1970) moral rules are: don't kill, don't cause pain, don't disable, don't deprive others of freedom or opportunity, don't deprive others of pleasure, don't deceive, keep your promise, don't cheat, obey the law, and do your duty. As these examples show, moral principles can be stated in either a positive or a negative form. Table 1-1 displays positive forms of typical principles on the left and negative forms on the right. It is useful to recognize that moral principles can be at different levels of specificity. In the Christian Bible, warnings to refrain from carving images of gods and from coveting a neighbor's spouse (*Holy Bible,* 1611, Exodus, chap. 20) are far more specific than the proposal that people should treat others as they themselves wish to be treated (*Holy Bible*, 1611, Matthew, chap. 7).

Table 1-1

Typical Moral Principles

Virtues to Be Encouraged	**Transgressions to Be Avoided**
Protection of the Society: People should act in ways that protect the structure and operation of the society.	*Destruction of the Society:* No one should behave in ways that undermine the social order.
Respect for the Law: Everyone should obey formally constituted laws and should support the laws' implementation.	*Disregard or Disdain for the Law:* No one should break formally constituted laws or hold the laws in contempt.
Responsibility: Everyone should fulfill obligations that by custom are considered duties in keeping with the individual's stage of life or roles that he or she assumes in the society.	*Irresponsibility:* No one should avoid carrying out obligations incurred by the nature of one's roles in life.
Concern for Human Life—Physical: Everyone should protect others from physical harm and should seek to enhance their physical well-being.	*Disregard for Human Life—Physical:* No one should exploit or harm others physically.
Concern for Human Life—Psychological: Everyone should protect others from intellectual and emotional harm and should seek to enhance their psychological well-being.	*Disregard for Human Life—Psychological:* No one should exploit or damage others either mentally or emotionally.
Honesty: Everyone should tell the truth whenever the welfare of others is at stake.	*Deceit:* No one should deceive others by lying or by deviously withholding the truth when the welfare of others is concerned.
Respect for Property: Everyone should protect others' right to hold and use property to which they have legal claim.	*Stealing and Vandalism:* No one should take or use others' property without their permission. No one should damage others' property.

Table 1-2

Conditions Affecting the Application of Sanctions in Cases of Wrongdoing

Conditions Warranting Less Severe Aversive Consequences	Conditions Warranting More Severe Aversive Consequences
Good Character: The individual is generally a good person.	*Bad Character:* The individual is generally a bad person.
Absence of Malevolence: In committing the offense, the person bore no ill will toward the recipient, so did not act out of animosity or malevolence.	*Malice:* The person committed the offense out of hatred or spite and with the desire to do harm.
Knowledge of Right and Wrong: The person did not realize that the behavior violated a rule or custom, because the person was either uninformed or was not in a rational mental state.	*Informed Violation:* The person was aware of the rule or custom and purposely violated it without any redeeming reason.
Role Suitability: The transgressor's behavior was in keeping with his or her role in life.	*Role Unsuitability:* The offender's behavior was not in keeping with any legitimate, assigned role.
Societal Determinism: The offender should not be blamed, for he or she is simply a product of the society, so the society is responsible for the offense.	*Personal Determinism:* The offender has a free will, is responsible for his or her own behavior, and thus deserves the consequences warranted by such irresponsibility.
Inadequate Social Support: The person did not receive the personal/social support that would encourage law-abiding behavior (inadequate parental guidance, poor models of behavior, or lack of reinforcement of good behavior).	*Adequate Social Support:* The person has had the kinds of personal/social support that would reasonably foster good behavior. People cannot blame their social background for their antisocial behavior.
Accidental Violation: The person was cognizant of the rule or custom but violated it unintentionally. It was simply an error, a kind of accident.	*Intentional Violation:* The person was aware of the rule or custom and intentionally violated it without any redeeming reason.

Conditions are characteristics of a particular event in life that influence the moral significance of that event. I would claim that rarely, if ever, does anyone apply a moral principle in an identical manner in all situations. Conditions will probably always affect the application of moral principles. Hence, in order to understand a theory's version of moral development, we need to identify not only the principles it espouses but also the patterning of conditions it employs when applying principles to events involving morality. A sample of conditions that a theory may include is offered in Table 1-2. Some theories would endorse certain conditions from the left column, whereas others would subscribe to certain of those in the right column.

With the above conceptions of moral values, principles, and conditions in mind, we are prepared to consider the question of morality versus immorality.

Moral behavior—or as some people to call it, *promoral behavior*—consists of thought or action that conforms to the principles and conditions advocated by the theory at hand. *Immoral behavior* consists of thought or action that violates those principles and conditions. Thus, it is important to know the principles and conditions advocated in a theory, since the decision about the morality of an action is arrived at by judging how well the action accords with that theory's set of values.

Good and Bad Development

How is good development distinguished from bad development?

For the purposes of this book, the word *development* will refer to change in a given direction. The phrase *good moral development* identifies a person's moral character changing in a way that more closely approximates a particular theory's conception of desired morality. The term *bad moral development* signifies thought and action that depart from the path of desired morality. In other words, bad development deserves the label *regression, retrogression, deviance, backsliding,* or *deterioration.*

Distinguishing good from bad development consists of a rather obvious two-step process. The first step is to identify the moral values (principles and the conditions of their application) prescribed by the theory. These values represent the ultimate goal of good development, the target at which development is aimed. The second step is to determine at different junctures of the person's life how closely that individual's thoughts and behavior conform to those values. Development is judged to be good to the extent that, with the passing of time, the person's values more satisfactorily approximate the goal.

Sources of Evidence

From what kinds of evidence and modes of investigation does the theory draw its substance?

Proponents of a theory can derive its structure and content from one or more sources and investigative techniques. The most familiar source on which models from religious traditions are based is divine revelation or its close relative, divine inspiration. Divine revelation takes place when a god or cosmic power directly transmits the theory to an earthly seer or prophet delegated to announce the doctrine to the populace. Divine inspiration is a flash of insight into the meaning of life, an insight that is intuitively recognized as the truth. Although theorists who attribute their ideas to divine inspiration do not claim to be any more than the conduits through which the divinity or cosmic power speaks, they still contend that such revelations are the unmistakable truth.

Another source of theories involves the logical analysis of empirical data. This is sometimes referred to as a *scientific approach.* In the realm of moral development, such an approach can consist of alternating phases of induction and deduction. To begin, a theorist observes how people behave toward each other. From analyzing the results of this observation, the theorist draws generalizations about how and why the people acted as they did. This initial phase has involved induction—deriving principles from empirical study. The next phase consists of deduction—applying the principles, in the form of hypotheses, to groups of people other than the ones originally observed. The purpose is to see if the principles hold true with a wider sample of individuals and under different environmental conditions. On the basis of this empirical testing, the original generalizations may be confirmed, rejected, or revised. This process of inductively deriving principles, testing them, revising them, and testing them again can go on indefinitely.

An important distinction between divine inspiration and scientific method is in the way the two sources can affect the permanence of theory structure and content. Theories derived from an omniscient supreme power via divine inspiration are immutable and everlasting. Theories derived through induction followed by deductive testing are always subject to change because of the underlying tenets of scientific method. The word *science* is typically used to identify both a general method of seeking the truth and a body of information compiled through use of that method. Although there is no single, specific scientific method, what scientists do hold in common is a set of precepts and attitudes that guide their efforts. Here are two such convictions as reflected in the above discussion:

1. Conclusions about moral development should be founded on empirical evidence, that is, on evidence derived from the direct study of people's behavior—on observations of people's social interaction and opinions and on the logical interpretation of those observations.

2. All conclusions are subject to revision as the result of additional empirical evidence and analysis. Consequently, from a scientific perspective, no answers to questions about moral development should be regarded as final and definitive.

Each answer, and thus each theory, is assumed to be no more than an approximation of the truth, an approximation that requires further evaluation and refinement.

Theorists dedicated to a scientific approach often differ significantly from each other in the techniques they employ to collect the empirical data on which to base their model. Such methodological differences can influence the nature of theories in important ways, as illustrated in later chapters. For example, the materials on which Freud erected his psychoanalytic theory were primarily dreams and memories of childhood that neurotic patients in his medical practice recounted to him during therapy sessions (Chapter 6). Piaget's model was built on the answers children offered to questions an experimenter asked about the rules of games and about what should happen to people who committed various kinds of misdeeds (Chapter 4). Gilligan generated her theory chiefly from interviews regarding how personal moral conflicts were perceived by (a) pregnant women contemplating abortion, (b) college students in a class on morality and political choice, and (c) matched pairs of males and females from ages 6 through 60 (Chapter 9).

In summary, the task of understanding why a theory assumes its particular form includes recognizing the kinds of evidence on which it has been founded.

Moral-Development Reality

What is the theory's conception of reality?

In the philosopher's lexicon, people's conceptions of reality belong in the field of ontology, that branch of metaphysics which concerns reality itself as apart from the subjective impressions of the person who is experiencing it. However, one of the knottiest problems confronting philosophers over the centuries has been that of determining what the "real world" outside of a person's mind is truly like. Or, indeed, is there actually anything outside the individual's mind that can be considered a "real world," because all knowing and all communication of knowledge necessarily flow through individual minds? Although logicians and theologians have argued this matter at length, no one has come up with a method for producing a universally accepted answer.

Yet, despite this recognition that comprehending reality is dependent on characteristics of the individual experiencer, probably no one operates as a thoroughgoing solipsist, believing that the only reality is what the individual person imagines, so that there is no "real world out there." Instead, people appear to believe that there is indeed an objective "real world" and that each of us has in mind a conception—a mental map—of that reality. However, most thoughtful people apparently are not *naive realists*, assuming that (a) their impressions of what they see and hear are true mirrors of the objective world and (b) that all people's impressions are thus identical. Rather, they believe that (a) their perceptions are only approximations of an objective world and (b) one person's impressions can differ from another's. Such a *conditional realist's* version of reality is the one I employ throughout this book.

As the contents of later chapters will attest, all of the models included in this book assume a reality outside the individual's mind. However, exactly what constitutes that reality can differ dramatically from one theory to another.

In the context of comparing theories of moral development, the significance of a conditional-realism viewpoint is twofold. First, it helps account for why one theory differs from another, because a theory is a statement of someone's belief about how moral thought and action develop in the real world. The statement is absolute if the theorist believes that his or her own model is accurate. The statement is no more than tentative if the theorist assumes that the model is simply an estimate of reality that probably needs elaboration and revision before it is confirmed. In effect, different theories offer different views of how the real world of moral development operates.

Second, from a conditional-realist's perspective we can infer that people do not behave on the basis of objective reality but, rather, they act on the grounds of what they believe is real. An individual who believes that lawbreakers will inevitably be caught is apt to behave differently than one who believes most lawbreakers are never apprehended. A person who thinks that most people are honest can be expected more often to trust strangers than does an individual who thinks most people are potential cheats.

Moral Human Nature

What is the natural moral condition of human beings?

A matter that has been debated for centuries is the issue of whether people are, by their very nature, morally prone to be good or to be bad. In other words, do infants enter the world with an innate tendency toward promoral rather than immoral behavior? Or, perhaps, do they come with no moral disposition at all; in effect, are they amoral?

In answer to such questions, the 18th-century social critic Jean Jacques Rousseau (1955) contended that children are born innocent and morally good; but during their growing years children's character is sullied by an evil society. Thus, in Rousseau's view, proper moral upbringing consists of protecting the young one's innate goodness from damage as the child advances to adulthood.

The Harvard University philosopher-psychologist William James in 1891 declared that a person's moral principles are a combination of values acquired through experience and ones that must be inborn.

> The feeling of the inward dignity of certain spiritual attitudes, as peace, serenity, simplicity, veracity; and of the essential vulgarity of others, as querulousness, anxiety, egoistic fussiness, etc.—are quite inexplicable except by an innate

preference for the more ideal attitude for its own pure sake. . . . Purely inward forces certainly are at work here. (James, 1992, pp. 597-598)

In more recent times, the humanistic psychologist Abraham Maslow (1968) concurred with Rousseau by proposing that the young child has a kind of intrinsic feeling of the right thing to do. This feeling is an intuitive knowledge of one's true self. Good moral development consists of nurturing the inner sense of propriety and integrating it with the rules of the society within which the child is raised.

In contrast, one variant of Judaic-Christian tradition holds that children are innately prone to act in evil ways (Hartman, 1990; Thomas, 1990). The task of child rearing consists of blocking the evil propensity and convincing children to adopt morally constructive values as guides to their behavior.

As a third alternative, most secular theories, either by outright statement or by implication, regard the child's initial nature as amoral, with children prone to be neither moral nor immoral. To account for moral differences among people, secular theorists typically assume (a) that people's behavior is motivated by needs or drives and (b) that people acquire their methods of fulfilling needs by what they see and hear in their daily experiences. Some of those methods will be socially acceptable (promoral, because they accord with the values espoused in the theory) and others will be unacceptable (immoral, because they conflict with the values endorsed by the theory). From such a perspective, people are seen as acquiring their moral tendencies from the environments they inhabit, not from their inborn nature. Child rearing thus involves placing the young in settings that teach promoral rather than immoral methods of satisfying needs.

Length of Development

How is the length of a person's moral development calculated, and is such development more intense at one time of life than at another?

In most secular theories, the length of human life extends from (a) biological conception (the joining of a sperm and an ovum) about nine months before birth to (b) the moment the heart stops beating on the occasion of physical death. The life span of the body coincides with the life span of the mind or personality. Although within the major religions the length of life for the physical self is quite the same as in secular theories, for the spiritual self the length is different. In the Judaic-Christian-Islamic tradition, a person's spiritual essence, the soul, is implanted in the body at some point between conception and birth, and that essence will continue to exist in a noncorporeal form for an indefinite period following physical death. According to Hindu lore, each person's soul or *atma* was first created out of an all-encompassing cosmic soul at some unknown point in the distant past. Over the centuries, each individual soul inhabits one body after another, abandoning one organism's shell after that organism's physical being dies; and the soul thereafter dwells within another body until that body also expires. This transmigration of the soul can continue indefinitely. Within such religious conventions, moral development concerns the soul rather than the body, so that one's moral essence is transported within the soul over multiple lifetimes.

In each of these views of the length of life, whether secular or religious, two important questions to ask are: (1) During what period of the life span does moral development take place? (2) Is the intensity or significance of development greater during some parts of that period than during other parts?

Personality Structure

What components of personality are important for moral development, and how do these components function?

Each theory of development includes an explicit or implied vision of the elements that comprise the human personality and of how these elements function in concert with each other. The following three examples illustrate contrasting conceptions of personality structure and function.

Within attribution theory (Chapter 3)—which is designed to explain the commonsense beliefs on which most people seem to base their moral judgments—five important components of personality are those of *ability, intention, motivation, conscience,* and *emotional dispositions.* An individual's behavior in moral-decision situations is believed to result from the interaction among (a) skills (ability), (b) plans (intention), (c) strength and direction of expended energy (motivation), (d) beliefs about what is morally right and morally wrong (conscience), and (e) feelings (emotional dispositions).

The psychoanalytic version of personality structure (Chapter 6) features three chief functionaries—*id, ego,* and *superego*—that operate at different levels of consciousness. The id is an unconscious source of needs that seek fulfillment. The ego is a decision maker attempting to negotiate between the id's demands and the environment's rules about acceptable ways to behave. The superego is the person's conscience, an internal representative of society's moral values that causes the individual to feel guilty when violating the values and to feel proud when abiding by them.

In Hindu doctrine, the human personality includes *soul, mind, will,* and *karma.* The soul is the person's spiritual essence, the mind serves the soul by coordinating impressions that the sense organs receive from the environment, the will orders the organs (speech, hands, feet) to act, and the karma records both the positive and negative effects of the person's actions in the world.

Directions, Processes, and Stages

How is development defined in terms of directions, processes, and/or stages of growth?

Three ways that theorists have pictured the course of moral development have been (a) in terms of direction, that is, tracing the path from moral immaturity to moral maturity, (b) as a growth process, and (c) as a hierarchy of stages. Some authors have employed only one of these approaches. Others have combined two or all three.

Directions of Development

In Piaget's theory (Chapter 4), the direction of moral growth is charted as progress from an ignorance of the rules of life toward a sophisticated, realistic knowledge of the rules. In Kohlberg's scheme (Chapter 4), the direction is from self-centered hedonism toward principled social concern. In a traditional monotheistic religious perspective such as Judaism (Chapter 10), moral development is pictured as advancing from a self-centered ignorance of God's commandments to a comprehensive understanding and acceptance of God's law.

Processes of Development

A growth-process approach consists of identifying the patterns of interaction among forces that bring about changes in a person's moral condition. In the radical behaviorism espoused by B. F. Skinner (Chapter 5), a person's future moral behavior is altered by the influence of consequences which followed that person's actions in past moral situations. Actions that were accompanied by rewards in the past are likely to be repeated in the future, and actions that were accompanied by no rewards are likely to be abandoned. Social-learning theorists not only agree that consequences are important, but also regard *modeling* (one person copying another's behavior) as a significant agent of moral change (Chapter 5).

Piaget (1973) advanced four principal factors as determinants of development —inherited potential, the person's direct experience with the environment, social transmission (learning from others' teaching), and a mediating variable called *equilibration* or *equilibrium* that maintained a proper balance among the other three. Piaget's theory has also included the functions of *assimilation* (fitting environmental experiences into what one already knows) and *accommodation* (altering what one already knows to more closely match environmental stimuli).

In Kohlberg's system, the process of development involves relationships among (a) the individual's level of logical reasoning, (b) motivation, that is, desire or will, (c) opportunities to assume social roles, and (d) the dominant justice structure of the social groups or institutions with which the individual interacts (Kohlberg, 1971, pp. 188-191).

Stages of Development

A continuing debate among theorists involves the question of whether development is best viewed as proceeding by gradual, almost imperceptible small increments or, in contrast, by occasional steep advances interspersed between plateaus of relatively slight growth. This is the *continuity-versus-stagewise* debate.

Social-learning theories typically portray moral development as a continuous, gradual process. In contrast, cognitive-structuralist theories, psychoanalytic models, and such religious conceptions as Hinduism depict development as a succession of stages. In the cognitive-structuralist models proposed by Piaget and Kohlberg (Chapter 4), stages are periods into which the life span is divided, with each period identifiably different from the others. Furthermore, the stages are universal (everyone goes through the same periods), sequential (the stages follow a set order), and irreversible (once a person advances to a stage, he or she does not return to any earlier period).

Causal Factors

What factors determine people's moral thought and action?

From the viewpoint of promoting morality and combating immorality, the most vital portion of a theory is its specifying the elements that contribute to moral development and its explaining how those elements interact. Understanding matters of cause equips people to decide what they can do to foster desirable moral thought and behavior.

Heredity and Environment

The most common way of categorizing the forces that fashion people's development is in terms of heredity and environment. Cast as a question, the issue becomes: How do inborn factors compare with environmental factors in contributing to a person's moral progress? The task of describing the way a given theory answers this query can be guided by two pairs of more specific questions. The first pair focuses on the influence of heredity and the second pair on the influence of environment.

1. In what ways does a person's genetic endowment affect moral development?
2. What conditions determine the direction, strength, and timing of genetic endowment influence?
3. In what ways do different physical and social environments affect a person's moral development?
4. What conditions determine the direction, strength, and timing of environmental influences?

A brief examination of these questions can illustrate the sorts of information about a theory that each question can imply.

As intimated in question 1, there are a number of conceivable ways biological inheritance might affect people's morality. For instance, a theory may propose that a particular combination of genes directly endows individuals with a moral trait, such as bravery or cowardice, honesty or mendacity, altruism or selfishness. Or, rather than directly producing a moral trait, a person's genetic structure may be seen as equipping the individual with greater or lesser analytical skill (intelligence, cognitive acumen) that influences how well the person can make wise judgments in moral-decision situations. Or, as a third possibility, a person may inherit physical characteristics that predispose other people to draw conclusions about that person's moral character because they associate certain physical attributes (skin color, facial contours, posture, eye contact) with stereotypical moral traits (honesty, furtiveness, aggressivity).

Question 2 suggests that the influence of biological inheritance is governed by various conditions. Three types of conditions are identified. First is direction, meaning whether the effect of an inherited predisposition is positive, thereby encouraging promoral thought and action, or is negative, thus conducive to immoral behavior. To illustrate, a theory that postulates the inheritance of a propensity to abuse and exploit others may also suggest conditions under which such a tendency will result in abusive behavior. One such condition may be the extent to which the people who control the individual's immediate environment will permit abusive behavior. Another condition may be the individual's physical prowess; a small and weak person will perhaps be less successful in administering physical abuse than will a large, strong person.

The second variety of influence is strength. One theory may picture a genetic effect as a dominating determinant of moral thought or action, whereas another may portray such a factor as having little influence. For instance, a person's level of analytical intelligence may be seen either as extremely important in guiding moral action or else viewed as no more than one among many subsidiary causes behind moral behavior—emotions, motivation, needs, environmental pressures.

Third, *timing* refers to the period in a person's life span when genetic endowment exerts its influence. Most theorists, if not all, assume that not all genetically determined effects on development appear at birth. Instead, the effects reveal themselves at determined junctures in the life span at a rate dictated by a genetically controlled timing mechanism. For example, in the realm of physical growth the primary and secondary sex changes that occur with the advent of puberty are among the obvious instances of genetic timing. Thus, theories can differ both in the types of moral characteristics that are conceived to be affected by a genetic clock and in the conditions that influence the appearance of those characteristics.

As noted on page 16, the foregoing set of questions about heredity is matched by a similar set about environment. In regard to question 3, theories can vary in the importance they attribute to different types of environments and to ways those environments are believed to affect moral thought and action. Examples of environment types are a one-parent home versus a two-parent home, a family with one child versus a family with six children, an inner-city ghetto neighborhood versus a wealthy suburban community, a street gang versus a church-sponsored club, and the like. As for ways that environments are believed to affect development, attribution theory views advice giving as a significant method of influence, social-learning theory stresses the importance of individuals serving as models to imitate, and Kohlberg's proposal emphasizes the importance of people having opportunities to try out multiple roles in life.

Like heredity, environmental factors can be viewed in terms of direction, strength, and timing (question 4). In regard to direction, an environmental episode such as a television program or a lesson in school can be interpreted by one theory as fostering positive values and by another as promoting negative values. In strength of influence, theories can differ in the comparative power they attribute to different agents in the environment (parents, siblings, age peers, priests and pastors, teachers, club leaders, movies, and the like). Furthermore, theories vary in their proposals about the time of life at which a particular environmental encounter exerts its most potent effect. For instance, Erik Erikson's version of psychoanalysis pictures environmental events during adolescence as more significant than does the original Freudian form of the theory (Chapter 6).

Supernatural Intervention

All varieties of theory, secular and religious alike, include both hereditary and environmental factors in accounting for moral development. However, theories derived from religious doctrine also posit another type of influence, that of supernatural, mystical forces. Each of the religious theories inspected in Part III is founded on the conviction that one or more invisible entities—gods or spirits—influence moral thought and behavior by establishing moral values and rules of conduct, by intervening in moral events, and by applying sanctions as a means of enforcing the rules. The religion's rules and sanctions are typically described in the faith's spoken and written doctrine, which is accepted as the supreme authority governing matters of morality.

Hence, theories of moral development that are embedded in religious traditions propose that moral thought and action result not only from the interaction of genetic and environmental factors but also from the participation of supernatural entities.

Free Will

Over the centuries, philosophers and theologians have debated the question of whether people's moral behavior is entirely determined by transactions among inherited and environmental factors (including supernatural forces, in the case of religious and mystical theories). Or do individuals also enjoy some measure of free choice in deciding how to act? This issue has never been settled to everyone's satisfaction. It continues to be a matter of significance in accounting for moral thought and action, since what people believe about the operation of free will becomes part of their theory of moral development. For instance, if wrongdoers are forced into their immoral acts by a particular combination of genetic and environmental forces, why should they be held personally responsible for how they behave? Or, if they have been driven into wrongdoing by mystical evil forces ("The devil made me do it"), then should they not be held blameless?

Chance and Luck

If people cannot adequately account for the causes behind moral acts, they may seek to explain the behavior in terms of chance or luck. When they appeal to chance, they usually mean one of two things, either that "Such things just happen for no particular reason" or that "Something's causing it, but I don't know what." The first of these reactions reflects a belief that some moral events occur spontaneously, without cause. Thus, we are permitted to abandon any attempt to explain the event. The second reaction reflects a belief that all moral incidents are the result of causal factors, but in the case at hand it is not at all clear what those factors may be. Hence, more thought and investigation are necessary.

The term *luck* can carry either of the meanings proposed for chance, but the notion of luck is usually accompanied by a value judgment. Luck is typically deemed either good or bad, fortunate or deplorable.

To summarize, theories can differ in their proposals about what factors contribute to moral thought and action and about how those factors are related. All theories give some consideration to biological inheritance as it interacts with environmental influences. In addition, some models include supernatural forces as important determinants of moral development. Theories can also recognize the operation of free will and chance, although such recognition is more often by implication than by forthright assertion.

Individual Differences

What sorts of differences among people are regarded as significant, and what are the causes of those differences?

People obviously are dissimilar in many aspects of their moral development. Thus, when we analyze a theory, it is useful to discover which differences the theory recognizes, how often they appear and in what degree, what importance is attributed to each kind, and how the theory explains the way such differences arise. It is the case, however, that theorists seldom address individual differences in any formal, systematic manner, so the significance of differences must be inferred from other features of their theories, such as the proposed causes of development and the types of moral values advocated.

Nomenclature

What terminology used in the theory is especially important?

Significant, unique features of a theory can be reflected in special words or phrases that are used. Understanding such terms often goes a long way toward revealing core characteristics of the theory. The following are examples of key concepts found at different points throughout the book: *ought forces, task difficulty, primary process, defense mechanisms, identity crisis, reinforcement schedule, modeling, leading activity, zone of proximal development, sin, redemption, moksha, karma, nirvana, jen,* and *kami.*

Popularity

Who subscribes to the theory and why?

In any attempt to estimate the extent of a theory's audience, it is helpful to recognize different meanings that can be assigned to the term *popularity*. One meaning is limited to "acquaintance with" or "knowledge about" a theory. The question becomes: How many people are aware of, or informed about, the contents of the theory? Thus, the number who are cognizant of a psychoanalytic model of development will be the measure of the popularity of psychoanalysis.

A second meaning refers to "nominal advocacy of" or "nominal belief in" a theory. In this case we ask: How many people say they are Christians, how many label themselves Piagetians, or how many say they prefer a social-learning perspective? But within this collection of people who thus identify themselves with a theoretical position, there are subgroups representing different degrees of fealty to that position. Hence, we can find highly dedicated and knowledgeable Buddhists as well as ones who subscribe to only limited aspects of Buddhist theory. Likewise, under the Marxist banner, there will be traditional Marxists, neo-Marxists, and partial Marxists. Therefore, gauging the popularity of a theory can involve distinguishing between the broad, overarching class of nominalists (people who say they subscribe to the theory, at least to some degree) and the subclass of fundamentalists (people who adhere to an original or authentic version of the theory).

Not only is it useful to recognize levels of acquaintance with and dedication to a theory, but it is also important to distinguish among types of indicators used for estimating popularity. One indicator is the number of members in an organization that subscribes to the theory, such as the membership of Islamic sects or of a Piagetian society. Another measure is the amount of attention accorded the theory in spoken or written discourse—in lectures, discussion groups, the public press, and scholarly journals. Furthermore, within such discourse, it is instructive to note how much of the attention is dedicated to extolling the theory rather than denigrating it. A third way to judge a theory's popularity is to observe people's expressed beliefs and actions in moral situations. Thus, even though individuals may not identify themselves as Hindus or Freudians, their words and deeds may accord with a Hindu or Freudian conception of moral development.

CONCLUSION

The purpose of Chapter 1 has been to introduce the questions that directed the selection of the material that comprises Parts II and III, where representative secular and religious theories of moral development are analyzed and evaluated. Chapter 2 describes the criteria adopted for guiding the evaluations.

2

Evaluating Theories

The purpose of this book is not only to describe representative theories but also to evaluate them, to identify their strengths and weaknesses as judged by a set of criteria or standards. Chapter 2 introduces the eight standards and explains each in some detail. Then in Parts II and III, the final section of every chapter offers an assessment of that chapter's principal theory in terms of the standards.

THE EIGHT CRITERIA

From the viewpoint of the eight criteria, theories are judged satisfactory to the degree that they are understandable, explanatory, practical, verifiable/falsifiable, adaptable, fertile, lasting, and self-satisfying. Each of the following standards is phrased in the form of a question that an evaluator seeks to answer.

Understandable

To what extent is the theory explained in a manner that makes it clearly understandable to anyone who is reasonably competent, in other words, anyone who has an adequate command of language and logical analysis?

Anybody with reasonable competence should be able to comprehend (1) what events in the real world the theory refers to, (2) the meaning of terms used, (3) the key assumptions on which the model is founded, and (4) how the theory's explanations and predictions are logically derived from its definitions and assumptions.

This criterion may appear simple and forthright, but in practice it can be quite controversial. If we find that we cannot understand a theory, there is a question about who is to blame. Is it the theorist's fault for being obscure or confused, or is it our own fault for lacking the ability to grasp what most people would judge is an entirely rational presentation?

Explanatory

How adequately does the theory equip a person to explain past moral incidents and to predict people's future moral behavior?

Humans seem driven by a need to make sense out of the happenings in their world. In the realm of morality, they are constantly trying to explain why all sorts of deeds have occurred, deeds of altruism, courage, integrity, mendacity, abuse, exploitation, and more. People also seek to predict how they themselves and others will likely behave in future moral encounters. Thus, they value a theory that enables them to comprehend the "why" behind moral incidents—a theory that depicts how people reason in moral situations and how such reasoning determines the way they act.

Theories are typically better at accounting for how people "generally" or "on the average" think and act than they are at clarifying how a particular person in a particular situation will behave. Thus, users of theories tend to value more highly one that can explain the moral reasoning of a particular Ms. Maria Garcia or Timmy Carmichael than one that only accounts for the reasoning of *women in general* or *preadolescents on the average*.

Practical

How satisfactorily does the theory provide guidance for coping with moral development issues in everyday life?

Many people believe that a theory's chief value lies in its ability to provide advice about handling daily moral encounters. Thus, a theory is valued not only for its ability to explain moral thought and action, but also for the practical guidance it can offer for dealing with moral questions. Parents in particular are interested in help with child-rearing problems. Practical applications are likewise a key concern of others responsible for promoting moral development—teachers, counselors, club leaders, religious leaders, pediatricians, social workers, law-enforcement officers, athletic coaches, and the like.

However, it is also the case that some theorists and readers of theory are not especially concerned with translating theoretical proposals into advice on child rearing or the treatment of wrongdoers. Rather, they are seeking to understand the processes involved in moral development. Whether a knowledge of these processes empowers people to treat matters of disobedience or crime is entirely incidental.

Verifiable/Falsifiable

How readily does the theory lend itself to determining whether its proposals are true or false?

Among scientists, a theory is generally conceived to be an estimate of the truth rather than an unquestionable revelation of the truth. Hence, researchers are constantly generating ways of testing the validity of a theory's proposals, either by collecting additional empirical evidence or by analyzing the logic of the theory's structure. If hypotheses derived from a theory can be tested to determine whether they are true, then the reverse should also obtain—it should be possible to test that a hypothesis is false, thereby suggesting that it needs some revision. In other words, many scientists believe that the validity of a theory should not only be confirmable through logic and the analysis of data, but it should also be falsifiable or disconfirmable.

However, some moral development models do not display this characteristic of falsifiability. In effect, investigators cannot conceive of a way to gather information that would determine whether some aspect of the theory is actually true. Among the theories reviewed in this book, the ones that pose the greatest problems of falsifiability are those related to religious persuasions, because such beliefs depend so heavily on faith in a respected authority rather than on observable evidence. For instance, what publicly available evidence can be offered to test the proposal that punishment for misdeeds as well as rewards for virtuous acts will be meted out in "life after death"? How can the notion of a human soul existing for eternity in a heavenly or hellish condition be either accepted or rejected on the grounds empirical data?

The problem of verifying or disconfirming a theory is complicated by the fact that not everyone agrees about which sources of evidence are most trustworthy. Some people are convinced if the proof derives from a respected authority. That authority may be a highly regarded publication—the Christian Bible, the Islamic Qur'an, an encyclopedia, a scientific journal, or a popular periodical. Or it may be a distinguished scientist, philosopher, Nobel Prize recipient, religious leader, or television personality.

Preferences for types of evidence also vary. For some people, the authority's testimonial is sufficient confirmation of a theory's worth. Others are persuaded by records of individual case studies, such as those compiled by Sigmund Freud in his psychiatric practice. Whereas some readers are satisfied with narrative accounts of moral development, others require statistical analyses, complete with the numbers of individuals studied and of how likely those individuals accurately represent the population about whom generalizations are being drawn.

In summary, people are most likely to approve of theories that are supported by large amounts of the types of evidence they prefer that are derived from the types of sources they esteem.

Adaptable

How readily does the theory accommodate new evidence?

Proponents of a theory can respond to new evidence in at least three ways—by reinterpreting, by revising, or by rejecting.

Reinterpreting means explaining how data that seem incompatible with the theory can actually be adapted to the theory quite satisfactorily. This can be illustrated with the concept of *free-floating anxiety* in Freud's psychoanalytic theory. Such anxiety is a persistent feeling of dread and distress that does not result from any apparent threat in the person's life. Freudians typically explain that the anxiety is the result of painful memories that have been forced into the individual's unconscious because such memories are too agonizing to be tolerated in the person's conscious life. To dispel such anxiety, the sufferer must go through psychoanalytic therapy, during which the repressed, "forgotten" material is brought into consciousness and relived in an emotionally acceptable manner. However, in recent decades the invention of drugs that relieve anxiety has cast doubt on this Freudian explanation. But proponents of psychoanalysis can still maintain the integrity of their theory be reinterpreting the drugs' apparent effects. Psychoanalysts can claim that the drugs have done no more than temporarily block the anxiety, leaving the disturbing hidden memories unresolved, thereby permitting the persistent psychic distress to rechannel itself into other forms of deviance, such as headaches or compulsive behavior.

Revising means altering the theory in order to reconcile the conflict between it and the new facts. In way of illustration, over the centuries the forms of conduct identified as sins under Catholic moral theory have periodically been augmented with further types of transgression that accompany changing social conditions. For example, in the early 1990s a new edition of the Catholic catechism added these four acts to the list of sins: (1) driving a car or piloting a commercial jet airplane while intoxicated, (2) cheating on taxes, (3) peddling illicit drugs, and (4) committing fraud in business transactions (Castro, 1992).

Rejecting can be either passive or active. Passive rejection consists of denying the possibility that the new data might have any bearing at all on the validity of the theory. Active rejection, on the other hand, involves discrediting the data by exposing flaws in the way the evidence was collected, reported, or interpreted.

In conclusion, evaluating a theory's adaptability consists of judging how reasonably the theory's advocates have reinterpreted, incorporated, or rejected potentially contradictory evidence.

Fertile

To what extent has the theory stimulated the creation of new research techniques and the discovery of new knowledge?

Some theories have been remarkable for the number of new vistas they have opened and the amount of research, analysis, and discussion they have engendered. Other theories have been far less fertile, leading to relatively little debate, new interpretations, or further data collection. Among the secular models reviewed in Part II, the one that has prompted the greatest amount of empirical study and argument in recent decades has been Lawrence Kohlberg's version of cognitive structuralism (Chapter 4). Considerably less research has been generated by Carol Gilligan's proposal about the differences between females and males in the values on which they found their moral judgments (Chapter 9). However, the amount of study and discussion generated by any of the secular theories in Part II pales in comparison to the enormous amount of study and controversy stimulated over the centuries by the religious theories in Part III.

Among researchers, a theory's fertility is often considered its most important feature, since models of moral development that stimulate many new ideas are considered to be the most effective devices for expanding and refining people's understanding of moral matters.

Lasting

Over what period of time has the theory attracted attention and enlisted adherents?

This question concerns a theory's durability and historical significance. Long-lasting theories are usually esteemed for having stood the test of time, for having weathered the vicissitudes of social change. Among those inspected in this book, the ones deriving from religious doctrine far outstrip the secular theories in longevity. Whereas the religious varieties measure their age in centuries and millennia, the secular forms can trace their beginnings back only a few decades, since all of them are products of the 20th century.

Self-Satisfying

Overall, does the theory seem to make good sense?

This is the self-affirmation criterion. It depends not only on a combination of the other seven standards but also on emotional and intuitive factors that we cannot readily identify. The operation of these factors is reflected in our general feeling that a theory "Doesn't quite ring true" or, in contrast, "It sounds pretty close to the way moral development seems to work."

Including a self-affirmation standard allows us to acknowledge instinctive tendencies that influence our judgments but do not lend themselves readily to logical examination. These nonanalytical inclinations apparently underlie the "faith that exceeds understanding" which people sometimes cite in accounting for their particular philosophical or religious convictions.

CONCLUSION

The eight assessment criteria introduced in this chapter will serve as the standards for evaluating the principal theories described in Parts II and III, where verbal judgments of theories' advantages and disadvantages are accompanied by charts summarizing those judgments.

Part II

Secular Theories

The word *secular*, as used throughout Part II, refers to models not derived from religious doctrine but, rather, ones intended to be the products of scientific inquiry. In contrast to theories extracted from religious traditions, secular proposals lack many of the elements that typically distinguish religious conceptions. Such elements usually include a belief in one or more supernatural beings that dictate the values to be pursued in moral development, that oversee people's behavior, and that reward morality and punish immorality.

Chapters 3 through 7 illustrate five major types of secular theory—an attribution perspective, cognitive structuralism, social-learning proposals, psychoanalysis, and Marxist views. Each of these can be found in more than one version.

Chapter 8 illustrates a method of extracting selected components from various theories and reassembling them to produce a composite, integrated theory.

Chapter 9 focuses on distinctive features of five additional theories so as to broaden the purview of secular models beyond the major types depicted in Chapters 3 through 7.

3

Attribution Theory

The contents of this chapter are founded on the proposition that the beliefs underlying people's understanding of moral development are not random, disparate notions that lack any coherent organization. Instead, the beliefs are linked together in a unifying network of logic, a network seldom apparent to the people who hold the convictions. In effect, people automatically assemble their commonsense ideas about moral thought and action on a subconscious theoretical framework. A psychologist's depiction of this framework is sometimes called *naive psychology* or *commonsense psychology*. As A. L. Baldwin (1967, p. 38) noted:

> It is important to realize . . . that naive psychology is not a stated theory but a body of beliefs about human behavior. Only the systematic description of naive psychology gives it the look of a theory.

In essence, naive psychology involves the analysis of the ways people attribute causes in moral encounters. Thus, the product of such analysis can be labeled *attribution theory*. Such a product is the focus of Chapter 3, which offers a description of the mental mechanisms people seem to employ for intuitively interpreting matters of moral development. The chapter opens with an illustrative version of attribution theory, next considers the answers that an attribution model offers for the questions posed in Chapter 1, and closes with an appraisal of naive psychology in terms of the assessment questions in Chapter 2.

ONE VERSION OF ATTRIBUTION THEORY

Present-day attribution theory owes much of its original form to Fritz Heider (1896-1988), a University of Kansas psychologist whose self-appointed mission was to discover the underlying structure of the way most people account for human behavior (Weiner, 1980, p. xv). Heider's analysis of how people explain human events was founded primarily on people's conversations, that is, on how they attributed causes. Over the decades since Heider introduced his approach in *The Psychology of Human Relations* (1958), other psychologists have followed his example of extracting the underlying thought system reflected in discourse. To suggest how such an investigative method works, I begin the following portrait of attribution theory with an envisioned conversation between a pair of friends discussing two moral incidents—a teenage girl arrested for theft and a banker accused of fraud. The friends' remarks subsequently serve as the source of examples illustrating components and functions of the attribution model.

A Conversation About Moral Matters

Two mothers, Ellen and Rosita, chat while waiting their turn in a beauty salon. Their comments reveal their perceptions of two moral episodes. The task of the attribution theorist is to identify the underlying structure of these perceivers' modes of reasoning about moral events.

Ellen: I suppose you heard about Francie Smith getting arrested?

Rosita: Arrested? What for?

Ellen: Shoplifting, and they found her carrying drugs, too—marijuana or cocaine or something.

Rosita: What a shock. Her family must be terribly upset, having their 16-year-old arrested. She should have been afraid to do such things.

Ellen: Not only that, she's pregnant.

Rosita: How awful. She's from such a nice family. I'd think she would have learned better. Her older brother and sister have turned out great. They've always been very capable—can really get things done.

Ellen: It's hard to understand why it happened to Francie—just fate or bad luck, I suppose. But I hear she's been running with a bad crowd and picked up their ways.

Rosita: Her folks should have kept her away from such a gang. If she'd been in the Young Life group at our church, she'd never have taken drugs or started shoplifting.

Ellen: Well, it's hard to blame the parents. You can't watch a teenager every minute of the day. And Francie probably lied to them about who she was with and what she was doing. My daughter says Francie's best friend is that Martin girl, Lila.

Rosita: That explains it. Any of those Martins would be a bad influence. Just look at the mother. What a role model she is—hanging around bars and sleeping with all kinds of men. She's forever on welfare and never seems to mind being a public burden that the rest of us have to support.

Ellen: Well, Francie's not entirely at fault. Her parents should have been there to help her resist the peer pressure.

Rosita: That's true. It isn't easy for a kid to stand against the crowd.

Ellen: It's clear that she's in no shape to care for a baby. She ought to have an abortion.

Rosita: Oh, no, not abortion—that's murder. But she could put the child out for adoption. Who's the father?

Ellen: My daughter says he's an 18-year-old who dropped out of school before graduating. His name's something like Cheswark or Cheswick.

Rosita: Fred Cheswick? I know about him. He's no good. He'd certainly have no intention of marrying Francie. I hear he sleeps with every girl he can. The kids call him The Big Stud. He's on some kind of macho kick.

Ellen: Every time he gets a girl pregnant, he probably brags, "Look what I did." He obviously can't care what happens to the girls or their babies.

Rosita: More likely he says, "Look what I gone and done." He's terribly incompetent—couldn't hold a job even if he wanted one. But he certainly can get girls to do what he wants. I'm sure he doesn't want real work. He just peddles drugs and gets money from his girlfriends.

Ellen: Why do they put up with him?

Rosita: I suppose he has some kind of sex appeal, or maybe they're afraid not to do what he wants. I hear he can be violent.

Ellen: I never thought of Francie as being stupid.

Rosita: You're right. She always seemed very bright, a good student till lately. It's a bad lapse of judgment that got her into this mess—like temporary insanity.

Ellen: Well, her family now has to decide what to do about the arrest.

Rosita: I don't see her getting off very easy. Maybe she could plead that the shoplifting was just a misunderstanding—that she didn't do it on purpose but just forgot to pay. But the drugs—that had to be on purpose.

Ellen: If she wasn't drunk or raped when she got pregnant, she deserves the blame for that, too. Whatever the judge does about her had better be painful enough to make her change her ways.

Rosita: Solving her problem will be expensive.

Ellen: I know her brother really cares for her, so he can be counted on to find the money for her defense. From what I've heard about him, he'd go to great lengths to get her straightened out.

Rosita: Speaking of defense, what do you think of this banker who's on trial for fraud?

Ellen: He's as guilty as sin, but he'll get off with a light sentence or none at all because of his money and political connections.

Rosita: It's strange that he turned himself in to the police even before anybody suspected he was stealing all that money.

Ellen: He said he turned himself in because couldn't stand feeling guilty any longer.

Rosita: I can understand that. If I'd stolen depositors' money, I'd be tortured by guilt.

Ellen: For a greedy person, being around all that money is a great temptation. It'll be interesting to see how the trial comes out.

Rosita: If he stole a few thousands, then some months in jail might be enough; but if he stole millions, he should be in there for years. If he gets off too easy, he'll probably be out there doing something like that again.

Ellen: And he's got to pay back the money somehow, so they should assess him a big fine. If he's so anxious to get rich, then the best way to fix him is to hit him where it hurts—make him poor by taking away everything he owns.

Rosita: But he must not be all bad. When they sentence him, they should recognize that he voluntarily turned himself in, and he seemed sincerely sorry for what he did.

Ellen: That's true, but they still shouldn't let him off too easy.

Rosita: If the court doesn't do what's right, I trust the good Lord will eventually see that he gets his just deserts.

With this dialogue in mind, we next consider how an attribution theorist might analyze the thought processes underlying the two women's remarks.

Dissecting Attribution Theory

As already noted, attribution theory focuses on how people, in their use of common sense, account for their own and others' thoughts and actions. In the present instance, our concern is with commonsense explanations of moral development.

Over the decades since Heider's book *The Psychology of Human Relations* (1958) introduced his rendition of naive psychology, a number of other theorists have added features to his original scheme, converting Heider's pioneering effort into a gradually expanding paradigm of several related varieties. Notable contributors have included E. E. Jones and K. E. Davis (1965), H. H. Kelley (1971, 1972, 1992), K. G. Shaver (1975), and B. Weiner (1974, 1980). The following version of the theory is one I have assembled from the work of such authors and from my own observations of the way people talk about morality. The discussion begins with components that undergird commonsense accounts of moral reasoning and action. It next turns to the processes by which those components interact, then closes with a proposal about how the components and their interactions change with the passing of time.

Components of an Attribution Model

Figure 3-1 summarizes the aspects of the individual person and of the social environment that commonsense explanations consider significant in accounting for how people think and act in moral situations.

The *perceiver* in Figure 3-1 is anyone who intuitively employs the theory's components when proposing causes for moral events. The box at the left displays characteristics attributed to each person who participates in a moral incident. The box at the right identifies features of environments that the perceiver believes influence moral actions. In effect, the left side represents personality structure as it relates to moral matters, whereas the right side represents important aspects of moral environments. The rectangle at the bottom portrays unidentified and supernatural forces to which people appeal when they are unable to explain moral events in terms of personality properties and aspects of the environment.

Figure 3-1

Components of a Commonsense Attribution Theory

The Perceiver's Concept of Personality Characteristics	**The Perceiver's Notion of Environmental Influences**

1. Personal power
  1.1 Abilities
    1.1.1 Intelligence
    1.1.2 Maturation rate
    1.1.3 Experience
  1.2 Attitudes (emotional)
  1.3 Social status
  1.4 Temporary conditions
2. Conscience (moral values)
3. Intention/motivation
4. Empathic capacity
	1. Opportunities and restrictions
	2. Models of behavior
	3. Rewards and punishments
	4. Task difficulty
	5. Environmental coercion
	6. Situational pressures
	7. Role prescriptions

Unidentified and Supernatual Forces

1. Luck, chance, fate, destiny, "it just happens"
2. Supernatural forces: God, Satan, spirits, astrological configurations

Characteristics of the Self. The phrase *perceiver's concept of person-*
ality characteristics refers to traits individuals believe are important determinants of how people act in moral situations.

Personal Power. A key variable proposed by Heider is the can-do or personal-
power aspect of personality. Beliefs about personal power are revealed in how
people use the concepts *can* and *cannot.*

> "Her older brother and sister have turned out great. They've always been very
> capable—can really get things done."
> "He's terribly incompetent—couldn't hold a job even if he wanted one. But he
> certainly can get girls to do what he wants."

Among several factors that contribute to personal power, the most important
is *ability*, which rests on three assumptions:

1. Abilities are rather stable, permanent attributes that do not change over the
   short term.
2. Abilities increase, either gradually or in spurts, over the period of childhood
   and adolescence.
3. Abilities are determined by both heredity and environment. However, the
   proportion that each of these two sources contributes to various abilities is
   often unclear.

Most people appear to believe that at least three factors contribute to mental
ability—intelligence, maturation rate, and experience. The term *intelligence* is
typically used to identify a person's inherited potential for being "smart" or
"clever."

> "I never thought of Francie as being stupid. . . . She always seemed very bright, a
> good student till lately."

This potential is recognized as maturing over time, with some children's
maturation rate faster than others'. As intellectual potential advances, experience
with the world is necessary to equip the child with a storehouse of knowledge,
particularly knowledge about the effects that different actions will produce and
about the presumed desirability of those effects (Shaver, 1975, pp. 45-46).

> " I'd think [Francie] would have learned better."

Beyond ability, other factors that are believed to affect personal power in
minor ways are *attitudes*, *social status*, and such *temporary conditions* as
fatigue, illness, and distraction. Attitudes influence personal power by
emotionally disposing a person to act in a given manner.

> "I suppose he has some kind of sex appeal, or maybe they're afraid not to do
> what he wants."
> "I know that Francie's brother really cares for her, so he can be counted on to
> find the money for her defense."

The term *social status* refers to the degree of respect that people accord an individual as a result of the person's position in society. Social status can result from one's socioeconomic level (wealth, lifestyle), educational attainment, position in an authority hierarchy (the world of business, politics, sports, the arts, entertainment, the military), family reputation, ethnic origins, and the like.

"[The banker is] as guilty as sin, but he'll get off with a light sentence or none at all because of his money and political connections."

Such temporary states as fatigue, illness, and being distracted by competing concerns may hamper a person's performance on a given occasion but do not diminish the true ability attributed to the person.

"It's a bad lapse of judgment that got her into this mess—like temporary insanity."

To summarize, from the viewpoint of attribution theory, an individual's personal power in moral situations is believed to result from a combination of ability, of attitudes (emotional dispositions), of social status, and of temporary conditions (illness, fatigue, distraction) that diminish the exercise of power on certain occasions.

Conscience and Moral Values. Conscience is the repository of a person's moral values—the *thou-shalts* and *thou-shalt-nots* of human relations. For many people, moral values also concern relationships between the individual and one or more supernatural beings—God for Christians and Jews, spirits of departed ancestors for Confucianists and Shintoists. Conscience, in effect, is an internalized set of social rules or standards, dos and don'ts that Heider called *ought forces* (1958, pp. 218-243). When people violate standards of what they think they ought to do, they "feel bad" or "feel guilty" or "feel ashamed." When they abide by the standards, they "feel good" or "feel proud." In brief, conscience is composed both of moral principles and of accompanying emotions.

Whereas naive theory holds that everyone has a conscience, the theory does not assume that the particular contents of conscience—the moral values—are identical from one person to another. One individual's dos and don'ts need not be the same as another's.

"She ought to have an abortion."
"Oh, no, not abortion. That's murder."

Most people believe that the values residing in the conscience are not innate but, instead, are gradually acquired from the environment over the years of childhood and adolescence—from older acquaintances, from peers, and from mass communication media.

"She's from such a nice family. I'd think she would have learned better."
"I hear she's been running around with a bad crowd and picked up their ways."

Conscience functions both as a stimulator of action ("He said . . . he couldn't stand feeling guilty any longer") and as an inhibitor ("She should have been afraid to do such things").

Intention and Motivation. Judgments of whether someone deserves blame for wrongdoing or credit for good deeds are strongly influenced by the apparent intentions of the participants in a moral episode. Individuals who misbehave on purpose invite greater censure than ones who misbehave by accident, by dint of a misunderstanding, or by being unaware of the rule they have violated. Wrongdoers may also avoid blame if their transgression was committed while they were not in control of their faculties or when they were under threat or duress, as can happen when they act out of fear for their own safety or for the safety of others.

> "Maybe she could plead that the shoplifting was just a misunderstanding—that she didn't do it on purpose but just forgot to pay. But the drugs—that had to be on purpose."
> "If she wasn't drunk or raped when she got pregnant, she deserves blame for that, too."
> "Maybe they're afraid not to do what he wants. I hear he can be violent."

Culpability is often implied in what people say about wrongdoers' motives.

> "She's forever on welfare and never seems to mind being a public burden that the rest of us have to support."
> "He obviously can't care what happens to the girls or their babies."
> "He'd certainly have no intention of marrying Francie."
> "I'm sure he doesn't want real work. He just peddles drugs and gets money from his girl friends."

Shaver (1975, pp. 28-29) has suggested that

> from the psychologist's point of view, to be attributionally valuable, an action must be judged to have originated from an intention. . . . Ultimately, the careful perceiver will rely on his assessment of the circumstances surrounding the action, on his other knowledge of the actor, and on his own past experience as an actor in similar situations to arrive at a choice of an intention behind the action.

Shaver's proposal can apply to several remarks in Ellen and Rosita's conversation.

> "He's on some kind of macho kick. . . and probably brags, 'Look what I did.'"
> "From what I've heard about [her brother], he'd go to great lengths to get her [Francie] straightened out."

Empathic Capacity. The term *empathic attitude* refers to people's potential for seeing and feeling things from the perspective of someone else—what George Mead (1934) referred to as "taking the role of the other." Thus, how empathy will affect people's moral appraisals depends on their capacity to project themselves into others' lives and imaginatively share their experiences. Shaver (1975, p. 23) has suggested that "individual differences in perceivers' ability to make interpersonal judgments accurately are probably related to differences in experience, intelligence, and empathic ability."

"Her family must be terribly upset, having their 16-year-old arrested."
"I can understand that. If I'd stolen depositors' money, I'd be tortured by guilt."

Characteristics of the Environment. In this version of attribution theory, the seven features of the environment regarded as significant influences on moral behavior are (1) opportunities and restrictions, (2) models of behavior, (3) rewards and punishments, (4) task difficulty, (5) environmental coercion, (6) situational pressures, and (7) role prescriptions.

Opportunities and Restrictions. Environments can open opportunities for particular types of moral behavior.

"I hear she's been running with a bad crowd and picked up their ways."
"For a greedy person, being around all that money is a great temptation."

Or else environments can restrict the opportunities that a person has either to misbehave or to do good deeds.

"Her folks should have kept her away from such a gang. If she'd been in the Young Life group at our church, she'd never have taken drugs or started shoplifting."

From a commonsense-attribution perspective, one of the key responsibilities in child rearing is that of controlling the environments that the young experience. Parents are cautioned to monitor the television programs children see, to inspect the books they read, to chaperone their parties and dances, and to know where they go and what they do during their free time.

Models of Behavior. Commonsense theory proposes that people often acquire moral values through imitation, copying the values that others display. In effect, the most influential elements of environments are believed to be the people who serve as models of desirable and undesirable values.

"Any of those Martins would be a bad influence. Just look at the mother. What a role model she is."

Consequently, two ways that parents, teachers, and counselors can foster the development of children and youths are (1) by trying to control the kinds of models the young will see and (2) by praising the constructive qualities and condemning the destructive qualities of potential models that the young encounter.

Rewards and Punishments. A further pair of environmental features considered crucial in moral development are the rewards and punishments that agents in the environment assign people for their good and bad deeds.

"Whatever the judge does about her had better be painful enough to make her change her ways."

The degree of punishment that a transgressor should suffer is usually intended to be proportionate to the degree of harm done by the transgressor's misdeed.

"If [the banker] stole a few thousand, then some months in jail might be enough; but if he stole millions, he should be in there for years."

Punishment can have one or more purposes: (1) to prevent further wrongdoing ("If he gets off too easy, he'll probably be out there doing something like that again"), (2) to compensate the victims of the misdeed ("He's got to pay back the money somehow, so they should assess him a big fine"), or (3) to avenge the wrong ("The people who lost money deserve the satisfaction of knowing he's been properly punished").

Task Difficulty. Some tasks that people face are more difficult to accomplish than others. Hence, if a person cannot perform a task or can do so only with great effort, the task can be blamed for being too difficult and the person incurs less censure or perhaps none at all.

"Well, it's hard to blame the parents. You can't watch a teenager every minute of the day."
"Francie's not entirely at fault. It isn't easy for a kid to stand against the crowd."

Environmental Coercion. Linked to task difficulty is the notion of environmental coercion, meaning pressures (ought forces) exerted by people's social surroundings that impel them to act in approved ways. People who do the approving can be either ones who encourage law-abiding behavior ("Her parents should have been there to help her resist the peer pressure") or ones advocating illicit acts ("I hear she's been running with a bad crowd and picked up their ways").

Situational Pressures. Commonsense theory proposes that people often base their estimates of cause on their belief about the way situations affect moral behavior. This is the idea that if people had not happened to find themselves in a particular environmental setting, their behavior might have been quite different.

"If she'd been in the Young Life group at our church, she'd never have taken drugs or started shoplifting."
"For a greedy person, being around all that money is a great temptation."

Role Prescriptions. Finally, opinions about cause in moral development include judgments of how people's social roles define how they should behave in moral situations.

"Her folks should have kept her away from such a gang."

"Her parents should have been there to help her resist the peer pressure."

"[That Fred Cheswick is] no good. He'd certainly have no intention of marrying Francie."

Unidentified and Supernatural Forces. Besides locating causes within an individual's personality or in the environment, people often include two further factors in their causal ascriptions. The first is an amorphous category representing a person's quandary about what actually was responsible for an event. They may signify that a moral episode is inexplicable by using such phrases as "Who knows?" or "That's the way things go" or "It's all a mystery."

"It's hard to understand why it happened to Francie—just fate or bad luck, I suppose."

Sometimes a lack of apparent personality or environmental factors prompts people to locate cause in supernatural forces—gods, spirits, nature, planetary configurations (astrology), relationships among numbers in a person's life (numerology), and the like. Someone not only may attribute past moral episodes to ethereal forces, but also may estimate the outcome of future moral events on the basis of faith in how supernatural forces operate.

"I trust the good Lord will eventually see that he gets his just deserts."

In summary, the version of attribution theory offered in the foregoing pages includes three major sources of causes for moral events—personality characteristics, social-environment variables, and unidentified/supernatural forces. None of these components operates alone. Instead, the factors exert their influence by interacting in complex ways, as demonstrated in the following paragraphs.

Interactions Among the Model's Components

The way elements of the attribution model operate in coordination with each other can be illustrated with the relationship between personal power and the environmental factor of task difficulty. The first clue to the degree of an individual's personal power is the proportion of other people who can perform the task at hand. If only a few people can perform it, then any individual who can do it is credited with extraordinary power. That person is accorded respect because the main cause of success is thought to reside in the person's ability and motivation. For instance, a teenager who successfully resists peer pressure to use drugs is judged to have strong character, since so many other teenagers have yielded to peer influence. But if nearly everyone can perform a task, then the task is judged to be easy, and those who perform it are not credited with much ability or strength of motivation. Consequently, success is not attributed to the person at all but to the environment.

Common sense also connects environmental consequences—rewards and punishments—to people's intentions by designing punishment that prevents wrongdoers from fulfilling their aims and by providing rewards that further the goals of "rightdoers."

> "If the banker is so anxious to get rich, then the best way to fix him is to hit him where it hurts—make him poor by taking away everything he owns."

In addition, common sense links conscience to environmental consequences by reducing the severity of punishment in response to displays of admirable moral values.

> "But [the banker] must not be all bad. When they sentence him, they should recognize that he voluntarily turned himself in and that he seemed sincerely sorry for what he did."

Developmental Trends—Changes Over Time

Commonsense observations of child growth have produced a variety of widely accepted beliefs about moral development, beliefs that assume the status of *growth principles*. The principles derive from people's impressions of how increases in intellectual maturity from infancy to adulthood can influence children's understanding of moral events and can affect their ability to act in morally acceptable ways. Here are six such principles. Younger children, as compared with older children and adults:

1. Have more difficulty in understanding the nature and social significance of moral values and in recognizing ways different values interact in daily human relations.
2. Are less skilled in distinguishing between harm done by accident and harm resulting from the intentional violation of moral values.
3. Are less adept at estimating other people's motives in moral situations.
4. Have command of fewer morally acceptable techniques for satisfying their wants and needs.
5. Deserve less blame when they violate moral rules or customs, because of their shortcomings in regard to principles 1 through 4.
6. Are more pliable, that is, more readily influenced by efforts to guide their moral convictions, because they are less set in their ways.

Having now reviewed the details of our illustrative attribution model, we next consider the answers that attribution theory offers for additional questions posed in Chapter 1.

ATTRIBUTION THEORY—FURTHER ANSWERS

Thirteen questions to guide the analysis of theories were introduced in our opening chapter. Answers to several have been implied in the early pages of the present chapter, including attribution theory's conception of personality structure, causes of moral thoughts and actions, nomenclature, practical applications, and the directions and processes of development. The purpose of the following section is to answer the remaining eight questions from Chapter 1.

The Moral Domain

Three of the questions are so closely interlinked that they can conveniently be considered together: (1) defining the moral domain, (2) distinguishing moral from immoral, and (3) differentiating good from bad development.

There are several sources of the kinds of behavior that people's commonsense judgments locate in the moral domain. One source is the particular society's collection of criminal and civil laws. Another source is the list of sins and virtues identified in the religious doctrine to which people subscribe. A third source is the body of unwritten ethical practices that children reared in a given culture are commonly taught to respect. Thus, behavior that conforms with the dictates of law, religious or philosophical doctrine, and custom is judged to be moral. Behavior that breaches law, doctrine, or custom is deemed immoral.

It is apparent that societies can vary in the extent to which their populations agree about which values to include in the moral domain. In other words, some societies are more homogeneous than others in their moral standards. More controversy over what constitutes morality can be expected in societies characterized by greater mobility, more immigration, and greater ethnic and religious diversity than in societies not so variable in those respects. Consequently, children raised in cohesive traditional societies have an easier time learning commonsense values and reaching moral decisions than do children who grow up in environments that confront them with a wide array of competing beliefs.

Moral-Development Reality and Human Nature

From the perspective of commonsense theory, the real world of moral development consists of the components of the model portrayed in Figure 3-1. For example, people who subscribe to such a version of attribution theory are convinced that *intelligence, punishment, conscience,* and *modeling* are real things, not just products of someone's imagination. The reality of moral development also includes assumptions about the way such components function, as illustrated by the following statements.

Some people are more intelligent than others and therefore are more likely to make wise judgments in moral situations.
Punishment is a useful device for making people change their way of thinking and acting in moral encounters.

The contents of individuals' consciences are revealed by which of their thoughts and actions make them feel bad (guilty, ashamed) and which make them feel good (proud, self-satisfied).

A lot of people's ways of behaving in moral situations have been copied from someone else. That is, they have learned how to behave by imitating models they have observed.

Many of the attribution model's components and their functions are accepted as real by the entire body of attribution-theory adherents. This is apparently the case with such notions as personal power, intelligence, conscience, social status, rewards and punishments, and task difficulty. However, certain proposed components—particularly the so-called supernatural forces—are held as real by only a portion of commonsense psychology's followers. And even when devotees agree on the existence of a given component, they may disagree about how that component functions in moral matters. For instance, one person who conceives of God as a real entity in the moral domain may believe God intervenes in daily moral affairs by imposing immediate punishment for immoral behavior. However, another person who also includes God as a feature of reality may believe that God imposes punishment only in "life after death," with "life after death" being a component that not everyone would agree is real.

Within the attribution-theory camp, one controversial issue is the question of children's inborn moral nature. Some people's common sense convinces them that children are innately good, others believe children are naturally inclined to wickedness, and still others think children are born with neither of those moral tendencies.

Length of Development

From the viewpoint of naive psychology, it is apparently possible for moral development to continue throughout the life span. However, people's opinions about when during a lifetime such development is most pliable and intense is reflected in the adage "You can't teach old dogs new tricks." In other words, attempts to form an individual's moral character are expected to be more successful during childhood and early adolescence than they are in later youth and adulthood.

Growth Stages

Widespread cultural practices suggest that moral development, from a commonsense perspective, can be divided into at least four stages.

1. The first stage, that of early infancy, covers the first year or two of life, before the child is able to walk, understand many words, or talk. Very little is expected of infants in the way of understanding right from wrong.

2. Over the years of childhood, from about age 2 to 10 or 12, children are thought capable of gradually learning rules of social behavior, but they are still not believed to display mature judgment in moral matters. This view of the childhood years is typically reflected in criminal law, in which preadolescent wrongdoers are not held as responsible for their moral behavior as are teenagers and adults.

3. According to long-standing belief, with the advent of puberty young people enter "the age of reason," signified by such rites of passage as formal membership in a church or synagogue and the inclusion in the school curriculum of complex, abstract subject matter. However, teenagers under age 18 are still identified as *minors*, and their lawbreaking is adjudicated in juvenile courts rather than in criminal courts for adults. Their names are withheld from the public press so they will not incur a bad reputation, and they are held in juvenile detention centers rather than in jails or prisons. In effect, they are still considered to be promising candidates for moral rehabilitation.

4. The last stage begins around age 18 to 21, when youths' errant ways are no longer treated lightly or with forgiveness. After age 18 or 21, they are treated as adults, both in the privileges they enjoy (buying liquor, voting in elections) and the responsibilities they bear (obliged to join the armed forces in time of war, fully prosecuted as adults under both criminal and civil laws).

Individual Differences

In attribution theory, what sorts of differences among people are emphasized, and what are the causes of those differences?

Figure 3-1 identifies the two general types of differences among individuals considered particularly important in moral development. The first is composed of such personality characteristics as intelligence, intention/motivation, conscience; and more. To illustrate, differences in intelligence affect how efficiently people learn from moral events and how logically they can reason in moral-decision situations. In addition, differences in the contents of people's consciences influence which sorts of moral behavior cause them feelings of guilt and shame. The second general category of differences is made up of the seven kinds of environmental influences listed in Figure 3-1, including models of behavior, rewards and punishments, task difficulty, and the rest. The ways such environmental features vary in the lives of different people will influence the values they acquire and the methods they adopt for pursuing their goals. For instance, the moral character developed by a youth who selects drug-dealing gang leaders as proper heroes to imitate will differ from the moral character of another youth who models his life on that of a religious luminary.

Thus, explaining why two individuals differ in their moral values and behavior involves describing how the two differ in key aspects of their personalities and in several, if not all, of the seven environmental influences.

Attribution Theory's Popularity

The popularity of attribution theory can be judged from at least two viewpoints. The first is in terms of the quantity of people whose explanations of moral development rest on the sorts of implicit beliefs identified in the first half of this chapter, even though few if any of those people have a formal conception of the structure of their beliefs. In this sense of widespread dependence on such beliefs, attribution theory is extremely popular; in fact, it is the most popular of all moral-development models, since nearly everyone depends on common sense for interpreting people's moral thought and action.

The second viewpoint is that of professional psychologists, philosophers, sociologists, and theologians who make it their business to create or adopt formal theories of moral development. Such scholars are quite limited in number. And among that number, only a small portion invest their principal allegiance in attribution theory. Far more of them appear dedicated to cognitive-structuralist, psychoanalytic, and social-learning theories than to commonsense models, as evidenced by the amount of attention accorded different types of theory in books and journal articles. The number of academics writing about a commonsense attribution approach to moral matters is very small indeed.

Thus, there is a great disparity between the quantity of people in general and of academics in particular who subscribe to commonsense views of development.

AN ASSESSMENT OF ATTRIBUTION THEORY

The chart on page 47 summarizes my estimate of how commonsense attribution theory fares when judged by the eight assessment standards described in Chapter 2. On the scale line to the right of each criterion, I have placed symbols to suggest how well I believe the theory meets that particular standard. In the following paragraphs, I explain my reasoning behind each appraisal

The word *understandable* can carry at least two different meanings. First, it can refer to how well people comprehend the collection of intuitive presumptions they use in accounting for moral thought and action in daily life. Their beliefs are not intentionally organized in any formal pattern, so that seldom will they recognize the framework of relationships on which their convictions may be assembled in their minds. Yet people's conversations about moral matters suggest that they generally understand each other's meanings, or at least they think they do. For example, they seldom stop to demand that those participating in a discussion precisely define the terms they use or explain the unstated assumptions behind their utterances.

The second meaning for *understandable* is the one illustrated in this chapter—an analysis of the underlying structure of commonsense psychology. This second level of understanding is much less common than the first. It requires that people follow a line of logic about theory construction and agree that such a

Commonsense Attribution Theory

How well do I think the theory meets the standards?

The Standards	Very Well	Moderately Well	Very poorly
1. Is clearly understandable	I*	F§	
2. Explains past and predicts future moral behavior		X	
3. Offers practical guidance in coping with moral matters		X	
4. Is readily verifiable and falsifiable		X	
5. Accommodates new evidence		X	
6. Stimulates new discoveries	X		
7. Is durable	I		F
8. Is self-satisfying		X	

*I = Intuitive set of beliefs   §F = Formal theory

line represents at least one reasonable way to dissect the anatomy of moral reasoning.

Thus, on the *understandable* scale in the above chart, I have rated attribution theory very high for its intuitive version and lower for its status as a formal theory. In effect, far fewer people recognize the anatomy of naive psychology than actually use naive psychology in their daily lives.

Standards 2 (explains past, predicts future) and 3 (guides child rearing) can conveniently be considered together. Naive theory is better prepared to explain past events than to anticipate future ones. Its weakness in predicting people's moral actions derives to a great extent from two of its prominent features. First, it fails to specify all of the conditions or causes that interact to bring about an event or a phase of development. Hence, people's commonsense interpretations tend to oversimplify causes. For this reason, if their cited cause is not the most powerful force actually operating, then their prediction will be in error.

Second, naive theory assumes that people have a *free will.* The issue of free will is an old one in philosophy, one that has never been resolved satisfactorily. The concept of free will is usually discussed in connection with *determinism,* which is a belief that everything that happens has been absolutely preordained by preceding conditions, so that an event could not have turned out any other way. In effect, if you know all of the causal factors and their comparative strengths, you can make an exact, error free prediction of what will happen. In contrast, the concept of free will usually holds that determinism may be true for strictly physical phenomena, such as thunderstorms and the growth of violets, but events involving human decisions are partly influenced by each individual's freedom to make a choice. Consequently, in human events, our knowledge of preceding conditions or causal factors enables us to estimate likely outcomes, but we still must consider individuals' free will and therefore can never predict exactly what they will do.

Therefore, even though naive theory contains a lot of folk truths that, over the generations, have enabled people to guide children's moral development with some measure of success, commonsense theory also has shortcomings that limit the accuracy of its predictions and child-guidance suggestions. Hence, I rate attribution theory in the moderate range for items 2 and 3.

As for item 4, some parts of naive theory are verifiable or falsifiable and some parts are not. For instance, the influence on development of models, of consequences of behavior, and of a person's empathic capacity appear testable. However, the operation of free will and the effect of different emotions seem difficult to assess. Therefore, I have rated the theory in the "moderately well" range on item 4.

In regard to adaptability (item 5), I believe naive theory also deserves a "moderately well" rating. This estimate is based on the observation that long-held convictions about why people develop morally are often resistant to data that would suggest those ideas are in error. This is particularly noticeable in cases of people citing unduly simplistic causes of moral thought and action. It is easier for them to conclude that "She's a born liar" or that a member of a particular ethnic group is apt to be dishonest than it is to ferret out multiple causes contributing to a given individual's moral behavior. On the other hand, if enough evidence is forthcoming from apparently reputable sources, common sense is apt to change. A case in point is the matter of the misconduct of people diagnosed as suffering from manic-depressive psychosis, certain forms of schizophrenia, or attention-deficit disorder (ADD). Whereas the antisocial acts of such individuals in the past have frequently been judged to result from faulty moral character, in more recent times drug therapy has often succeeded in alleviating their objectionable behavior. As a result, common sense today is more likely to convince us that a chemical imbalance rather than meanness of spirit or a flawed moral character has caused the morally unacceptable acts.

I have rated attribution theory high on fertility (item 6), since commonsense beliefs have been the stimulators of virtually all scientific theories. It is when theorists are dissatisfied with naive interpretations of moral development that they seek to furnish new alternatives. So the seeds of innovation in moral-development theory arise from the inadequate answers offered by traditional beliefs. New theories are intended to correct, expand, or render more precise the public's naive notions of moral development.

In *durability*, commonsense theory as a set of intuitive assumptions can hardly be surpassed, since over the centuries people's naive interpretations are the ones that have dominated their belief systems in virtually all cultures. Commonsense convictions continue on and on from one generation to another. However, the durability of the particular formal version of attribution theory offered in this chapter, or others of similar nature, is a very different matter. As scientists address further attention to analyzing people's commonsense notions of moral matters, we can expect that the description in this chapter will undergo significant changes. To reflect this distinction between naive psychology as people's collection of beliefs and naive psychology as a formal method of analyzing those beliefs, I have placed the set of intuitive notions much higher on the durability scale than I would locate any formal version of attribution theory.

Finally, I consider naive theory, overall, moderately self-satisfying. Although much of my own interpretation of people's development is based on commonsense notions, in many ways common sense fails to answer my moral-development questions adequately, so I am left discontented with naive theory. This discontent serves as a sufficient stimulus for learning what more formal theories, such as the ones in the following chapters, have to offer.

4

Cognitive Structuralism

The phrase *cognitive-structuralist theories of moral development* refers to a cluster of proposals founded on three basic convictions:

1. Each time someone encounters a moral incident, that individual's cognitive structures fashion the meaning that he or she will assign to—or derive from—the incident. Cognitive structures, in effect, serve as mental lenses that cast life's experiences in particular configurations. Because one person's structures differ in some degree from another's, the interpretation that one person places on a moral episode is expected to differ somewhat from the interpretation that another assigns to the same episode.

2. During the years of childhood, cognitive structures change with advancing age. The characteristics of anyone's cognitive structures are determined by a combination of that individual's genetic inheritance and environmental encounters. In effect, the composition of a person's mental templates at any point in life is the product of transactions between that individual's genetic code and daily experiences. The genetic timing system establishes the time in life that a given structure can be activated; then experience in the world fashions the exact way the structure evolves.

3. The development of moral reasoning consists of a sequence of changes in a person's cognitive structures (the interpretive mechanisms of the mind) and in the contents of the mind (memories, beliefs) that have been forged by the operation of those structures.

Among the recognized variants of cognitive-structuralist theory, the two inspected in this chapter are ones proposed by the Swiss child psychologist Jean Piaget (1896-1980) and by a Harvard University professor, Lawrence Kohlberg (1927-1987). The chapter's topics are presented in the following order: Piaget's version of moral development, Kohlberg's contributions, and an assessment of Kohlberg's theory.

PIAGET'S VERSION OF MORAL DEVELOPMENT

The following overview of Piagetian theory opens with (1) a definition of the moral domain, (2) Piaget's stages and moral development, (3) the elements of personality, (4) Piaget on causation, and (5) moral development reality.

The Moral Domain: Piaget's Definition

As noted in Chapter 1, Piaget wrote that "All morality consists in a system of rules, and the essence of all morality is to be sought for in the respect which the individual acquires for these rules" (Piaget, 1965, p. 13). Because children have no innate sense of right and wrong, they must acquire the rules from their experiences with other people.

> . . . most of the moral rules which the child learns to respect he receives from adults. . . . In the case of the very simplest social games, on the contrary, we are in the presence of rules which have been elaborated by the children alone . . . handed down, just like so-called moral realities, from one generation to another. (Piaget, 1965, pp. 13-14)

However, as suggested in our later analysis of Piaget's ideas of the causes of people's moral development, he also believed that certain moral propensities—such as tendencies toward retribution or toward equity—were a part of people's biological nature. These tendencies would subsequently be either enhanced or diminished by people's experiences with the world.

The period of development of moral reasoning implied in Piaget's writings extends from infancy through old age, with the greatest changes occurring over the years of childhood and adolescence.

Piaget's Stages and Moral Development

From his extensive studies of children's intellectual development, Piaget derived two sorts of progression in mental growth: (a) stages in general cognitive development and (b) a variety of separate sets of stages, with each focusing on a particular thought process, such as children's conception of numbers, the causes of physical events, how dreams develop, how forms of play evolve, and how moral judgment advances. The two sets important for understanding cognitive-structuralist views of moral development are Piaget's general stages of mental growth and his specific stages in the progress of moral judgment.

General Stages of Mental Growth

In Piagetian theory, general stages of mental development are significant because a particular level of general intelligence is the foundation on which children's specific stages of moral judgment are erected. In one popular version of Piaget's scheme, mental growth advances through four principal levels: sensorimotor (birth to about age 2), preoperational thought (about age 2 to 7), concrete operations (about 7 to 11), and formal operations (about 11 to 15). Beyond the midteens, thought patterns move from a condition of egocentrism and idealism to a growing recognition that people do not operate solely on the basis of pure logic but that they also are influenced by life's social realities. The following are principal characteristics of the stages:

Sensorimotor Period (Birth–2). The infant advances from performing only reflex actions to finally representing objects mentally and thereby cognitively combining and manipulating them.

Preoperational-Thought Period (2–7). This period is divided into two levels. The first (ages 2–4) is characterized by egocentric speech and primary dependence on perception, rather than on logic, in problem solving. The second (5–7) is marked by an intuitive approach to life, a transition phase between the child's depending on perception and depending on logical thought in solving problems.

Concrete-Operations Period (7–11). In this stage children can perform logical mental operations on concrete objects that either are directly observed or are imagined. An important feature of this period is the child's developing greater ability to recognize which aspects of an object remain unchanged (are *conserved*) when the object changes from one form to another. For example, when a large ball of clay is divided into a series of small balls of clay, the typical preoperational child will not recognize that in this transformation the weight and mass of clay remain the same. The concrete-operations child, in contrast, will understand that weight and mass have been conserved.

Formal-Operations Period (11–15). During adolescence the typical child is no longer limited by what he or she directly sees or hears, nor is he or she restricted to the problem at hand. The adolescent can now imagine various conditions that bear on a problem—past, present, and future—and devise hypotheses about what might logically occur under different combinations of such conditions. By the end of this final stage of mental development, the youth is capable of all the forms of logic that the adult commands. Subsequently, further experience over the years of youth and adulthood fill in the outline with additional, more complex concepts so that the adult's thought is more mature and freer of lingering vestiges of egocentrism than is the thought of the adolescent. (summarized from Piaget & Inhelder, 1969)

In conclusion, these general modes of thought are intimately connected with successive levels of reasoning specific to moral matters. Each stage represents a significant change in the cognitive structures that serve as the mental lenses adopted for interpreting events in the environment.

Piaget's Moral-Reasoning Stages

Piaget's conclusions about the evolution of moral judgment derived from moral dilemmas—brief anecdotes—that he posed for children ranging in age from 6 through 12. These studies led him to decide that such development involves two successive domains, the *heteronomous* and the *autonomous* (Piaget, 1965). People operating from a heteronomous perspective accord unilateral respect for authorities (such as parents, teachers, the clergy, the police) and for the rules they prescribe. People operating from an autonomous perspective base their moral judgments on mutual regard among peers or equals and respect for the rules that guide their interaction. He suggested that development in reasoning tended to progress from heteronomous to autonomous morality through three periods that he observed among children during the elementary-school years. Within the first period, typically found up to age 7 or 8, children believe justice is whatever has been prescribed by adult authority—justice means abiding strictly by rules formulated by adults. This conception is gradually altered over the age range 8 to 11 by a belief in justice as equality. Justice means treating everyone alike—reciprocity and equality among peers. Finally, at a higher level of morality that appears around ages 11 and 12, "purely equalitarian justice is tempered by considerations of equity" (Piaget, 1965, p. 315).

> Instead of looking for equality in identity [with everyone treated alike], the child no longer thinks of the equal rights of individuals except in relation to the particular situation of each. In the domain of retributive justice it means no longer thinking of a law as identical for all by taking account of the personal circumstances of each (favouring the younger ones, etc.). . . . Even if this evolution does not consist of general stages, but simply of phases character-izing certain limited [mental] processes, we have said enough to elucidate the psychological origins of the idea of justice. (Piaget, 1965, p. 317)

In effect, Piaget identified a succession of three modes of cognitive structures that determined children's interpretations of moral incidents between middle childhood and early adolescence.

The Elements of Personality

In Piagetian theory, personality—or more accurately, the architecture of the mind—comprises three kinds of components: cognitive structures, schemes, and operating mechanisms.

Cognitive structures are the perceptual capacities—the lenses or templates—that determine the person's interpretation of what the world's sights and sounds mean. As noted above, during the years of childhood and adolescence, these structures change from one period to another in a predictable pattern. And because that pattern is common to all children, it must be a reflection of human nature—the way people are biologically designed.

In Piaget's system, the purpose of all thought and all action is to equip people to adapt to the environment in ever more satisfactory ways. Piaget called the techniques of adaptation *schemes.* A scheme or technique of adjustment can be biological or mental or both. "A scheme is the . . . organization of actions as they are transferred or generalized by repetition in similar or analogous circumstances" (Piaget & Inhelder, 1969, p. 4). The *grasping* movement of the infant's hand is a scheme, a physical organization of actions that the infant can generalize to grasp a bottle, a toy, or the edge of a blanket. On the intellectual level, the concept of *addition* is a scheme that the schoolchild can generalize to find the sum of a group of pennies in a dish, cars parked along the curbing, or children in the classroom. Such a moral value as *abiding by the rules* is a scheme the adolescent can apply in judging the propriety of people's behavior when they are playing basketball, driving a car, and voting in elections. The entire storehouse of knowledge that children accumulate from their encounters with the world consists of a collection of schemes.

To account for how schemes are acquired, Piaget posited two principal mechanisms that he labeled *assimilation* and *accommodation.* He called these *functional invariants* to signify that they operate continuously throughout the life span.

Assimilation is taking place when a person interprets a new experience as an example of a scheme (a type of experience) already in mind. The scheme *spousal abuse* comes to the mind of a police officer who hears of the way a husband has treated his wife. When a woman sees the operators of a soup kitchen feeding homeless people, her mind categorizes that behavior as *altruism, kindheartedness,* and *philanthropy.* In effect, assimilation is the process of taking in or understanding events of the world by matching the perceived features of those events to one's existing schemes. "To assimilate an object to a scheme means conferring to that object one or several meanings" that the person already has in mind (Piaget, Jonckheere, & Mandelbrot, 1958, p. 59). This process of matching environmental stimuli to existing mental patterns is not simply a matter of ingesting objective reality as it exists in the world. Rather, the person reshapes and bends the events of the world somewhat to fit the form of his or her existing schemes.

However, sometimes the perceived events do not reasonably fit the person's available schemes. It is thus necessary for the person to alter a scheme or create a new one in order to effect a match.

New objects which present themselves to consciousness do not have their own qualities which can be isolated . . . they are vague, nebulous, because unassimilable, and thus they create a discomfort from which there emerges sooner or later a new differentiation of the schemes of assimilation. (Piaget, 1963, p. 141)

Therefore, schemes, under pressures from recognized realities of the environment, can be changed in form or multiplied into new variants to reconcile the lack of an acceptable match. Piaget used the term *accommodation* to identify this process of adjusting existing schemes to permit the understanding of events that would otherwise be incomprehensible.

In short, whereas assimilation reshapes environmental stimuli to fit existing schemes, accommodation revises or adds to the present schemes so as to readjust for environmental features that cannot conveniently be ignored or distorted.

Piaget on Causation

Piaget's academic training was in biology, an emphasis that prompted him to assign genetic factors a prominent role in accounting for why development occurs as it does. He proposed that intellectual growth results from four causal factors: (1) heredity (biologically determined internal maturation), (2) the child's direct experiences with the world, (3) social transmission (instruction), and (4) equilibration.

First, heredity sets the basic conditions for how and when each phase of development can occur. That is, the potential for a new variety of mental structure to appear is determined by a genetically controlled timing system. When speaking of moral development, Piaget frequently revealed his conviction that people's moral reasoning is heavily influenced by genetic propensities. For example, in writing about retribution as a response to wrongdoing, he asserted:

> It cannot be denied that the idea of punishment has psycho-biological roots. Blow calls for blow and gentleness moves us to gentleness. The instinctive reactions of defence and sympathy thus bring about a sort of elementary reciprocity which is the soil that retribution demands for its growth. (Piaget, 1965, p. 321)

In like manner, when considering children's progress toward autonomous reasoning, Piaget contended "it cannot be denied that the idea of equality or of distributive justice possesses individual or biological roots which are necessary but not sufficient conditions for its development" (1965, p. 318).

Thus, genetic timing cannot alone ensure that a new cognitive structure—a new way of interpreting the world—will materialize. Experience with the world is necessary for the fruition of this potential. Piaget suggested that such experience is of two principal types—the physical and the socially transmitted.

Physical experience consists of the person's direct and generally unguided encounters with the world. In the realm of moral development, the individual interacts with other people—either directly or vicariously (viewing a television program or reading a novel or a newspaper)—and draws conclusions about the moral propriety or impropriety of what occurred. The child on the playground, the secretary in the office, the labor-union leader meeting with management, and the baseball pitcher all make judgments about the fairness, compassion, courage, and loyalty of the events they witness. Piaget saw these physical encounters as the foundational experiences on which social transmission can build.

Social transmission is education in a broad sense—conveying knowledge to the person from without, usually as some form of intentional instruction. Parents' advice on how to behave, lessons in school about rights and responsibilities, the pastor's sermon about following the Lord's commandments, the coach's admonitions about playing by the rules—all these qualify as social transmission.

Finally, Piaget applied the label *equilibration* or *equilibrium* to the fourth variable in his quartet of causal factors. Equilibration's role is to maintain a balance among the other three factors, fitting the genetic (maturational), direct experience, and social transmission influences together harmoniously, because "a whole play of regulation and of compensation is required to result in a coherence" (Piaget, 1973, p. 29).

Although Piaget paid little or no specific attention to individual differences among people in their moral development, it can be assumed that the variability among them results from the differences in their genetic composition, their physical experiences, and the kinds of instruction they have received.

Moral-Development Reality

Piaget's theory was grounded in empirical data—in young people's expressed judgments of moral episodes that were described to them or of episodes in which they took part. Thus, to Piaget, moral-development reality consisted of observable events in the daily world and of people's moral interpretations of those events. His theory made no use of supernatural forces, such as God or spirits, since he viewed himself as a scientist bent on providing logical analyses of empirical data.

In summary, Piaget's pioneering investigations of moral development during the latter 1920s furnished the general framework on which subsequent cognitive-structuralist theorists would erect their models. The best known of these latter-day scholars has been Lawrence Kohlberg, who accepted Piaget's basic scheme, then extended and embellished it with a variety of features derived from a host of empirical studies of moral reasoning among adolescents and adults.

KOHLBERG'S MORAL-REASONING HIERARCHY

Following Piaget's lead, Lawrence Kohlberg (1984) devised the best-known moral reasoning theory to appear in recent decades. He used Piaget's set of general cognitive growth stages as a foundation for erecting a six-stage hierarchy of moral judgments that refined Piaget's original conception of ideal heteronomous and autonomous types. Kohlberg expanded that scheme with his own proposals and with those of a variety of philosophers and psychologists, ranging from Aristotle, through Immanuel Kant and James Mark Baldwin, to Jurgen Habermas. Among the elements of Piagetian theory that Kohlberg adopted were the concept of cognitive structures, Piaget's stages of mental development, the length of the moral-development period, the importance of a genetically controlled timing system for arousing the potential for each successive stage, the necessity of suitable environmental experiences for the fruition of a stage, and assimilation and accommodation as functional invariants. Among Kohlberg's innovations were his definition of the moral domain, his specifying six stages that carried children from heteronomous to autonomous moral reasoning, his conception of the causes for progress up the hierarchy of stages, and his cross-cultural studies of moral development.

The following sketch of Kolhberg's views opens with his conception of the moral domain, then continues with the hierarchy of stages he devised and his beliefs about cause.

The Moral Domain: Kohlberg's Definition

Kohlberg labeled his theory a "rational reconstruction of the ontogenesis of justice reasoning" and not, as people have often assumed, a complete depiction of moral development.

> I have always tried to be clear that my states are stages of justice reasoning, not of emotions, aspirations, or action. Our data base has been a set of hypothetical dilemmas posing conflicts between the rights or claims of different persons in dilemma situations. (Kohlberg, 1984, p. 224)

The dilemmas are moral episodes drawn from a set of nine standard incidents. The first eight are unfinished anecdotes that respondents are expected to complete, while the ninth describes a completed event that respondents are to evaluate. To illustrate, the essence of four of the anecdotes is as follows (Kohlberg, 1984, pp. 640-651):

1. A husband (Heinz) cannot afford an expensive drug to treat his wife's cancer, so he must decide whether to steal the drug from a pharmacy.
3. A son (Joe) has earned money to go to camp, but his father asks for the money so the father can go on a fishing trip; Joe must decide whether to give his father the money.
7. In a military unit during wartime, one man must remain behind to blow up a bridge if the unit is to retreat safely. But that man will thereby risk certain death. Thus, the officer in charge must decide whether to order one of the men to blow up the bridge or to do it himself.
9. Two brothers want to get $1,000 each before they sneak out of town. One gets money by stealing it, and the other by feigning illness and begging an

elderly man to "lend" him $1,000 for an operation. Which of the brothers did the worse thing, and why is that worse than the other brother's action?

A Hierarchy of Stages

Kohlberg postulated six stages in the development of moral reasoning from early childhood into adult life. The following brief glimpse of the stages in their mid-1980s version suggests several of their distinguishing characteristics. The presentation advances from the earliest levels, indicative of the thinking processes of young children, to the higher levels, which can be achieved by individuals who are intellectually more mature (Kohlberg, 1984, pp. 621–639). Kohlberg linked his scheme to Piaget's stages of logical reasoning by contending that the growing child had to reach a suitable level of logical thought before being able to advance to a comparable stage of moral reasoning. For example, Kohlberg proposed that an individual must be capable of Piaget's concrete-operational thought in order to adopt Kohlberg's Stage 2 (individualistic, instrumental morality) approach to moral judgments. An older child needed to command Piaget's full formal-operations thought processes before reaching Kohlberg's Stage 4 (social-system morality) (Kegan, 1982, p. 86).

Stage 1: Heteronomous Morality. Kohlberg refers to the perspective at this initial stage as *moral realism* in which a person assumes that moral judgments are so self-evident that no justification is needed beyond simply stating the rule that has been broken. Failing to tell the truth or using an object that belongs to someone else is absolutely wrong and automatically warrants punishment. There are no such things as extenuating circumstances, such as people's intentions or their knowledge of right from wrong. This stage represents Piaget's heteronomous justice—absolute obedience to authority and the letter of the law.

Stage 2: Individualistic, Instrumental Morality. At this second level, the person recognizes that different people can have different points of view toward a moral incident. "Since each person's primary aim is to pursue his or her own interests, the perspective is pragmatic—to maximize satisfaction of one's needs and desires while minimizing negative consequences to the self" (Kohlberg, 1984, p. 626). Thus, the participants in a moral incident seek to negotiate a deal with each other as the instrument for coordinating their efforts for mutual benefit. No general moral principles guide their action, so that each case is handled separately. However, such a pragmatic approach "fails to provide a means for deciding among conflicting claims, ordering or setting priorities on conflicting needs and interests" (Kohlberg, 1984, p. 626).

Stage 3: Impersonally Normative Morality. The notion of justice advances beyond the individual-interest level to a conception of shared moral norms that guide everyone's moral behavior, regardless of the particular situations or particular people involved. In contrast to Stage 1, where rules are handed down by authority, the shared norms at Stage 3 are the result of general agreement about what constitutes suitable social behavior. Individuals operating from a Stage 3 perspective are concerned with playing their social role in a positive, constructive manner, with good compared to bad motives as evidence of one's general personal morality. The guide to action is provided by the Golden Rule —do unto others as you would have others do unto you. People at Stage 3 are especially concerned with maintaining mutual trust and social approval.

Stage 4: Social System Morality. People at this level look beyond informal, commonly agreed upon rules for individuals' interactions and now encompass the entire social system in their purview of moral behavior. "The pursuit of individual interests is considered legitimate only when it is consistent with the maintenance of the sociomoral system as a whole. . . . A social structure that includes formal institutions and social roles serves to mediate conflicting claims and promote the common good" (Kohlberg, 1984, p. 631). This perspective recognizes a societal, legal, or religious system that has developed codified rules and practices for adjudicating moral conflicts. In some settings, the laws may be ones representing an overarching philosophical or religious conviction embedded in the individual's conscience, a conviction that can be in conflict with the society's dominant legal system. In summary, moral judgments at Stage 4 are founded on legal or religious institutions and belief systems.

Stage 5: Human-Rights and Social-Welfare Morality. In contrast to accepting the rules of a society as they are already constituted, Kohlberg posits at Stage 5 a perception of morality that people would rationally build into a social system to promote universal values and rights. This prior-to-society viewpoint asks what rules would guide a society that fosters equality, equity, and general welfare for all. Upon answering this question, people are then obligated to make moral choices in keeping with those rules, even when their choices conflict with the society's present codes. Stage 5 provides a concern for the protection of the rights of the minority that cannot be derived from the social system perspective of Stage 4, since "social institutions, rules, or laws are evaluated by reference to their long-term consequences for the welfare of each person or group in the society" (Kohlberg, 1984, p. 634).

Stage 6: Morality of Universalizable, Reversible, and Prescriptive General Ethical Principles. Kohlberg describes this stage as *the moral point of view* that "all human beings should take toward one another as free and equal autonomous persons" (Kohlberg, 1984, p. 636). Such morality is universalizable in being applicable at all times and in all places among all peoples. It is reversible, in that the plaintiff and defendant in a moral incident could exchange places and the decision for resolving the issue would not be affected—a kind of "moral musical chairs" or second-order application of the Golden Rule. Each person understands and respects the point of view of every other person. "General principles are distinct from either rules or rights, first, in being positive *pre*scriptions rather than negative *pro*scriptions (don't kill, don't steal or cheat)" (Kohlberg, 1984, p. 636). One general principle can be respect for human personality or dignity. Another can be benevolence or universal compassion and care. Or moral decisions can derive from a cluster of principles—maximum quality of life for everyone, maximum individual liberty in relation to like liberty for others, and the equitable distribution of goods and services. (summarized from Kohlberg, 1984, pp. 621–639)

Empirical studies of moral reasoning in a variety of societies have confirmed that people do apply the perspectives of the first five stages in their responses to hypothetical moral dilemmas. However, there remains a question about whether Stage 6 might perhaps be an ideal condition never actually achieved in practice (Colby, Kohlberg, Gibbs, & Lieberman, 1983, p. 5).

An earlier investigation revealed that only about 30% of adults could be classified as having reached Piaget's formal-operations level in logical judgment (Kuhn, Langer, Kohlberg, & Haan, 1977). Thus, not everyone within an age group would be expected to display the same level of moral reasoning when facing moral decisions.

In his description of moral reasoning stages, Kohlberg suggested the way three kinds of justice are typified at each stage—distributive, commutative, and corrective. The term *distributive justice* refers to the way desirable assets (honor, wealth) are allotted to people of a society in terms of equality or merit and need. *Commutative justice* concerns issues deriving from voluntary agreements, contracts, and equal exchange. *Corrective justice* aims at repairing private transactions that have been unfair and call for restitution or compensation. Corrective justice also concerns crimes and torts that violate the rights of involuntary participants and thus call for restitution or retribution (Kohlberg, 1984, 621–622).

Kohlberg on Causation

When asked what caused people to pass from one stage to another and what determined how high they would advance up the stage structure, Kohlberg adopted an interactionist position in which heredity and environment played equally essential parts. He did not believe a person's progress was produced entirely by genetic inheritance or entirely by factors in the environment. Instead, he proposed that four principal factors interact to determine how far in the six-stage hierarchy a person will progress and when he or she will arrive at each stage. The first factor, and the one with the greatest genetic component, is the individual's *level of logical reasoning* as identified in Piaget's basic mental-growth stages. The second, a personal factor that probably has both genetic and environmental elements, is the individual's desire or *motivation*, sometimes referred to the person's needs. The remaining two factors are entirely environmental: (a) opportunities to learn *social roles* and (b) the *form of justice* in the social institutions with which the person is familiar.

In regard to roles, Kohlberg agreed with many social psychologists that children become socialized by learning to take the roles displayed by people around them. As children interact with others, they imagine themselves in the others' shoes and see life from others' perspectives. This ability increases with advancing age as children increasingly abandon a completely egocentric mode of perceiving life and become more adept at adopting other people's viewpoints. Thus, mature moral judgment "is based on sympathy for others, as well as on the notion that the moral judge must adopt the perspective of the 'impartial spectator' or the 'generalized other'" (Kohlberg, 1971, p. 190). How well children learn to assume others' roles depends to a great extent on the conditions of their social environment. Some environments encourage role-taking and thus hasten children's advance up the moral judgment ladder. Other environments limit opportunities to learn role-taking and thus slow children's progress in moral reasoning and may prevent them from ever reaching stages 4 or 5.

> In four different cultures, middle-class children were found to be more advanced in moral judgment than matched lower-class children. This was not because the middle-class children heavily favored a certain type of thought which corresponded to the prevailing middle-class pattern. Instead, the working-class children seemed to move through the same sequences, but the middle-class children seemed to move faster and farther. (Kohlberg, 1971, p. 190)

Kohlberg's fourth variable that contributes to growth in moral judgment is the justice structure of the social groups or institutions with which the child interacts—the family, the school, the church, and local and national governments. At all stages of moral growth, the individual has some sort of concern for the welfare of other people. But only at stage 5 is this concern based on what Kohlberg regarded as principles of true justice, those of *equality* and *reciprocity*. The principle of equality holds that we "treat every man's claim equally, regardless of the man" (Kohlberg, 1967, p. 169). The principle of reciprocity means equality of exchange—"punishment for something bad, reward for something good, and contractual exchange" or fulfilling one's bargain. In each society the groups or institutions with which the growing child is intimately involved vary in their justice structures. A family dominated by an autocratic father differs from a family in which children are encouraged to make decisions, to take responsibility, and to be rewarded in accordance with how they carry out their self-imposed commitments. A dictatorial government that allows no voicing of contrary opinions differs from a multiparty democracy that permits freedom of expression. Kohlberg proposed that people who participate in social groups that operate on a high level of equality and reciprocity will advance to higher levels of moral judgment than will individuals whose main participation is in groups that display less equality and reciprocity.

Although Kohlberg's attention focused chiefly on group trends rather than on individual differences, it can be assumed that the variations among people in moral reasoning result from the differences among them in the four causal factors described above. A child whose genetic endowment leads to slower than average mental development, who lacks the will to abide by societal rules, who has few opportunities to adopt social roles, and who is raised in an autocratic social setting will exhibit a lower level of moral judgment than a child whose native endowment, motivation, and social environment are quite the opposite.

AN ASSESSMENT OF KOHLBERG'S THEORY

Lawrence Kohlberg's proposal, as a representative of cognitive-structuralist theory, is evaluated in the following paragraphs in relation to the appraisal standards introduced in Chapter 2.

In judging how clearly Kohlberg explained his ideas (item 1), I placed his theory in the "moderately well" position. On the positive side are the many specific examples he cited from children's answers to moral dilemmas to clarify some terms Kohlberg used (*instrumental relativist orientation, social-contract legalistic orientation*) and that distinguish one stage from another. However,

---

Kohlberg's Cognitive-Structuralist Theory

How well do I think the theory meets the standards?

The Standards	Very Well	Moderately Well	Very Poorly
1. Is clearly understandable		X	
2. Explains past and predicts future moral behavior	X		
3. Offers practical guidance in coping with moral matters	X		
4. Is readily verifiable and falsifiable		X	
5. Accommodates new evidence	X		
6. Stimulates new discoveries	X		
7. Is durable		X	
8. Is self-satisfying		X	

other terms were not delineated so clearly. R. S. Peters (1971, pp. 246-248) chided Kohlberg for being vague and unsophisticated in comparing *character traits* (honesty, courage, determination) unfavorably with *principles* (a sense of justice). Critics have also noted that the scoring system used for determining a person's dominant stage of moral reasoning involves a substantial amount of subjective judgment on the part of the scorer, thus casting doubt on the reliability of the stage that a person is assigned.

The theory provides both for explaining people's past moral judgments and for predicting their future judgments (item 2) by proposing four interacting determinants (mental maturity, motivation, role opportunities, societal justice structure) that can be used to assess an individual's mode of thought (if proper measures of the four variables are available).

In putting his theory to practical use in child rearing, Kohlberg based two educational applications on his model. The first application involves using moral dilemmas as group discussion topics. Members of the group are expected to tell how they would solve the dilemmas and to explain the moral principles underlying their solutions. During the ensuing discussion, individuals who base their judgments on reasons lower in Kohlberg's stage hierarchy are expected to advance in their reasoning when they hear the arguments of group members who apply principles representing a higher stage. The second application, labeled *the just community*, consists of conducting a secondary school in which moral issues that arise during the daily school routine are resolved cooperatively by students and staff members in open discussion sessions (Hersh, Miller, & Fielding, 1980). Thus, I would rate the theory relatively high for its providing practical guidance in coping with moral matters (item 3).

Is the theory verifiable and falsifiable (item 4)? In answer, I would say that many aspects of Kohlberg's scheme can indeed be tested. Such is the case with his proposed sequencing of the six developmental levels, the relationship of people's judgment to the dominant justice structures of the social groups in which they participate, and the ability of a moral education program to foster one's progress up the stage hierarchy. However, other aspects do not lend themselves to empirical testing. One is Kohlberg's contention that his scheme represents a hierarchy of absolute, universal values appropriate for all cultures. Another is the assertion that even handed justice based on an individual's personal convictions is morally superior to other possible ultimate aims of moral development, such as obedience to God's will or compassion for people who suffer misfortune. Weighing these considerations against each other, I have marked the theory in the "moderately well" position along the verifiability/ falsifiability dimension.

I judge Kohlberg's model to be somewhat more than moderately satisfactory in accommodating to new evidence (item 5). The earliest forms of the theory were subsequently changed to account for different age levels of moral judgment found in different cultures, with the varied levels perhaps the result of differences among cultures in opportunities to adopt social roles and in the dominant justice structures of the society. In addition, the results of empirical studies prompted Kohlberg to concede that the highest level of his six-stage hierarchy was unduly idealistic and not actually found in real-life settings. In response to Gilligan's (Chapter 9) charge that Kohlberg erred in defining moral development solely in terms of even handed justice, Kohlberg willingly admitted that compassionate caring was also an important aspect of moral thought and action (Kohlberg, 1984).

For its durability (item 7), I have located the theory in the "moderately well" region. Over nearly four decades since its creation, Kohlberg's model has consistently been the most discussed secular theory of moral development, and it will likely retain its position in the years ahead. The standard psychological journal literature over the 1970-1995 era reports more than 770 investigations based on Kohlberg's work. Such lively interest in the theory suggests that Kohlberg's model deserves a high mark for its fertility (item 6).

Finally, Kohlberg's theory displays both strengths and weaknesses, with some of the weaknesses addressed in our next chapter—"Social Learning, Social Cognition." However, despite its ostensible shortcomings, Kohlberg's proposal remains one of the most stimulating and potentially fertile models of moral development in current psychological and philosophical circles. Balancing the strengths against the weaknesses, I have rated the theory as moderately self-satisfying overall (item 8).

5

Social Learning, Social Cognition

Social-learning theorists, who often march under the more inclusive *social-cognition* banner, show greater concern for the process of moral development than they do for the content. In other words, they are more interested in how people acquire moral values than in what those values are. Whereas Piaget traced the progress of values from the heteronomous to the autonomous, and Kohlberg commended youths' advance from accepting society's laws to developing their own moral principles, social-learning proponents are less likely to suggest which of these bases of values is more admirable than another. And whereas religious theories typically describe specific behaviors that are moral and ones that are not, social-learning models offer no such lists.

In their analysis of the moral-development process, social-learning theorists usually share in common four foundational assumptions.

1. People's moral values and their habitual modes of behavior are not inborn, nor do they naturally evolve over the advancing years. Instead, they are learned during the social encounters of daily life.

2. People either engage directly in these significant social encounters or else they witness others participating in such episodes. Moral values and ways of behaving can be learned either from participating directly in, or from simply observing, social transactions.

3. From among the multitude of values and modes of behavior that people experience, the decision about which ones to adopt and which to avoid is governed by the nature of the consequences that follow each social interaction. Expressions of value and ways of acting that are accompanied by rewarding consequences are adopted. Ones accompanied by undesired consequences or no apparent consequences at all are rejected.

4. Moral development is a gradual, day-by-day process of accumulating and refining one's values and ways of acting. In other words, moral development does not progress in a stage wise fashion, with a sudden advance followed by a period of relatively no change until another sudden advance occurs.

Among a variety of proposals that qualify as social-learning theories, the best-known is one devised by a Stanford University psychologist, Albert Bandura (born 1925). This chapter draws heavily from Bandura's theory but includes features offered by other proponents of social-cognition models. The chapter's topics are addressed in the following order: (1) sources of moral behavior, (2) the nature of moral values, (3) processes of development, (4) answers to guide questions, and (5) assessing social-learning theory.

SOURCES OF MORAL BEHAVIOR

Social-learning theorists generally appear to believe that moral behavior results from a combination of rational (cognitive) and irrational (affective) sources. The three most prominent rational sources are moral values, prudential considerations, and ego-protection techniques.

Moral values are convictions a person holds about good and bad ways to act in moral situations. Examples of typical values, in their simplest form, are *don't kill, don't cheat, don't steal,* and *help people who are in need.*

Prudential considerations are beliefs about how a contemplated action could influence one's own welfare, particularly in terms of what other people might think about the action and what undesirable social consequences could thus result. Prudential concerns conflict with moral values whenever a value is set aside in favor of one's immediate welfare.

> "If I told Cynthia's parents where she really spent the night, Cynthia would never speak to me again."
> "Testifying in court against the drug dealers could get me killed."
> "If I included on my income tax all the tips I received as a waiter, I'd be out a lot of money."

Whereas prudential considerations involve a person's consciously disregarding a moral value, an ego-protection technique consists of excusing oneself for what might appear to be a violation of a moral value. This is kind of rationalization that morally justifies behavior that, at first glance, could be considered wrong. Ego protection usually consists of citing ameliorating conditions that ostensibly warrant the person's actions.

> "I knew he'd try to hit me, so I hit him first."
> "While I've been getting unemployment insurance payments, I've worked in my sister's beauty salon for ten dollars an hour, and that's cash. I know it's not quite going by the letter of the law, but everybody does it, so why shouldn't I? You can't live decently on unemployment insurance—it's not enough."

The primary irrational source of moral behavior is strong emotion—fear, rage, lust, shame, affection, sympathy, or the like—that can alter or overwhelm rationality in moral-decision situations.

"He was so startled that he pulled the trigger without thinking."

"Overcome with sympathy for the woman's story, the officer let her go free before realizing her story was no more than a fabrication."

"The mother knew her son had raped the girl, but the mother still refused to tell where her son was hiding."

To accommodate all of these facets of moral development (cognition, emotion, and behavior as affected by the social environment), Bandura explains that

Social cognitive theory adopts a cognitive interactionist perspective to moral phenomena. Within this conceptual framework, personal factors in the form of moral thought and affective self-reactions, moral conduct, and environmental factors all operate as interacting determinants that influence each other bidirectionally. (Bandura, 1991, p. 45)

In comparing social-learning theory with cognitive-structuralist interpretations of development, Bandura has faulted cognitive-structuralists for failing to account for the discrepancy that often exists between a person's highest stage of moral reasoning (as in Kohlberg's scheme) and the way people actually behave in moral encounters (Kupfersmid & Wonderly, 1980). The error, according to the social-learning camp, is that cognitive structuralists center their attention solely on people's reasoning about the values they find in rather simplistic moral dilemmas they are asked to judge. This is the error of proposing that rationality dictates moral behavior, a proposal that fails to recognize other factors (prudence, emotions, complex environmental influences) that participate in determining how people conduct themselves in moral situations.

THE NATURE OF MORAL VALUES

In a typical social-cognition theory, moral values can be both individual and shared. An individual value is a conviction a person holds about good and bad ways to act toward others. A shared value is such a conviction that is held in common by a variety of people. Shared values are often codified in the form of laws or, in a less formal fashion, maintained as customs that members of a group have come to honor. Social-learning theorists usually do not attempt to argue which moral values are philosophically superior to others. Instead, their chosen psychological task is that of explaining the processes by which people acquire the values they adopt.

A distinction is sometimes drawn between (a) theorists who envisage acceptable moral values as being universally applicable to all peoples and (b) theorists who regard acceptable values as ones relative to a particular culture, group, or individual. Such cognitive structuralists as Piaget and Kohlberg, as well as virtually all religious theorists, endorse a universal-values position. Their rationale is that certain moral precepts—either by the command of a supreme being or other authority, or else by virtue of the nature of humans and their social systems—are proper guides to behavior in all places at all times. In contrast, typical social-learning advocates appear to subscribe to a cultural-relativist position, a position that may be combined with some degree of individual relativism. They declare that (a) the moral precepts widely held in one society may legitimately differ from those of another society and (b) the values people hold are ones they have learned or devised during their encounters with their culture. It is also the case that individuals or small groups may differ in their beliefs from the values endorsed by most members of their society. Thus, we can usefully recognize individual relativism—the belief that one individual can acceptably subscribe to values different from those of other individuals or those of the society in general. Such can be true with revolutionaries, including ones cited later in this book—Sigmund Freud, Karl Marx, Moses, Jesus, Mohammed, the Buddha, Guru Nanak, and Mahavira. Furthermore, the fact that a person subscribes to cultural relativism does not rule out the possibility that there are indeed some universal values. For instance, precepts embraced by a great many people in a great many cultures can be referred to as virtually *universal*. Prohibitions against murder, incest, lying, and stealing are of this sort. However, the reason that these tenets are universal is not because they are issued by an authority but, rather, because people have discovered over the centuries the pragmatic sense of such prohibitions—abiding by those values has promoted the welfare of more people more of the time than otherwise would be the case.

> A shared morality . . . is vital to the humane functioning of any society. . . . Without some consensual moral codes, people would disregard each others' rights and welfare whenever their desires come into social conflict. Societal codes and sanctions articulate collective moral imperatives as well as influence social conduct. (Bandura, 1991, p. 46)

In brief, social-cognitive theorists recognize the necessity for people to hold moral values and the need to have most, if not all, values widely endorsed by the members of the society. But such theorists do not usually insist on what those values must be. This is not to say that these theorists lack personal preferences regarding which moral values are the best guides to behavior. Instead, it means they recognize (a) that differences in normative moral values can exist between one society and another and can also be found to some extent between individuals within a society and (b) that most people adopt, through a social-learning process, the dominant values of their particular culture.

PROCESSES OF DEVELOPMENT

From a social-learning perspective, moral development does not consist of the periodic unfolding of successive stages of moral reasoning common to all children and identical from one culture to another. Instead, development involves the young gradually learning moral values and behaviors during transactions with their social surroundings. While Bandura rejects the notion that moral growth occurs in "discrete lock-step stages," he does acknowledge that "there are some universalities in the order of development" because of the similar types of biopsychosocial changes that appear in all cultures as children increase in age. Those similarities include the maturing of children's intellectual abilities, expanding circles of social experience that require more generalized and complex moral values, the changing behavior expectations and sanctions that society applies to transgressors of different ages, and the growing ability of the young to internalize moral standards (conscience) to guide their actions (Bandura, 1991, p. 52).

From various authors' conceptions of social cognition, I believe it possible to create a brief, suggestive, generic sketch of elements that participate in the social-learning process as it bears on moral development (Bandura, 1977, 1986, 1990, 1991; Rotter, 1982; Eisenberg & Fabes, 1988; Kurtines & Gewirtz, 1991a, 1991b; Musser & Leone, 1986). One version of such a description is charted in Table 5-1.

The chart traces typical individuals' moral progress through the first quarter-century of life. For convenience of discussion, the 25 years are divided into six segments labeled newborn (birth to 1 month), the infant (1 month to 18 months), the young child (18 months through year 5), the school-age child (years 6 through 11), the adolescent (years 12 through 17), and the young adult (years 18 through 25). These divisions are not intended to be stages in the sense that *stage* is employed by most cognitive-structuralists. In other words, there is no intention in Table 5-1 to suggest that movement from one age period to the next involves an abrupt transition from one moral-development condition to another. Instead, progress is viewed as a gradual accumulation of learning experiences.

Throughout the chart the left-hand pages describe the status of the person at each age period, whereas the right-hand pages portray the accompanying aspects of the environment that influence the individual's moral condition. On the first left-hand page, at the outset of infancy, the newborn is pictured as entering the world with six undeveloped potentials or capacities—potentials for gradually acquiring (1) differentiated needs, (2) intellectual maturity (reasoning skills and a store of knowledge), (3) physical skills, (4) internalized moral values (conscience), (5) differentiated emotions, and (6) responses to consequences. Over the upcoming years, these potentials are progressively actualized as the result of the internal maturation of the growing child's nervous system in coordination with the child's interactions with an expanding environment.

The right-hand pages depict agents (individuals, groups, institutions) that provide services for the developing child and that stipulate rights, privileges, and responsibilities (requirements) the child is expected to acquire. The term *rights* means opportunities people receive simply as a consequence of their being a member of a particular demographic category—age group, physical size, citizenship, school attended, club or team membership, and the like. A four-year-old has the right to receive food and shelter by virtue of her young age. A teenager has the right to apply for an auto driver's license because he has reached age 16. The term *privilege* identifies earned opportunities, that is, rewards an individual acquires by virtue of accomplishment. The 16-year-old is not accorded the privilege of actually driving a car legally until he demonstrates the ability to drive safely. *Responsibilities* are obligations people are to assume. In the realm of morality, the obligations are chiefly in the form of moral standards or values the person is expected to adopt as guides to behavior.

As children grow up, the rights and privileges they receive are frequently linked to the responsibilities they incur. This matter of coordinating rights and privileges with responsibilities is often the cause of friction between the young and their caretakers, particularly during the years of adolescence. Teenagers are often prone to claim rights and privileges before parents are willing to grant them, and parents are apt to impose responsibilities on their adolescent offspring before the youths are fully willing to accept those burdens.

In social-learning theory, as illustrated on the right-hand pages throughout Table 5-1, two critical environmental factors affecting moral development are (a) the models of behavior that different environments provide and (b) the consequences that people directly experience from their actions in moral-decision situations and also the consequences they see other people experience.

The Importance of Modeling

According to Bandura, people rarely create a new behavior in a hit-or-miss fashion. Instead, most of their novel acts result from imitating someone else. Such an innovative act can be either an exact copy of the model or else a unique combination of segments of other people's actions.

> When exposed to diverse models, observers rarely pattern their behavior exclu-sively after a single source, nor do they adopt all the attributes even of preferred models. Rather, observers combine aspects of various models into new amal-gams that differ from the individual sources. . . . Different observers adopt different combinations of characteristics. (Bandura, 1977, p. 48)

Although such observational learning is far from completely understood, some of the conditions influencing it have been identified. Bandura proposes that the main reason people learn from seeing or hearing a model is that the information they acquire helps them decide how the observed behavior might help or hinder them in fulfilling their needs on some future occasion. This information is stored in memory in symbolic form, as images or as verbal symbols, for future use.

In Bandura's opinion, the process of learning moral conduct from models consists of five main functions: (a) paying *attention*, (b) *coding* for memory, (c) *retaining* in memory, and (d) *carrying out the action*. All four steps require (e) *motivation* (Bandura, 1977, pp. 22-29).

First, when people observe a model, they must *attend to the pertinent clues* in the episode and ignore aspects of the model and the setting that are merely incidental. Missing crucial features of the act and including nonessential aspects leads to disappointing results when the observers try the behavior in the future.

Second, people must accurately record the event in memory as a *visual image* or *semantic code*. Without a proper coding system, a person fails to store the essentials of the witnessed event. There are obvious developmental trends in the ability to remember and recall episodes. For example, older children learn more readily from observing others' performances, primarily because of the older child's more advanced ability to use symbols. Bandura points out (1977, p. 30) that the infant's use of modeling is confined mainly to instantaneous imitation. The very young child will imitate the adult's gesture or word immediately instead of reproducing it after a period of time. But as children mature and gain more experience in associating words or images with events, they can store these symbols in order to recall and reproduce events after extended periods of time. Thus, the development of language skills and of schemes for coding observations enhances children's ability to profit from models.

Third, if the knowledge gained from models is to be available for future use, it must be *permanently stored* in memory. Memories fade or disappear with time. Therefore, much that people learn from observing others is forgotten and is thus no longer available when needed in moral-decision situations (Bandura, 1969, p. 202). Such memory aids as rehearsal (review or practice) and attaching multiple codes to an event (associating a variety of interlinked words or images with the episode) serve to render the stored information readily retrieved when needed.

Fourth, people need to *express the behavior in actions*. It is not enough simply to get the general idea of an act. Instead, if the behavior is to be of use, it needs to be produced in full. Before going to court, the lawbreaker should rehearse—at least mentally—the explanation he intends to give the judge. Before risking her safety on the city street, the woman needs to demonstrate the karate moves she will use if accosted by a mugger.

The fifth requirement in the process of learning from models is that the learner be *motivated* to carry through the steps of the process. This motivational function is embedded in the crucial role of the consequences of behavior.

Table 5-1
The Developing Individual
Potentials and Status

The Newborn
Differentiated needs

The potential for evolving a variety of socially conditioned (learned) needs, drives, or motives that influence which aspects of the environment attract the individual's attention and what the person tries to do about those aspects.

Initial status. The neonate is energized by basic physiological needs (for food, drink, warmth, elimination of bodily wastes) and psychological needs (for affection and protection from overwhelming stimuli).

Intellectual maturity

The potential for sophisticated reasoning, for accumulating a large store of memories of events, and for communicating through the use of complex oral and visual symbols.

Initial status. Almost no reasoning skill; few if any vague memories of a prenatal state; communication chiefly though cooing, distressed crying, and random arm and leg movements.

Physical skills

The potential for acquiring great muscular strength and coordination that permit a wide variety of bodily and manual movements.

Initial status. Very little strength and coordination of body parts. Movements limited to wiggling the arms and legs.

Internalized values

The potential for incorporating into the personality standards of behavior displayed in the individual's social environment. This function is called "developing a conscience."

Initial status. No internalized standards; in effect, the neonate has no conscience or sense of social right and wrong.

Differentiated emotions

The potential for acquiring a wide range of feeling tones identified by such terms as joy, sorrow, relaxation, anxiety, pride, shame, friendliness, anger, and more.

Initial status. Only gross sensations of comfort and discomfort.

Responses to consequences

The potential for abandoning behaviors that are followed by unpleasant feelings and for repeating—in future circumstances similar to one's present situation—those behaviors that are followed by pleasant feelings.

Initial status. Extreme difficulty in recognizing exactly which behaviors are accompanied by pleasant consequences or accompanied by unpleasant outcomes.

Table 5-1 (continued)
The Developing Individual
Agents, Services, Rights, and Responsibilities

The Newborn's Social Setting
Agents

The most important people composing the neonate's social environment are such immediate caregivers as the biological mother, surrogate mothers, hospital nurses, the father, and siblings. They are the initial models whose actions the newborn will soon begin to imitate.

Services

Because neonates' skills are so meager (limited to such automatic acts as breathing, digesting, wiggling the limbs, and crying), it is necessary for other people to provide the services needed for the babies' survival and development. Older people most ensure that the newborns have proper food, drink, warmth, bodily cleanliness, a comfortable resting place, medication, and protection from injury and irritation.

Rights, privileges, and responsibilities

Since newborns' mental and physical abilities are so slight, people are obliged to free them from all responsibilities. Neonates typically are excused for violating all manner of social custom that older members of the society are expected to observe. In households with understanding and tolerant caregivers, newborns with impunity soil themselves and their resting places with bodily excretions and they wail at all hours of the day or night, regardless of any distress such behavior causes others. In households whose occupants are less tolerant of these disturbances, neonates must bear postponement or neglect in satisfying their needs. Or, under the worst circumstances, newborns must endure physical punishment at the hands of irate older children or adults who find the disturbances inexcusable.

In the immediate days after birth, the baby is not expected to display any sense of moral or prudential values.

Table 5-1 (continued)
The Developing Individual
Progressively Improving Status

The Infant (1 month to 18 months)
Differentiated needs

Status. Needs, as reflected in preferences, become more specific as the months pass. Infants increasingly express selective tastes among foods and playthings without regard for sharing or for others' rights of ownership. Infants display preferences among people without regard for people's feelings.

Intellectual maturity

Status. Recall of objects and events, the understanding of language, and the ability to reason rapidly improve. Meaningful speech begins around age 9 to 14 months, with speaking vocabulary by 18 months ranging from a few words to several dozen.

Physical skills

Status. Infants change from immobile beings at age 1 month to ones that can walk, run, and manually manipulate objects with growing skill by age 18 months. The increasing mobility and manual dexterity enable them to reach places and handle objects that can threaten their own and others' safety and can encroach on others' rights (Osofsky, 1978).

Internalized values

Status. Infants appear to have few, if any, internalized values. They begin to connect certain events, places, objects, and people with pain or unpleasantness and other events, places, objects, and people with pleasure. However, the connection may be weak and ill defined.

Differentiated emotions

Status. Emotions become increasingly differentiated beyond a sense of comfort and discomfort, so that by 18 months a typical young child's affective responses suggest different degrees of joy, despair, amusement, disgust, fear, eagerness, anger, and more.

Responses to consequences

Status. The maturing infant increasingly recognizes which events are likely to bring pain and which are likely to bring pleasure. However, infants are so new to the world that a great many events are novel; thus, young children find it difficult to predict the consequences that are apt to occur from different sorts of behavior. Likewise, their limited skill at generalizing from one instance to another constrains their ability to foresee what sorts of reactions their behavior is likely to elicit from a particular environment.

Table 5-1 (continued)
The Developing Individual
Agents, Services, Rights, and Responsibilities

The Infant's Social Setting (1 month to 18 months)
Agents

The most important people composing the infant's environment are typically such immediate caregivers as the biological mother, the father, siblings, a grandmother, and baby-sitters or nannies. In North America since the middle of the 20th century, two changes in social organization patterns have yielded particularly significant consequences for child-rearing practices. First has been the growing number of mothers who work outside the home, so they are not available to look after their offspring full time. Second has been the increase of one-parent families, principally of families in which there is no father in the home. This expansion of one-parent homes has resulted primarily from a rapid increase in the divorce rate and a growing number of infants born to unwed mothers, especially to unwed teenagers. The changes have meant that young children's moral environments (a) are less likely to have a permanent male adult in the home and (b) are more likely to find the chief care of an infant alternating between a biological mother and some sort of baby-sitter or nanny, with two such caregivers often differing in the moral standards they hold for the growing child. Those differences can be expected to cause a measure of confusion for the infant, who is punished for (or at least discouraged from) certain kinds of behavior by one caregiver but not by the other.

Services

Because infants command only meager skills or internalized values (contents of conscience) to guide their actions, caretakers are obliged (a) to manipulate environments in ways that prevent infants from doing harm and intruding on others' rights and (b) to physically remove infants from settings in which they may breach social custom. Or people may resort to physical punishment—slapping, shaking, pinching, or the like. This physical force is typically accompanied by an angry shout—"No" or "Stop that" or "Don't do that"—in an attempt to connect the words with the punishment in the child's mind, so that in the future the words themselves may become consequences sufficient to control the infant's behavior (Bandura, 1991).

Rights, privileges, and responsibilities

Infants' rights are represented by the services they deserve. But even by age 18 months, infants are not considered morally responsible persons. They are barely learning to monitor their own actions. The people and the institutions in their immediate environment accept the entire responsibility for supervising the social behavior of the toddler.

Table 5-1 (continued)
The Developing Individual
Progressively Improving Status

The Young Child (18 months through 5 years)
Differentiated needs
     Status. Needs, as reflected in preferences, become more numerous and specific. Increasingly, needs are socially determined, in the sense that the young child acquires motives and desires from observing the sorts of things other people desire and obtain.
Intellectual maturity
     Status. The typical preschool child's concepts grow at a rapid pace, as reflected in a vocabulary of approximately 300 words at age 2, of 1,500 at age 4, and over 2,000 at age 5 (M. E. Smith, 1926; Bloom 1964).
Physical skills
     Status. Young children's advances in physical coordination and strength equip them to manipulate objects with increasing skill and to run, jump, climb, throw, push, pull, lift, and hit with growing accuracy. These abilities enable them to engage in a widening range of behaviors, including ones that may cause harm and violate society's rules about other people's rights.
Internalized values
     Status. As the result of the pattern of punishment and reward that their environment has imposed for different kinds of social behavior over the years, young children develop internal criteria for what is socially approved and disapproved. As part of their progress toward intellectual maturity, children can increasingly identify which actions are *good* or *right* and which are *bad* or *wrong*. This is the true beginning of a conscience.
Differentiated emotions
     Status. Internalized moral values are accompanied by positive and negative emotions. Acting in ways that comply with the standards of *good behavior* results in feelings of pride and self-satisfaction. Acting contrary to standards of *good behavior* brings feelings of guilt, shame, and diminished self-worth.
Responses to consequences
     Status. By dint of their increased intellectual maturity, children improve in recognizing connections between specific behaviors and the consequences those behaviors incur. Thus, they are more competent in predicting what will likely result from different ways to act in moral-decision situations. Furthermore, young children's rudimentary consciences begin to serve as monitors of moral action by creating pleasant emotions for abiding by internalized values and by imposing unpleasant emotions for violating those values. Hence, the young child's moral behavior increasingly invites internal as well as external consequences (Grusec & Lytton, 1988).

Table 5-1 (continued)
The Developing Individual
Agents, Services, Rights, and Responsibilities

The Young Child's Social Setting (18 months through 5 years)
Agents

The agents in the child's moral environment expand beyond the family and immediate caregivers to include agemates in the neighborhood, child-care center, or nursery school. In most homes in many societies, television now assumes a significant role in offering models of behavior for the young to emulate and moral values that may or may not be acceptable to children's family members. Hence, this period of life typically confronts children with a growing diversity of moral values from which to choose.

Services

Children continue to depend principally on their family for food and shelter, physical and psychological protection, forms of amusement, instruction in social rules, emotional support, and reward or punishment for abiding by or for violating moral and prudential precepts.

Rights, privileges, and responsibilities

The rights to which young children are entitled are found chiefly in the services they can expect. As the young appear more competent to care for their own needs, they are often provided more privileges in the form of freedom to carry out activities with minimal adult direction. At the same time, children are gradually delegated responsibility for dressing themselves, doing minor chores around the house and nursery school, and obeying customs and rules when not directly supervised by adults or older siblings (Winegar & Valsiner, 1992).

Table 5-1 (continued)
The Developing Individual
Progressively Improving Status

The School-Age Child (ages 6 through 11)
Differentiated needs

   Status. Needs and drives continue to grow more numerous and specific as influenced by an expanding social environment in which a greater range of people display their preferences for objects, activities, companions, and models to emulate.

Intellectual maturity

   Status. The typical elementary-school pupil's concepts continue to expand at an accelerating rate, so that by age eight, children have 50% of the vocabulary they will have at age 18 (Bloom, 1964). It becomes increasingly apparent that the advancing years bring marked differences among children in their command of concepts. For example, M. K. Smith (1941) found that among six-year-olds, individuals' vocabularies ranged between 5,500 and 32,000 words. In judging moral issues, school-age children grow in their ability to see moral episodes from different people's viewpoints, rather than solely from their own perspective. They also can cite a greater variety of possible causes behind moral events (Overton, 1983; Siegler, 1990).

Physical skills

   Status. Improved strength and agility equip children to engage in an wide range of activities, including team sports and competitive games played according to rules. Playing by the rules becomes a matter of great consequence.

Internalized values

   Status. The contents and power of conscience increase. As a result, school-age children's moral and prudential acts are more frequently influenced by their growing sense of right and wrong whenever they are not directly supervised by people in authority.

Differentiated emotions

   Status. Children advance in their ability to explain how and why they feel as they do about moral matters. They are often able to admit ambivalent emotions about moral events, simultaneously expressing both anger toward, and affection for, such people as parents who punish wrongdoing.

Responses to consequences

   Status. The behavior of school-age children is increasingly influenced (a) by verbal approval and disapproval rather than such physical consequences as sweets for a reward and spanking or isolation for a punishment and (b) by conscience. Externally applied consequences create the contents of conscience, in that "people's self-reinforcement is at least initially governed largely by external reinforcement" (Loevinger, 1987, p. 158).

Table 5-1 (continued)
The Developing Individual
Agents, Services, Rights, and Responsibilities

The School-Age Child (ages 6 through 11)
Agents

The greatest expansion in agents who affect children's moral development derives from the child's attending school. Throughout the elementary-school years, pupils are under the constant, systematic influence of teachers, of other pupils, and of instructional media (books, television programs, videotaped lessons, simulation games) designed to form learners' moral values and behavior. Teachers reflect moral beliefs fostered by the dominant socio-political forces in the community. In schools that feature considerable cultural diversity in their enrollments, the population of pupils confronts children with a greater variety of moral attitudes and practices than the children likely met during their preschool years. As a result, learners face a widening range of choices about what to believe and about how to act in moral situations, with some of the potential options endorsed, and others condemned, by school personnel. A child can become confused when the moral convictions represented by the school fail to match those of the child's home. Likewise, the moral attitudes and behavior of certain classmates may conflict with the school's position or that of the child's family (Rubin & Ross, 1982; Shantz & Hartup, 1992). Moral values and behavior that children adopt are ones most often reinforced by the people the children most esteem or perhaps most fear.

Services

Children still depend heavily on their family for food and shelter, physical and psychological protection, spending money, instruction in social rules, emotional support, and reward or punishment for abiding by or for violating moral and prudential precepts. The school bears the main burden of equipping the young with communication skills (reading, writing, calculating, culturally approved ways of speaking) and knowledge of history, of one's own culture as well as others' cultures, and of the world of nature. Embedded in these studies are moral values reflected in such terms as *environmental pollution, religious rights, the justice system, majority rule, freedom of speech,* and much more.

Rights, privileges, and responsibilities

Attending school is both a right and a responsibility in industrialized societies, but is a privilege in many developing nations that cannot afford to furnish everyone formal education. Where educational facilities are widely available, children are not only held responsible for attending school but also for doing well, that is, for achieving up to their potential. Failing to do well in school often leads pupils to neglect their studies, become truant, and engage in antisocial activities that may lead to a future life of lawbreaking.

Table 5-1 (continued)
The Developing Individual
Progressively Improving Status

The Adolescent (ages 12 through 17)
Differentiated needs
     Status. Needs and goals continue to grow more differentiated. Crossing the
threshold of puberty heightens teenagers' interest in ways of venting their sex
drives. The need for peer approval typically increases and may lead to behavior
intended to curry peer acceptance but that conflicts with traditional societal
rules and family values.
Intellectual maturity
     Status. Youths advance in their comprehension of complex moral issues.
Some adopt philosophical ideals that influence their moral decisions and are
apt to endorse social movements that feature religious and ethical precepts. By
the end of adolescence, they are capable of adult levels of moral reasoning.
However, there can be vast differences between individuals in their reasoning
skills and stockpile of knowledge (Sprinthall & Collins, 1984).
Physical growth
     Status. Puberty initiates bodily changes that accentuate differences in the
appearance of the sexes, such as breast development in girls and voice change
and facial hair in boys. In early adolescence the average girl is taller and
heavier than the average boy; but by the end of adolescence, boys have
surpassed girls in height, weight, and strength. Changing physical appearance
affects individuals' appeal to their peers and influences their self concepts. The
changes may affect moral behavior, such as by motivating teens to commit
antisocial acts in response to peer rejection, teasing, or seduction (Ketterlinus
& Lamb, 1994).
Internalized values
     Status. The contents and power of conscience continue to expand, so that
adolescents' behavior is increasingly guided by internalized moral values rather
than—or in addition to—the prospect of immediate rewards or punishments
(Pritchard, 1991).
Differentiated emotions
     Status. Emotions associated with sexual drives and peer approval (affection,
resentment, fear of rejection, joy, sadness) assume greater importance in
judgments and behavior during moral encounters.
Responses to consequences
     Status. As a result of their improved reasoning skills and greater store of
experiences, teenagers are better equipped than younger children to predict the
sorts of consequences they might expect from alternative kinds of behavior in
moral situations.

Table 5-1 (continued)
The Developing Individual
Agents, Services, Rights, and Responsibilities

The Adolescent (ages 12 through 17)
Agents

Peers and mass-communication media—television, movies, videos, popular songs, magazines—become stronger sources of influence on teenagers' moral values and actions. Peers are of special importance because they, rather than parents, are so often present on the occasions in which adolescents are obliged to make decisions about whether to try alcohol or drugs, to shoplift, to engage in sexual intercourse, to cheat on tests, to drive recklessly, and more. Mass-communication sources frequently offer models of behavior that promise such coveted rewards as popularity, sexual gratification, and emotional thrills. However, the behavior exemplified by the models may conflict with the society's or family's traditional moral standards. Formally organized youth groups—teams, clubs, church organizations—typically promote traditional moral values (Carlson & Lewis, 1988). Teenagers' moral behavior is increasingly affected more by social consequences than by physical consequences.

Services

Teenagers still depend heavily on their family for food and shelter, physical and psychological protection, spending money, emotional support, and reward or punishment for abiding by or for violating moral and prudential precepts. However, peers increasingly offer emotional support, partially replacing parents as confidantes with whom they share intimate thoughts. Peers assume a major role in providing the teenager's recreational pursuits and companionship. In the United States, society protects youthful lawbreakers from full prosecution as adults by providing juvenile courts and detention centers, by furnishing social workers, and by prohibiting the news media from publicizing transgressors' identities.

Rights, privileges, and responsibilities

Most societies practice rites of passage that signal adolescents' promotion to opportunities and obligations approaching those of adults. Typical privileges and responsibilities in industrialized societies include full membership in a church, chances for paid employment, permission to drive a car, and the option of dropping out of compulsory schooling programs. Teenagers are treated by law-enforcement bodies as being more liable for their behavior than are young children, yet not as liable as adults. Thus, adolescents are regarded as en route to adult status.

Table 5-1 (continued)
The Developing Individual
Progressively Improving Status

The Young Adult (ages 18 through 25)
Differentiated needs
　　Status. In addition to youths' continuing concern for social acceptance and sexual drives, their needs and goals shift more toward career plans, earning a living, and the matter of selecting a life long partner. The way these choices are made is influenced by the pattern of moral values that by now is a well-established component of the young adult's personality.
Intellectual maturity
　　Status. The young adult advances further in comprehending complex moral issues. By the mid-20s the idealism that perhaps marked the teen years may be moderated somewhat by the acceptance of life's realities that cause people's moral behavior to fall short of the ideal. Marked differences between individuals in their moral reasoning and their stockpile of knowledge tend to increase, partially because a portion of the young-adult population pursues advanced formal education that tends to enhance awareness of moral issues.
Physical growth
　　Status. Most young adults have reached their maximum growth in height. Their body shapes and facial features have reached the state that will be relatively fixed over the next two decades or so. This physical appearance and improved strength and agility can affect moral development by influencing the activities individuals pursue and by partially determining whether others accept or reject a person.
Internalized values
　　Status. The contents and power of conscience continue to expand, so that young adults' behavior is increasingly guided by internalized moral values rather than—or in addition to—the prospect of immediate rewards or punishments.
Differentiated emotions
　　Status. As in adolescence, emotions associated with sexual drives and peer approval (affection, resentment, fear of rejection, joy, sadness) continue to strongly affect the young adult's judgments and behavior in moral episodes.
Responses to consequences
　　Status. Their greater store of experiences enables young adults to predict more accurately than do adolescents the sorts of consequences they might expect from alternative kinds of behavior in moral situations. By age 25 people are usually considered more responsible than they were a decade earlier.

Table 5-1 (continued)
The Developing Individual
Agents, Services, Rights, and Responsibilities

The Young Adult (ages 18 through 25)
Agents

The diversity of agents that can influence individuals' moral development expands during the young-adult years, particularly as affected by the greater mobility and freedom afforded by the transition to adult status. Youths move away from home, enter an occupation, travel away to college, and enjoy greater opportunities for recreational pursuits, including admission to X-rated movies, adult bookstores, nightclubs, and bars.

Services

Services formerly furnished by others—principally by the family—are ones young adults are expected to provide for themselves. Thus, officially, youths are no longer expected to need parents' support for food, clothing, shelter, or general finances. However, in reality families are often obliged to continue furnishing such services, especially if youths are attending college, enter low-paying employment, or prove ill prepared to shoulder burdens they have incurred, as in the case of unwed mothers with one or more children. As they now are increasingly freed from the control of parents and teachers, some young adults are prone to breach laws or customs that formerly they were obliged by their care-takers to respect.

Rights, privileges, and responsibilities

Persons in the age range 18 through 21 are officially accorded rights available only to adults. In the United States those such rights include the opportunity to vote in public elections, purchase alcohol and tobacco products, wed or have an abortion without parents' consent, bear offspring without censure, and be tried in a criminal court before a jury (aided by a defense lawyer) rather than tried before a juvenile court judge (usually without counsel). The rights are accompanied by new responsibilities that were formerly borne by parents, such as providing for one's own financial support, being available for military service, and being held fully liable for indebtedness and for violating the law. Misusing the rights or failing to bear the responsibilities in a manner deemed proper by the society can be regarded as moral wrongdoing.

Functions of Consequences

In the field of psychology, such behaviorists as B. F. Skinner (1974) have stressed the importance of consequences as determiners of people's future actions. The formula for understanding why people act the way they do is rather simple. Every time someone acts, the action is followed by a consequence. The nature of the consequence determines whether the person will act in the same way in a similar situation in the future. If the consequence is pleasant and rewarding (reinforcing), then the person will tend to act in the same way in the future. If the consequence is not rewarding [punishing or merely nonreinforcing], then the person will subsequently tend to act differently in similar settings.

Social-learning theorists, like behaviorists, view consequences as important in molding behavior. According to Bandura (1977), the results that follow an individual's actions affect future behavior by providing *information* and by influencing the person's future *motivation*. Consequences in their informative function tell a person whether a given act will likely lead to pleasant or unpleasant outcomes on a later occasion. Those actions that promise positive, welcome outcomes are likely to be repeated. Those that have produced unwelcome results are likely to be avoided in the future. Furthermore, consequences in their motivational role help determine how enthusiastically a person will try to learn behavior exhibited by a model. For example, if a child observes that a classmate's apologizing to the teacher for having misbehaved has led to the teacher's providing attractive rewards for the apologizer, then the observer will be more highly motivated to learn techniques of apology than otherwise would be the case.

In summary, from Bandura's social-cognition perspective, moral development can be viewed as a process of (a) children's gradually expanding their repertoire of moral values and moral actions by means of both observing others as models and trying the actions themselves and (b) using information from the observed and directly experienced consequences to guide future decisions about whether one sort of moral behavior will be better than another in fulfilling one's needs and obtaining rewards.

Self-efficacy

An important element of Bandura's scheme is how people's actions are influenced by their sense of power and ability—that is, by their sense of self-efficacy. According to Bandura, a sense of self-efficacy is built up through past successful social encounters, producing an attitude that regulates subsequent moral functioning through four major processes: cognition, emotion, motivation, and selection. Cognitive processes involve people analyzing their own moral behavior in relation to (a) their personal values and (b) feedback (experienced consequences) from their surroundings on how well they have been able to cope with their moral encounters. These analyses (cognition) are then joined by the individuals' feelings about their experiences (emotion) to influence the behaviors they attempt (selection) and to determine how strongly they try to succeed (motivation) at those behaviors (Bandura, 1990).

With the foregoing discussion of moral development as a background, we turn now to summarizing how typical social-learning advocates respond to guide questions posed in Chapter 1.

ANSWERS TO GUIDE QUESTIONS

From a social-learning perspective, the moral domain is defined by the particular array of moral values to which the people of a given social group—a society, a clan, a family—are dedicated. Certain of these principles (prohibitions against murder, incest, lying, theft) are essentially universal since they promote the general welfare of the members of all, or nearly all, societies. Other values, or the conditions under which moral values are applied, can differ from one social system to another. Good moral development consists of individuals' adopting their reference groups' principles. People's observed behavior, rather than their verbal testimonials, shows the extent to which they have indeed internalized the desired values.

Social-learning theorists generally believe that children are born amoral, with no inclination toward either good or bad behavior. However, children do bring into the world a capacity to internalize moral values learned from their environment. The internalized representation of moral precepts (usually called *conscience*) provides emotional consequences that affect moral behavior— feelings of pride and self-satisfaction for abiding by adopted standards, and feelings of guilt, shame, and fear for violating those values.

Moral development is viewed as a life long process, in that the social environment at any time can affect an individual's values and behavior by the models it offers and the consequences that follow actions in moral encounters. However, experiences of children and youth during the first two decades of life are particularly potent influences on moral development since they form the basic convictions on which all subsequent moral experiences are founded.

Reality from a social-cognition viewpoint includes (a) people's personality characteristics (physical appearance, needs, physical and mental abilities, emotions, rate of maturation, self-concept) and (b) the physical/social environments that influence the models of behavior people witness and the types of consequences that follow different moral actions. No supernatural forces, such as invisible spirits that might affect moral events, are included in social-learning theories.

Differences between individuals in their moral thought and action result from permutations of people's personality characteristics and the diverse social settings they inhabit.

Evidence in support of the social-learning model derives from the interpretation of social experiments and of observations of people in moral situations rather than from doctrine issued by a seer or an ostensible authority.

In popularity, social-learning approaches have enjoyed the support of a substantial portion of the community of developmentalists and social psychologists and have led to a large quantity of empirical research. For instance, more than 200 research studies conducted from a social-learning perspective were reported in *Psychological Abstracts* for the years 1983-1994.

AN ASSESSMENT OF SOCIAL-LEARNING THEORY

As in previous chapters, the following assessment focuses on the eight standards described in Chapter 2.

To begin, I find descriptions of social-learning theory easy to understand (item 1). The key features of the theory are typically well illustrated with examples from life or with descriptions of the results of experiments.

Social-learning models are well equipped to explain the factors that apparently account for individuals' past and present states of moral development (item 2). However, the models' ability to predict future development is limited by a predictor's lack of knowledge of the kinds of social environments a person will experience in years to come and of the types of consequences resulting from those experiences. Cognitive-structuralist theories that propose a series of stages through which everyone is expected to pass are better suited to forecasting the nature of children's future moral growth.

Social-learning theories offer specific suggestions about how to promote desirable development and correct moral behavior that has gone awry (item 3). For example, Bandura's perspective has served as the foundation for widely adopted behavior-modification practices (Alberto & Troutman, 1986; Grabowski, Stitzer, & Henningfield, 1984; Morris & Braukmann, 1987; Thomas, 1989).

As the source of a host of hypotheses that can be empirically tested, social-learning theories render themselves amenable to verification and disconfirmation (item 4).

Such theorists as Bandura appear willing to incorporate new findings into their proposals (item 5), as suggested by their recognizing a wide variety of studies in their writings and by altering or refining their positions to accommodate others' viewpoints (Bandura, 1986, 1991). The fertility of social-learning approaches in stimulating new discoveries is affirmed by the large quantity of empirical investigations and theoretical alternatives deriving from those approaches over the past two decades or more (item 6).

Social-Learning Theory

How well do I think the theory meets the standards?

The Standards	Very Well	Moderately Well	Very Poorly
1. Is clearly understandable	X		
2. Explains past and predicts future moral behavior		X	
3. Offers practical guidance in coping with moral matters	X		
4. Is readily verifiable and falsifiable	X		
5. Accommodates new evidence	X		
6. Stimulates new discoveries	X		
7. Is durable		X	
8. Is self-satisfying	X		

Social-learning or social-cognition theories are not static models. Rather, they shift and grow as investigators identify putative weaknesses and propose new vantage points from which to view moral development. Thus, the durability of a given version of the theory is not great. However, the general conception —placing learning from models and from consequences at the center of moral development—continues to be popular in the world of secular theories. For this reason I have rated social-learning theories in the *moderately well* position for their durability (item 7).

Overall, I find the social-learning explanations of moral development quite convincing (item 8).

6

Psychoanalysis

As an approach to interpreting moral development, psychoanalytic theory is distinguished by four interlinked assumptions:

1. All human behavior is driven by inborn instincts. One of the most important of the instincts is the sexual drive—a motivating force that seeks satisfaction of sensual needs from the time of birth through old age.

2. Instincts express themselves through actions in the real world. In other words, people must find ways to fulfill their instinctual needs by interacting with their physical and social environments. However, not just any type of behavior is acceptable to the environment, since society has rules and customs that dictate which ways of expressing instincts will be permitted and which will not.

3. Agents in the individual's environment monitor the person's methods of fulfilling needs, informing the person about which methods are acceptable and which are not. As a means of influencing the person's methods of need fulfillment, such agents as parents, teachers, pastors, the police, and others reward approved methods and punish forbidden ones.

4. As children grow up, they gradually incorporate into their own personalities the expectations about behavior that have been imposed on them by significant agents. These expectations are the individual's moral values. As the values become internalized, it is no longer necessary for outside agents to apply sanctions to control the person's behavior. Instead, the individual's conscience now serves as the monitor, rewarding approved actions with feelings of pride and self-worth, and punishing forbidden acts with feelings of guilt, shame, and fear.

The first purpose of Chapter 6 is to describe the theory of personality that the creator of psychoanalysis, Sigmund Freud, devised to explain the process of moral development as founded on the foregoing assumptions. The second purpose is to identify variations of psychoanalysis proposed by proponents of psychoanalysis known as neo-Freudians. The initial, major portion of the chapter focuses on Freud's formulation of psychoanalysis. The second, shorter segment of the chapter sketches alterations in the theory advanced by two of his most prominent disciples, Erik Erikson and Erich Fromm.

FREUD'S PSYCHOANALYTIC THEORY

This description of a psychoanalytic version of moral development treats the following topics: (1) Freud's mission, (2) a psychoanalytic anatomy of personality, (3) stages of psychosexual development, (4) the nature of values, and (5) causes and individual differences.

Freud's Mission

In the final decades of the 19th century, Sigmund Freud's (1856-1939) psychiatric practice in Vienna, Austria, confronted him with some very puzzling cases. Patients came to him with symptoms that could not be explained in relation to the condition of their nerves. Neurological tests revealed no damage to their neural systems that could account for such complaints as paralysis of the arm, deafness, blurred vision, pain across a section of skin, and more. During this same period, Freud learned of experiments with hypnotism conducted in Paris by Jean Charcot, experiments that enabled Charcot to induce physical symptoms in people by suggesting, while they were in a hypnotized state, that they suffered such ailments. When Charcot's subjects were brought out of the hypnotic condition, they did indeed display the suggested disorders, even though they failed to recall anything that had occurred while they were hypnotized. In addition, Charcot demonstrated that people who came to his clinic with a variety of ailments—headaches, nausea, paralysis of limbs, and more—could often be rid of their complaints by means of suggestions he gave them under hypnosis.

Freud's experiences with his own patients, coupled with his study of hypnosis in Charcot's clinic in 1885-1886, impelled him to create a theory of human personality that would account for these strange phenomena. Moral development would be a central concern in the resulting theory. In devising his model, Freud sought to answer the question: What is the structure of human personality, and how does this structure evolve over the years of childhood and adolescence? In the following pages, we first inspect Freud's ideas about personality structure, then consider the stages through which he believed such a structure developed.

A Psychoanalytic Anatomy of Personality

Freud presumed that the adult personality consists of three operatives—*id, ego,* and *superego*—that have evolved over the first two decades of life and function at various levels of consciousness. To understand how this system works, it is useful to begin with the notion of *states* or *levels* of consciousness.

Levels of Consciousness

As a means of explaining the obscure symptoms he observed in his patients, Freud proposed that people's daily lives often confront them with moral dilemmas that they cannot readily solve.

A son finds himself sexually attracted to his mother, but he realizes that such cravings are highly disapproved by society.

A one-year-old is urged by her distressed parents to defecate in the toilet rather than in her diaper, but she does not have sufficient control of the sphincter muscles of her intestinal tract to comply with her parents' demands.

A teenage boy yearns for his parents' love and approval, yet highly resents the rules they set for how and with whom he spends his spare time.

A teenage girl is tempted to have sexual intercourse with her boyfriend, yet she fears the punishment that would be imposed by God if she yielded to that temptation.

A young woman, physically and emotionally exhausted while caring for her dying father, falls asleep at his bedside, then suddenly wakens with feelings of shame and guilt for having neglected her vigil and for resenting the burden of responsibility imposed on her by her father's illness.

Freud speculated that whenever such dilemmas became too painful to bear, people automatically dismissed the moral conflicts from consciousness, solving their problem by relegating the distressing thoughts to an unconscious state. However, in Freud's opinion, the dilemmas were not truly solved, only postponed by being *repressed* into an unconscious chamber of the personality. In this unconscious state the conflicts continued to seethe, expressing their agony in such disguised forms as the bodily ailments reported by Freud's patients. Not only were physical disorders, which he called *conversion hysteria symptoms*, the consequence of mental conflicts, but so also were all the neurotic symptoms that people suffered, including phobias, obsessions, compulsions, and anxieties.

To account for the neuroses and thereby cure patients of their distressing symptoms, Freud proposed that the unresolved moral conflicts needed to be brought into consciousness so that the afflicted individual might recognize their origin and relive the dilemmas in a realistic fashion, accepting them for what they were. Freud tried three main techniques for unmasking the vexing episodes from which the conflicts had originated. The techniques were those of hypnosis, free association, and dream interpretation. But he soon "came to dislike hypnosis, for it was a temperamental and . . . mystical ally" (Freud, 1910, p. 22), so henceforth he abandoned it in favor of free association and dream interpretation.

The process of free association consists of encouraging a patient to relax, usually on a couch, and to describe free-flowing thoughts without editing them. The psychoanalyst listens to hours of such narration in order to locate underlying themes of moral conflict that symbolize hidden problems. In doing so, the therapist assumes that "the repressed wishful impulse . . . is on the look-out for an opportunity to be activated, and when that happens it succeeds in sending into consciousness a disguised and unrecognizable substitute for what has been repressed" (Freud, 1910, p. 27). It is the analyst's task to unveil the tell tale elements of the patient's narration and reveal them for what they represent in the sufferer's earlier development.

In parallel with free association, Freud used dream interpretation as a window, albeit warped and misty, for viewing the contents of the unconscious. He believed that during sleep, a censor force, which seeks to prevent unconscious conflicts from entering consciousness, is not as alert as during the waking hours. Thus, dreams, in psychoanalytic theory, are products of people trying to satisfy wishes and solve problems during sleep. Dreams are symbols of unconscious urges pressing for expression into consciousness. The analyst endeavors to interpret dream images as tokens of repressed conflicts from the individual's past (Freud, 1900).

Freud not only conceived of both conscious and unconscious aspects of personality, but he also distinguished two levels of the unconscious. One level contains those ideas that are not in consciousness at the moment. They are latent, but can be recalled if we choose, even though it may take some effort. This first level Fred labeled the *preconscious*. The second level contains the truly repressed ideas, those buried intentionally by the personality's resistance forces because allowing them to enter consciousness would be too painful for the person to endure. This second level, deeper and less accessible than the preconscious, is the true, prototype *unconscious* in psychoanalytic theory. In effect, the preconscious is a shadow zone between the open, bright conscious and the closed, dark unconscious (Freud, 1923, pp. 4-5).

The Psychic Functionaries

In addition to defining levels of consciousness as the arena in which psychic life is lived, Freud equipped human personality with three principal functionaries whose interactions determine how people think and behave in moral situations. He named the three *id, ego,* and *superego.* In the course of a child's development, the three do not arise simultaneously. The id comes first—already present at birth. The ego begins to develop during infancy and early childhood. The superego appears some time later. In order to explain how the id, ego, and superego evolve in relation Freud's stages of psychosexual development, I first describe the functions of these three psychic operatives, then later describe their relationships to Freud's growth stages.

Instincts and the Id. Freud contended that the energy needed to activate all growth and behavior derived from instincts that reside in the unconscious. After experimenting with several conceptions of instincts, he finally settled on a fundamental pair of forces—the *life* and *death* instincts—which he said competed for dominance in directing psychic energy throughout the life span. The life instinct (*eros*) expresses itself in constructive acts of love, creation, self-sacrifice, and altruism. The death instinct (*thanatos*) displays its influence in destructive acts, hate, and aggression. Freud applied the word *libido* to the energy arising from the life instinct, but he coined no parallel term for the death-instinct energy (Freud, 1920).

From the perspective of instincts, the process of development consists of a constant struggle between the life and death forces—love against hate, life preservation against self-destruction. Although throughout childhood and well into the adult years the life instinct appears to be more prominent, the ultimate victory goes to the death force as the human organism ultimately loses all animation and returns to a state of inert chemicals.

In Freud's system, the id is the psychic agent representing the instincts. It is the single operating component in the newborn's personality. The id "contains everything that is inherited, that is present at birth, that is laid down in the constitution—above all, the instincts" (Freud, 1938, p. 2). Libidinal energy within the id builds up as a form of pressure searching for expression. The pressure represents needs demanding fulfillment. Release of the pressure is experienced by the infant as pleasure. The postponement or blocking of release is felt as pain. Thus, the id operates on the *pleasure principle* of getting as much enjoyment and avoiding as much pain as possible. Consequently, psychoanalytic theory pictures the neonate as all id, seeking only to satisfy its needs for food, for drink, for eliminating bodily wastes, and for affection. The newborn's view of the world is quite nebulous, making no clear distinctions between self and the environment. The baby is aware only of discomfort and pain, which signal unfulfilled needs that demand attention, and of pleasure and relief when those needs are satisfied.

As the days and weeks pass, the infant's increased experience with the world leads to a growing awareness of the environment, an awareness that produces the personality's *primary process*—the baby's act of creating in its mind the image of an object that will fulfill a need. To illustrate, when newborns feel hunger pangs, they cry until someone feeds them. The food reduces the tension of hunger, and the baby experiences pleasure. As the days pass, this cycle of hunger, feeding, and tension reduction is repeated time and again, so gradually the taste, smell, feel, and sight of the food and of the feeder are stored as images in the infant's memory. Consequently, the baby, by dint of the primary process, can now imagine those objects that will bring a particular kind of satisfaction through a particular means of expending libidinal energy.

From the viewpoint of moral development, it is important to recognize that the primary process is *amoral*. The id has no sense of society's concepts of right and wrong. From the id's hedonistic perspective, whatever gives pleasure is right and whatever gives pain is wrong. However, because the environment will not tolerate such a self-indulgent approach to life, the growing child's personality now requires a component that recognizes the requirements of the environment as well as the demands of the id. This new component is expected to provide morally realistic methods of investing instinctual energy. Freud gave the name *ego* to this second of the personality's operatives.

The Ego. Freud explained that "the ego is that part of the id which has been modified by the direct influence of the external world through the medium" of conscious perception (Freud, 1923, p. 15).

> It is to this ego that consciousness is attached; the ego controls the . . . discharge of excitations into the external world; it is the mental agency which supervises all its own constituent processes, and which goes to sleep at night, though even then it exercises the censorship on dreams. (Freud, 1923, p. 7)

Whereas the id resides entirely in the unconscious and displays no awareness of the reality of the world, the ego is conscious and well aware of the opportunities and restrictions of the environment. The ego thus serves as a go-between or referee that negotiates between the id's demands and the requirements of the physical and social environments, endeavoring to find realistic ways of satisfying the id's needs within the limitations imposed by the society in which the child is reared. The ego provides the child with an initial sense of morality, a recognition of the rules and customs that guide social relations, and an awareness of the penalties assessed for violating social custom.

Whereas the id operates according to the primary process (envisioning images that will fulfill needs), it becomes the ego's task to translate these images into actions that can actually be implemented. Freud called this function of the ego the *secondary process*.

As the months and years advance, children engage in a growing diversity of environmental encounters. They seek to satisfy their physical and psychological needs without unduly antagonizing the people around them, and they witness others in their immediate surroundings, in story books, and on television programs trying to resolve moral dilemmas. From these encounters children acquire an expanding repertoire of ways to act in moral situations, and they learn which of these ways are morally more acceptable than others. In effect, as the ego develops, it evolves techniques for accommodating to the conflicting demands made on it by the id and the environment. A strong, mature ego uses direct means to accomplish this. It frankly admits both the instinctual demands and the environment's rules. Then it adopts forthright, reasoned, morally acceptable ways to effect a solution that satisfies each source of demand to a reasonable degree. For example, when caught committing a mistake, a boy frankly admits the error and seeks to make restitution. In the realm of sexual behavior, a young woman outrightly acknowledges her strong sexual drives, then satisfies those drives in ways that do not exploit or offend other people. When judging cases of wrongdoing, a jury member bases decisions on a careful weighing of the evidence, then firmly defends the decisions in the face of criticism.

However, an ego that is weak and immature slips into using more devious techniques for accommodating both the instinctual demands and the expectations of the environment. Freud called these techniques *ego defense mechanisms* or *ego adjustment mechanisms.* When the ego feels unable to solve a moral conflict by direct means, yet it cannot admit this inadequacy, it substitutes a circuitous mode of addressing the problem. The most significant of these defense mechanisms, *repression*, has already been described. Repression is an automatic, nonconscious process of pushing disturbing matters out of consciousness into the unconscious. The phenomenon of repression demonstrates that the ego can operate at more than one level of consciousness. Not only may the ego's judgments be arrived at through intentional, logical, fully conscious thought, but judgments also can be performed below the threshold of awareness, performed as automatic functions that save the individual from the embarrassment of recognizing those functions' devious nature.

A second defense mechanism is *projection*, which consists of accusing other people of unworthy motives and feelings that the accuser actually harbors but is ashamed or afraid to acknowledge. Because the individual finds it too painful to admit having objectionable or offensive urges, the ego seeks to relieve this discomfort by attributing unacceptable id demands to other people rather than to oneself. A youth who harbors hate in his own unconscious will accuse others of hating him, claiming at the same time that he himself bears no malice. A woman who is repressing strong sexual desires of which she is ashamed will contend that others are trying to seduce or assault her.

Another device is *regression*—returning to an earlier, more primitive mode of adjusting to moral dilemmas. At the police station, a young man arrested for shoplifting breaks into tears and crumples to the floor. A woman apprehended passing forged checks explodes in a temper tantrum, knocking over furniture and screaming at her accusers.

Rationalization involves offering a socially acceptable reason for a behavior that actually was motivated by a less honorable intention. A passerby, when caught removing a wallet from the pocket of a drunk lying on the sidewalk, claims that he was simply trying to discover the inebriate's name and address so he could take the man home. A schoolgirl, who went to a movie instead of doing her homework, feigns illness the next day to avoid attending school without the completed assignment.

Escape consists of leaving the scene of a distressing situation. The escape can be either physical (a hit-and-run motorist, a truant student) or psychological (a day dreaming delinquent youth during a juvenile-court hearing, a witness at a murder trial who has "forgotten" what he saw the night of the crime).

Each of the foregoing adjustment techniques provides some temporary relief from the dilemmas people face but fail to solve the conflicts in a lasting fashion. Repression leaves conflicts buried in the unconscious, continuing to roil and vent their distress through neurotic symptoms. Regression returns the ego to a less mature stage of development. Escape usually does no more than postpone the task of resolving moral issues. Rationalization is simply self-deception that diminishes the individual's ability to cope with reality. However, two additional defense mechanisms—compensation and sublimation—are regarded as more constructive and thus morally superior to the others.

Compensation involves substituting success in a realm of life other than the realm in which the person suffers a weakness. A sickly adolescent boy, unable to participate in high-school sports, invests his energies in the study of science, thereby winning the plaudits of his teachers and earning a college scholarship. An ungainly high-school girl compensates for her lack of success in attracting boyfriends by excelling as a graphic artist.

Sublimation means replacing a less virtuous method of expressing instinctual drives with a culturally higher and socially more acceptable method. Such altruistic acts as caring for children or aiding the sick, or such artistic endeavors as writing poetry or performing a ballet, are viewed by Freudians as substitutes for direct sexual behavior that would be disapproved by society.

In summary, as the ego develops over the years of childhood and adolescence, it acquires a widening array of methods for negotiating between id demands and the opportunities and requirements of the world. A strong ego increasingly adopts direct means of solving moral conflicts. A weak ego depends more heavily on defense mechanisms that involve deluding oneself, distorting reality, and deceiving others about the true state of affairs. From the vantage point of one's ego, moral development consists of the ego's employing an expanding range of direct methods for satisfying instinctual needs and simultaneously meeting society's moral requirements. At the same time, the ego increasingly abandons defense mechanisms that avoid or misrepresent reality.

The Superego. In Freudian theory, no moral values are inborn. As noted earlier, infants arrive in the world *amoral*—with no sense of right or wrong. Although neonates are devoid of moral values, what they do bring into the world is the capacity to gradually incorporate into their personalities the values imposed on them by significant agents in their environment. The initial agents are parents and immediate caregivers. Subsequently, the growing child acquires values from ever-widening circles of acquaintances—age-mates, teachers, religious leaders, counselors, coaches, and mass-communication media.

Not only do children have the ability to ingest values, but they also automatically experience emotions evoked whenever they either abide by or violate those values. Acting in concert with their values induces feelings of pride, contentment, and self-righteousness. Acting in opposition to their values induces feelings of guilt, shame, fear, and self-reproach.

Freud applied the label *superego* to the child's proclivity to assimilate moral values and to employ those values as guides to behavior. How and why the superego evolves are matters intimately involved in the psychosexual stages of development and will be discussed in connection with them. For the present we will restrict our attention to the role the superego plays in the mental life of older children and youths.

Just as Freud pictured the ego as developing out of the id, so he saw the superego as emerging from the ego.

> This new psychical agency continues to carry on the functions which have hitherto been performed by the people in the external world: It observes the ego, gives it orders, judges it and threatens it with punishments, exactly like the parents whose place it has taken. (Freud, 1938, p. 62)

Freud portrayed the ego as having two facets, the *conscience* and the *ego ideal.* The conscience represents the "should nots" of society, the things for which the child will be punished. The ego ideal represents the "shoulds," the positive moral values the child has been taught. Whereas very young children must be punished for transgressions and rewarded for good behavior by their parents and guardians, older children and adolescents often do not need outside sanctions. For breaching the values they have now accepted as their own, their conscience metes out punishment in the form of distressing emotions. For abiding by their moral values, their ego ideal rewards them with approval and praise.

With the superego added to the id and ego, the psychoanalytic structure of personality is now complete. The moral behavior of older children, youths, and adults is thus the result of the way the ego negotiates a settlement among three conflicting sources of demands: (1) the id, which insists on immediate fulfillment of wishes, regardless of environmental circumstances; (2) the environment, which sets conditions under which wishes can be satisfied without penalties; and (3) the superego, which presses individuals to live up to a set of moral values they have learned from their parents and from other influential agents in their world.

Stages of Psychosexual Development

In Freud's opinion, each individual's personality structure evolves over the first two decades of life through a sequence of psychosexual stages. Each stage is characterized by a distinctive zone of sensual gratification, by attitudes of other people toward such gratification, and by implications for moral development. Freud grounded his series of stages on three assumptions:

1. Each stage represents a distinctive way that the principal driving force behind behavior—the sexual or life instinct—is expressed during a particular time of life.

2. How successfully the growing child masters the developmental task that a stage poses determines whether the child will move on to the next stage unencumbered by a residue of unresolved problems that can cause neurotic symptoms.

3. The body's zone of satisfaction that is associated with a stage, and the activities pursued for achieving that satisfaction, are normal for people who are in the age range suited to that stage. But for people who have passed beyond the stage's usual age range, concentrating on that zone and its related activities is neither normal nor mentally healthy. Thus, psychosexual growth that is arrested at such a stage is deemed abnormal, symptomatic of personality maladjustment and of deviant moral development. An exaggerated, obsessive fixation on the activities of a given stage, when carried into later periods of life, is indicative of a destructive, immoral personality.

Although the number of developmental periods identified between birth and adulthood may vary slightly from one psychoanalytic theorist to another, all of them cite at least five major stages: oral (ages 0-1), anal (ages 2-3), infantile-genital (ages 3-4 or so), latency (ages 4 or 5 to puberty), and mature-genital (from midteens to adulthood).

The Oral Period (Ages 0-1)

As already explained, the id of the newborn is seeking to invest libidinal energy in images of objects that will satisfy the instinctual needs and bring the pleasure of release. This act of investment (the primary process) is called *cathexis*. When the id channels energy into an image of an object, the id is said to be *cathecting* that object.

Following birth, the first natural object for cathexis is the mother's breast or a suitable substitute, because it is through the mouth that newborns must ingest life-sustaining nourishment. Neonates must also use their mouth and nose for breathing. The nerve endings in the lips and mouth are particularly sensitive and offer the infant special pleasure. Freud wrote:

> The baby's obstinate persistence in sucking gives evidence at an early stage of a need for satisfaction which, though it originates from and is instigated by the taking of nourishment, nevertheless strives to obtain pleasure independently of nourishment and for that reason may and should be termed *sexual*. (Freud, 1938, p. 11)

The success with which children fulfill the need for food, drink, and breath gives them their first impressions of the world and of their relation to it. Not only are their personalities influenced by how soon and how completely the pent-up libidinal energy is released, but the atmosphere associated with how these needs for release are either satisfied or neglected affects them as well. If their mothers hold them affectionately during the feeding process, children will pass through the oral period in a happier, more confident state than if they are never cuddled and if distressing sounds and sights disturb them while feeding.

Not only do infants use the oral zone for ingesting food and drink, they also use the lips and mouth to explore those parts of their world within reach. They examine most objects by putting them to their lips and into their mouths. Freud proposed that children mouth objects in order to control and master the objects by *incorporating* them.

The oral period can be divided into two substages—the early *receptive stage*, which occurs before the child has teeth, and the later *biting stage* that arrives when the gums are harder and teeth erupt. Each of these stages has its own implications for the type of moral character that the growing child may carry into adulthood.

The receptive stage extends over the first few months after birth, when erotic pleasure derives from sucking, swallowing, and mouthing. During this period, infants are mainly passive and are extremely dependent. If their feeding and other dependency needs are not adequately met or if great conflict is associated with those needs, then a residue of unfulfillment and conflict is repressed into the unconscious to reveal itself in later years, often as a neurotic overdependency or a compulsive habit of trying to "take in" or exploit other people. In psychoanalytic theory, adults who display extreme greed—an inordinate drive to acquire objects and status regardless of the harm done to others—have apparently been fixated at the receptive stage of the oral period.

In effect, Freudian theory sees the experience that children have with satisfying instinctual drives at a particular psychosexual stage as forming a model for attitudes or relationships with the world that may be carried over to later life. Freudians suggest that there are two ways children's psychosexual development can be arrested at a given stage. One way is for them to gain too little satisfaction at that stage, thereby leaving unfulfilled remnants of needs to be carried in the unconscious through subsequent periods of life. The other way is for children to gain too much satisfaction at the stage—to so completely relish overindulgence that they are unwilling to face the tasks of the next stage in the sequence. The resulting message for people engaged in rearing the young is that children (a) should have sufficient trauma-free satisfaction of each stage's mode of need fulfillment to avoid carrying a damaging residue of unmet needs into later periods of life, yet (b) the satisfaction gained at a given period should not be so long extended that children are unwilling to tackle the problems of subsequent stages.

Just as the receptive substage of the oral period holds implications for later moral character, so also does the biting substage. Unresolved conflicts during the biting phase may seethe in the unconscious to affect an individual's treatment of others in the years of later childhood, adolescence, and adulthood.

As the infant develops teeth, the dominant zone of gratification is still the mouth, but touching things with the lips is now less satisfying than biting and chewing. During this period infants develop their first *ambivalent* feelings. They recognize that one object, such as mother, can have both pleasure-giving and pain-giving functions. Mother gratifies hunger when the baby cries. But mother also has to carry out other activities in her life, so she cannot satisfy the baby's demands immediately all the time, and the baby finds this postponement painful. Hence, infants sense that they both love and hate the same object. Freudian theory proposes that children's early ambivalent feelings and sadistic tendencies are expressed in biting—biting mother's breast, people's fingers, toys, and the like. If progress through this stage is incomplete, so that the infant experiences insufficient satisfaction of biting needs and has inadequate opportunities to express ambivalence without unduly painful repercussions, then a residue of conflict remains in the unconscious to mar the individual's moral character in later life. An adult who became fixated at the biting stage will be excessively critical of others, "chewing them out" and attacking them with "biting criticism" at the least provocation.

The Anal Period (Ages 2-3)

In the second and third years of life, much of parents' attention is directed toward getting young ones to establish proper control of their bowels. In psychoanalytic parlance, this is the *anal period* or, more completely, the *anal-urethral period*, because control of the urinary function is also involved. The dominant zones of gratification or of libido investment become the anal cavity, the sphincter muscles of the lower bowel, and the muscles of the urinary system.

During the anal period, much of children's emotionally charged contact with adults is related to toilet training. Like the oral period, the anal period can be divided into two substages, the first concerned with pleasure in expelling feces and urine, and the second with retaining these materials.

During the *expulsion stage*, children meet their first serious experience with an external barrier (parents' concern to have the young control their bowels) to an instinctual cathexis (yearning to defecate). If children are to accomplish bowel and bladder control, the ego must apply resistance to their urge to eliminate at the moment they feel the need. Thus, the ego must borrow libido from the id to energize the resistance. Such a use of libidinal force by the ego— or at a later stage, by the superego—is called *countercathexis* or *anticathexis*. In brief, the cathexis or energy investment of the id in the pleasurable release of defecation must be countered by an opposing cathexis of the ego if the child is to meet the parents' demands for cleanliness and thus to retain their love.

This period is a critical time for children to learn to earn love, praise, and approval. If the period is not handled wisely by parents—if they harshly impose cleanliness standards before the child is physically prepared to control the bowels and bladder—then the child's personality will retain vestiges of fear, guilt, and defiance. The repressed conflict may produce an adult who is compulsively regular and clean, prone to damaging relationships with others by insisting that they adopt similar standards of regularity and tidiness. Or, in contrast, the lingering unconscious distress may be vented during adulthood as bitterness—a person disposed to symbolically voiding and urinating on others in social relationships. Such phrases as "I don't give a shit for him" or "Piss on them" or "They aren't worth crapping on" are interpreted as evidence of fixation at the anal expulsion stage.

During the *retention phase* of the anal period, children have learned to hold in feces and urine at will. They now gain sensuous satisfaction by keeping products they value. Freudians suggest that the child's idea of things having value evolves during this substage, and inadequate passage through the stage may show up in later life in acts of hoarding and collecting things. A compulsion to accumulate and hold worldly goods, symbols of status, or disciples becomes a moral problem when it involves exploiting others and employing devious means (lying, intimidating, bribing) for pursuing one's ambitions.

The Infantile-Genital Period (Ages 3-4 or So)

The boy's penis and the girl's clitoris and vulva become the focus of erotic pleasure during the third major psychosexual period. Like the previous periods, the infantile-genital phase can be divided into two phases.

During the first phase, called the *phallic stage*, the child discovers that fondling the genitals and masturbation (but without orgasm) give erotic pleasure. Next the child associates fondling the genitals with a love object with whom he or she wishes to have some sort of sexual relations. In the case of boys, Freud explained:

> The object that has been found turns out to be almost identical with the first object of the oral pleasure-instinct, which was reached by attachment (to the nutritional instinct). Though it is not actually the mother's breast, at least it is the mother. We call the mother the first *love-object*. (Freud, 1917, p. 329)

At this same time the boy realizes that he cannot have his mother all to himself, for his father has already won her affections. Freud applied the label *Oedipus complex* or *Oedipus conflict* to the resulting dilemma—the boy's wanting to possess his mother but being prevented by the powerful father. The girl finds herself in the opposite dilemma, yearning for her father as her love partner but being defeated in this contest by her mother. Freud labeled the girl's plight the *Electra complex.*

Children resolve this conflict by rejecting sexual feelings toward the forbidden object—the opposite-sex parent—and at the same time they identify with the parent of the same sex. By identifying with the same-sex parent, children relieve their fear of reprisal and incorporate the traits of the same sex, the traits which made that parent the victor in the contest for the opposite-sex parent's love. The girl identifies with her mother and seeks to develop her traits, and the boy likewise imitates his father.

Through this process of identification the superego evolves over the preadolescent years as the child adopts the moral values of the same-sex parent. These values equip children to reward and punish themselves psychologically and thus control their own behavior in the absence of outside authority figures. If the Oedipus/Electra conflict is not adequately resolved through repression of sexual impulses and identification with the like-sex parent, remnants of the conflict churn in the unconscious to distort the personality of the adolescent and adult. For example, homosexuality sometimes has been explained as children's identifying with the opposite-sex parent and thus modeling their subsequent sexual tastes after the other-sex parent rather than the same-sex one. Homosexuality as an adult sexual orientation was viewed by Freud as a personality disorder—even to the extent of being immoral—rather than as an acceptable alternative sexual preference.

The resolution of the Oedipus/Electra complex through the repression of sexual desires inaugurates the latency phase of the infantile-genital stage. Because this phase is so different in its manifestations from the early infantile-genital stage, I treat it as a separate period.

The Latency Period (Ages 4-5 to Ages 11-13)

Although the dominant zone of gratification is still the genital region, this focus is seldom displayed in children's behavior, since both girls and boys are repressing expressions of sex in order to control their unacceptable yearning for their parental love objects. Because children have adopted both the gratifying and punishing parental roles, they now consider talk and displays of sex to be vile and nasty. The boy stops masturbating because he is afraid of being punished by having his penis cut off, and the girl stops because she is afraid of losing parental love. Freud (1938, p. 10) asserted that children fall "victim to *infantile amnesia*" and forget (by dint of repression) the sex urges and activities of the previous half-decade of life.

This period has sometimes been called the *gang age*, because children seldom form groups that include the opposite sex. The recently evolved superego operates as a strong, moralistic internal representative of a parent, and thus of societal rules. Playing by the rules both in games and in other daily activities becomes a matter of great import to children during the latency period. On the playground, in the home, and in the classroom issues of justice are argued with such charges as "That's not fair" or "You're cheating" or "You can't change the rules in the middle of the game."

Children who fail to work through the Oedipus/Electra conflict successfully can become fixated at the latency period, so in adult life they never feel comfortable around the opposite sex. They may avoid sexual relationships with the opposite sex or else perform sexual activities in an emotionally detached or aggressive manner. Their antagonism toward members of the opposite sex may vent itself in efforts of males to violate females and of females to violate males in the form of physical or psychological rape. The antagonism may also be reflected in the use of sexual phrases with malevolent rather than affectionate intent, as in "Screw you" and "Fuck off, you bastard."

The Mature-Genital Period (Ages 14-16 to 18-21)

With the advent of puberty, girls begin to menstruate and to display such secondary bodily changes as the rounding of the breasts and the growth of pubic and underarm hair. Boy's maturation involves the growth of the genital organs, the appearance of sperm, nocturnal emissions of semen (often accompanied by erotic dreams), lowering of the voice pitch, and the growth of facial and bodily hair.

The principal zone of erotic pleasure is still the clitoral area in the girl and the penis in the boy, but now gratification involves sexual orgasm. Furthermore, the dominant erotic activity becomes copulation with a partner of the opposite sex. The transition from the rejection of sex in the latency period to the enthusiastic pursuit of heterosexual activity can be a psychologically demanding task, particularly in societies that have erected moral barriers against intercourse outside the bonds of marriage. Such was the case in the late-nineteenth-century Viennese society from which Freud drew so many of his patients on whose narratives he built his theory.

Freud saw the societal pressure on youths to abstain from sexual intercourse as a strong force motivating the young to substitute some form of sublimation for the direct expenditure of libidinal energy in copulation. Sublimation can assume any of a variety of artistic, athletic, scholarly, or philanthropic forms— composing music, playing the violin, painting landscapes, writing poetry or novels, engaging in sports, pursuing scientific inquiry, caring for children, aiding the homeless and handicapped, and more.

In summary, the first two decades of life confront children and youths with the task of progressing through the psychosexual stages. How successfully they resolve the conflicts encountered at each stage affects their personal-social adjustment in adult life, including the repertoire of values that direct their moral thought and action.

The Nature of Values

The moral values advocated in psychoanalysis are not stated outright but, instead, are implied in the general tenor of Freud's remarks about the expression of instinctual drives and the function of sublimation.

The deepest essence of human nature consists of instinctual impulses which are of an elementary nature, which are similar in all men and which aim at the satisfaction of certain primal needs. These impulses in themselves are neither good nor bad. . . . All the impulses which society condemns as evil—the selfish and cruel ones—are of this primitive kind.

Civilized society, which demands good conduct and does not trouble itself about the instinctual basis of this conduct, has won over to obedience a great many people who are not following their own natures. . . . [People] are constantly subject to an unceasing suppression of instinct, and the resulting tension betrays itself in . . . neurotic disorders. (Freud, 1968, pp. 240-241)

In effect, Freud criticized people's denying or condemning sexual motives in both children and adults, claiming that neuroses typically arise from people's preventing the id from expressing its instinctual drives. By adopting such a stance, Freud appeared to advocate libidinal freedom—the id's right to assert itself without societal restrictions. From this viewpoint, the underlying moral value becomes the id's pleasure principle: "If it feels good, just do it."

At the same time, Freud accounted for civilization's most laudable features by suggesting that such things as creativity and altruism result from sublimation—from people substituting socially acceptable acts for the unfettered assertion of their raw sexual drives. In sublimation, libidinal energy is redirected into constructive endeavors whenever society's rules or the superego's dictates make the open expression of sexual urges inadmissible. In this event, the foundational moral value becomes the ego's reality principle—the conviction that it is enlightened self interest to abide by society's moral rules by investing libidinal energy in activities that lead to greater ultimate satisfaction and less pain than would result from directly expending sexual and aggressive drives in a socially inappropriate manner.

Freud was convinced that "the masses [of people] are lazy and unintelligent, [with] no love for instinctual renunciation, . . . [and logical] arguments are of no avail against their passions. Therefore, it is only through the influence of individuals who can set an example [of moral behavior] and whom the masses recognize as their leaders that the masses can be induced to perform the work and undergo the renunciations on which the existence of civilization depends" (Freud, 1968, pp. 242-243).

Thus morality, from a psychoanalytic perspective, requires some compromise between the pleasure principle (you owe it to yourself to fulfill your libidinal needs) and the reality principle (you owe it to society not to violate others' rights). In short, Freud's psychoanalysis does not stipulate particular moral values to guide behavior but, instead, assumes that a rapprochement must be achieved between the pleasure principle and the reality principle, a compromise conducive to an individual's mental health, leaving the person free from neuroses or psychoses.

Causes and Individual Differences

A psychoanalytic explanation of the causes behind moral development can usefully be inspected in relation to inherited traits and environmental influences.

Heredity

Three ways that heredity influences moral development are in (a) the instincts that affect the aspects of the world to which people direct their attention and that motivate their behavior, (b) the sequence of stages through which the child and adolescent advance over the first two decades of life, and (c) the potential for merging society's values into the personality in the guise of a superego.

As described earlier, the id of the newborn child consists entirely of unconscious instincts that guide the individual's attention and drive all the infant's acts. Throughout the life span, Freud's postulated innate life and death instincts that serve as potent motivating factors behind moral behavior.

The psychosexual stages in Freud's scheme are also assumed to be inherited, since theoretically they are experienced by all humans, regardless of the culture into which they are socialized. Whereas all children and youths experience the same sequence of stages, the degree to which they master the developmental task posed by each stage is determined to a great extent by the environment in which they are raised, principally by the way their caregivers address children's concerns at each stage.

As explained earlier, psychoanalytic theory assumes that children are born amoral—tending neither to good nor to bad behavior. Instead, they acquire moral rules from their surroundings, initially from their parents and siblings, then later from their school, their companions, and the books they read and television programs they watch. Although people do not acquire any moral values via their biological nature, what they do inherit is the capacity to incorporate values from their environment into their personality in the form of conscience and an ego ideal. The superego becomes an important cause behind moral thought and action by punishing breaches of values with guilt and shame, and rewarding adherence to values with pride and self satisfaction.

Environment

Four ways that environments influence moral development are by (a) providing models, (b) furnishing values, (c) offering opportunities for the investment of libidinal energy, and (d) supplying strong leaders who apply rewards and punishments.

Identification as a ego-adjustment mechanism is assigned a key role in Freudian theory. The term *identification* means extending one's ego (sense of self) to encompass people, objects, beliefs, and events beyond one's own body. For example, in resolving the Oedipus conflict during the first decade of life, the child is expected to identify with the same-sex parent and therefore model his or her beliefs and behavior after that parent. In like manner, people throughout their lives identify with people, places, and beliefs that they find appealing. The resulting psychological bond affects their moral development in two important ways. First, the bond causes them to imitate the behavior of the admired models. Antisocial behavior results from copying a model's antisocial acts, and socially constructive behavior results from imitating an exemplary model. Second, the psychological bond causes individuals to be pleased by their models' successes and to feel sad and angry at the models' defeats and ill fortune. These emotions can lead a person into either promoral or immoral acts.

The moral values that an individual can adopt are ones displayed in the behavior of models that people witness in their daily lives. Values exhibited by models who appear to fulfill needs that the witness harbors are values which that individual is likely to adopt as his or her own. In effect, the ego adopts values that seem (a) to meet the id's demands, (b) to satisfy society's demands, and (c) to be acceptable to the superego.

Different environments offer different opportunities for satisfying one's personal adjustment attempts. The moral development of an infant whose parents are unreasonably demanding of bowel and bladder control will not be the same as the development of an infant whose parents tolerate incontinence in the young child. The boy raised by a single mother and her maiden aunt can be expected in Freudian theory to develop a different sexual orientation than one reared by a masculine father and feminine mother. A child from an inner-city ghetto where gang wars and illicit drugs are endemic may well subscribe to moral values different from those held by children in an Amish farm community.

A fourth causal factor consists of the rewards and punishments imposed on people to encourage moral behavior.

> There are two widespread human characteristics which are responsible for the fact that the regulation of civilization can only be maintained by a certain degree of coercion—namely, that men are not spontaneously fond of work and that arguments are of no avail against their passions. (Freud, 1968, p. 243)

The particular patterning of the foregoing variables in a person's life causes that individual to experience a different sort of moral development than does another individual whose life represents a different array of the variables.

Psychoanalytic Therapy

In Freudian theory, a further influence on moral development is psychoanalytic therapy. When development has gone wrong during the years of childhood and adolescence, the individual either suffers neurotic symptoms (phobias, obsessions, compulsions, psychosomatic ailments) or breaches society's rules in ways that invite continual social sanctions. These underlying developmental disorders can be corrected by psychoanalytic therapy in which the client, in cooperation with the analyst, psychologically relives the damaging events of earlier years, this time viewing those events in a mature, realistic, nondistressing manner that rectifies the client's distorted moral perceptions.

Conclusion

Psychoanalytic theory enjoyed its greatest popularity from the 1920s through the 1950s. Thereafter, the number of proponents declined until, by the 1990s, it was accepted by far fewer members of the scientific community than currently were attracted to cognitive-structuralist and social-learning theories.

During the hey day of psychoanalysis, numbers of Freud's disciples sought to improve the master's scheme either by altering some of his proposals or by embellishing the theory with additional features. The final pages of this chapter illustrate two of the more notable variations suggested by followers who are often referred to as neo-Freudians.

NOTEWORTHY VARIATIONS OF FREUDIAN THEORY

As the following section illustrates, Erik Erikson and Erich Fromm were two among a number of psychoanalytically oriented theorists whose contributions have extended or revised Freudian views in ways that bear on moral development.

Erik H. Erikson (1902-1994)

Erikson was a German-born psychoanalyst who began his professional career in Vienna, where he graduated from the Vienna Psychoanalytic Institute before emigrating to the United States in 1933 to teach at a number of universities, to provide psychoanalytic therapy, and to conduct research. His final academic appointment was at Harvard University.

From the viewpoint of developmental psychology, Erikson has been the most influential of the neo-Freudians. He focused attention primarily on stages of psychosocial development to accompany Freud's series of psychosexual stages, with Erikson's stages progressing from infancy and adolescence through adulthood and into old age. He proposed that people's interactions with their social environments produce a sequences of eight major *psychosocial crises* that must be worked through if individuals are to achieve ego strength and psychological health. The way a person experiences each crisis and seeks to resolve it yields moral/ethical consequences.

The first crisis, parallel to Freud's oral-respiratory stage (birth to age 1), features a psychosocial conflict between *trust* and *mistrust*. If the infant's caretakers are inconsistent, harsh, overly demanding, and unsympathetic with the young one's physical and emotional needs, then the infant will mistrust the world it has entered. On the other hand, if the caretakers meet the newborn's needs in a kindly, affectionate fashion, then the growing child will experience the world as nonthreatening and predictable. The moral development of two such infants—one who mistrusts and one who trusts—will be significantly different since their social encounters are founded on markedly different expectations about how other people will act.

The second crisis, related to Freud's anal-urethral period (ages 2-3), concerns *autonomy* versus *shame and doubt*. The manner in which caretakers deal with the child's toilet training can affect the child's sense of autonomy (feeling able to display initiative and to control oneself). Caretakers who treat toilet training in a constructive manner foster the development of a confident child who has the "determination to exercise both free choice and self-restraint" rather than a child who doubts his or her ability to cope with the world and is ashamed of this lack of control (Erikson, 1964, p. 118). Thus, in moral-decision episodes, the degree of a child's sense of autonomy and willpower influences the child's behavior.

The third psychosocial crisis, associated with Freud's infantile-genital stage (ages 3-6), pits *initiative* against *guilt*. This period builds on the previous one, with the preschool child whose sexual concerns are treated wisely by caretakers gaining a sense of purpose, "the courage to envisage and pursue goals uninhibited by the defeat of infantile fantasies, by guilt, and by the foiling fear of punishment" (Erikson, 1964, p. 120). Where the child is located on the scale between initiative and debilitating guilt affects how he or she will act in moral situations.

Crisis number four (Freud's latency stage) is experienced by the primary-school child (ages 7-12) as a conflict between *industry* and *inferiority*. As a result of their success in solving the Oedipus conflict and in mastering the learning tasks they face in school, children come to view themselves as either industrious and competent or else as inferior failures. The sense of competence that children develop at this stage influences the skill and confidence they bring to moral decisions they face in the years ahead.

Erikson viewed the fifth crisis, which appears with the advent of puberty and adolescence (ages 12-18) as particularly crucial in the person's advance toward maturity. The developmental task demanding the youth's attention is that of achieving a clear personal identity and repudiating unsuitable values and life styles. It is a conflict between *identity* and *identity diffusion*. The adolescent faces a new array of contrasting values offered by peers and the mass-communication media. In the struggle to find a true and trustworthy self, the youth is tempted to join cliques, gangs, groups, and movements and to identify with popular models. It is a period of experimentation with life styles, which may vary in the degree to which they are morally constructive or destructive. The individual's identity crisis is properly resolved when the youth displays fidelity to self and to valued others—sustaining freely pledged loyalties despite contradictions in contrasting value systems, such as the dicta of the church versus the beliefs of the street gang.

In a manner similar to the first five crises, Erikson identified three further psychosocial stages of adulthood that also bear implications for moral thought and behavior. During the age period of the 20s, the conflict is between *intimacy and solidarity* with a loved mate in contrast to *isolation*. The next stage, extending from the 20s into the 50s, concerns the responsibilities a person assumes for others, most immediately for one's children and other family members, but also extending to people and causes beyond the family. The crisis pits *generativity* against *self-absorption*. In terms of morality and ethics, generativity leads to altruistic acts, to obligations "generated by love, necessity, or accident" (Erikson, 1964, p. 128). In contrast, self-absorption leads to egocentrism and disdain for the misfortune of others.

The final stage, beyond the 50s, confronts the aged with a conflict between *integrity* and *despair*. This crisis is more psychic than social—more inner-personal than moral—since it involves the individual coming to terms with declining abilities and death. Erikson proposed that the chief virtue and quality of strength during this final period is that of wisdom—"detached concern with life itself, in the face of death itself" (Erikson, 1964, p. 133).

In summary, Erikson contended that crucial periods over the life span involved psychosocial crises that needed to be resolved properly if the person was to lead a life that was both personally satisfying and socially responsible. How people deal with each crisis affects their moral/ethical development, that is, how they think and act in moral situations.

Another of Erikson's contributions was his suggesting a distinction between *moral rules* and *ethical rules* by implying that morals are linked to the conscience aspect of the superego, whereas ethics are linked to the ego-ideal aspect.

> I would propose that we consider *moral rules* of conduct to be based on a fear of *threats* to be forestalled. These may be outer threats of abandonment, punishment and public exposure, or a threatening inner sense of guilt or shame or of isolation. In either case, the rationale for obeying a rule may not be too clear. It is the threat that counts. In contrast, I would consider *ethical rules* to be based on *ideals* to be striven for with a high degree of rational assent and with a ready consent to a formulated good, a definition of perfection, and some promise of self-realization. (Erikson, 1964, p. 222)

Erich Fromm (1900-1980)

Fromm was trained as a psychoanalyst in Berlin before moving in 1934 to North America where he taught at Columbia University, Bennington College, Yale University, and the New School for Social Research before accepting the directorship of the Instituto Mexicano de Psicoanálisis in Mexico City. He later joined the faculties of Michigan State University and New York University.

Although he agreed with much of Freud's theory, Fromm contended that Freud erred in asserting that the basic force motivating human passions and desires derived from the libido.

> Powerful as the sexual drive and all its derivations are, they are by no means the most powerful forces within man, and their frustrations are not the cause of mental disturbance. The most powerful forces motivating man's behavior stem from the conditions of his existence, the "human situation." (Fromm, 1968, p. 311)

That "situation," in Fromm's opinion, is the problem of humans having evolved from an animal state into a condition of self-awareness. As a result, people—unlike animals—are forever puzzling about their existence, about truth, and about the purpose of life. This striving to understand life is the principal motivator of human behavior, including moral behavior.

> Man is the only animal who finds his own existence a problem which he has to solve and from which he cannot escape. . . . Indeed, the tremendous energy in the forces producing mental illness, as well as those behind art and religion, could never be understood as an outcome of substrated or sublimated physiological needs; they are attempts to solve the problem of being born human. All men are idealists . . . striving for the satisfaction of [psychological] needs that transcend the physiological needs of the organism. The difference [between individuals] is only that one idealism is a good and adequate solution, the other a bad and destructive one. (Fromm, 1968, pp. 308, 312)

Fromm's humanistic perspective resulted in his espousing somewhat different moral values than those found in Freud's writings. In Fromm's credo that appears in the commemorative book of his writings, *On Being Human* (1994), he set forth his core beliefs about both the virtues he most admired and the principal means by which humans can adopt those virtues. He cast the values in both positive and negative forms.

The positive values include those of love, brotherhood, recognition of the equal worth of all human beings, personal integrity, responsibility, freedom to choose among alternatives, and independence of thought and action.

> Love is the main key to open the doors to the "growth" of the human person . . . to put oneself into relationships with others, to feel one with others, without limiting [one's] sense of integrity and independence. . . . I believe that *equality* is felt when, completely discovering oneself, one recognizes that one is equal to others and one identifies oneself with them   Every individual bears humanity inside himself; "the human condition" is unique and equal for all men, in spite of the inevitable differences in intelligence, talent, height, color, etc. (Fromm, 1994, pp. 101-103)

Fromm believed that modern industrialized societies fetter the human spirit by requiring people to hold dehumanizing jobs and by stimulating their desire to acquire increasing quantities of those products of technology that advertisers urge on a consumption-oriented populace. Envisioning a more hopeful future, he wrote:

> I believe in the possible realization of a world in which man can *be* much, even if he *has* little; a world in which the dominant motivation of existence is not consumption; . . . a world in which man can find the way of giving a purpose to his life as well as the strength to live free and without illusions. (Fromm, 1994, p. 104)

In speaking of negative values that damage moral development, Fromm found particular fault with *narcissism*, which he defined as "intense attachment to oneself, to one's own group, clan, religion, race, etc.—with consequent serious distortions of rational judgment" (Fromm, 1994, p. 101).

The chief instruments of moral development, in Fromm's opinion, are logical reasoning and knowledge, both of which are needed for controlling "irrational passions." Reason and knowledge free people to objectively understand their world and their place in it.

AN ASSESSMENT OF PSYCHOANALYSIS

In keeping with the practice of evaluating the theories in the previous three chapters, the standards of goodness described in Chapter 2 are adopted in the present chapter for assessing Freud's scheme for interpreting moral development.

On clarity of explanation (item 1), I judge that the theory deserves a mark slightly above the middle of the scale. Freudians explain the system's main components rather clearly. But when we move beyond the basic outline of the theory's structure, many puzzles appear, calling for more precise explanation. For instance, Nagel (1959, p. 46) asserted that Freud

> sometimes describes the main theoretical components of the mental apparatus [id, ego, superego] as "units of function," and suggests that unconscious drives are like dispositions. But he also declares that these components possess energies and conflict with one another—though without explaining in what sense functions can be charged with energies or dispositions can be engaged in conflicts.

The difficulty I faced in judging item 2 (explains past, predicts future) is reflected in the pair of appraisals on the assessment chart. The mark for specificity is at the high end of the scale, principally because Freudian explanations of what psychosexual events occurred earlier in an individual's life, and why they occurred, are quite specific. Psychoanalysis reveals a past history of the person's moral development by means of free association and dream interpretation and, in a general way, predicts what is likely to happen to the person's moral condition in the future, often in terms of possible deviant development that might result if the person's needs during up coming psycho-sexual stages are not dealt with wisely by a child's caretakers. In view of the theory's very specific explanations of the past and more general predictions of the future, I have given it a relatively high mark for specificity. However, the theory's *accuracy* of explanation and prediction is far more questionable, as we may recognize when considering item 4 (verifiability,).

Probably the main reason psychoanalytic theory has been difficult either to verify or to refute is not that its adherents are stubbornly defensive or are inept researchers (though in some instances they may be), but that many of the scheme's key elements seem to render it nonfalsifiable. Such is the case with the concepts of unconscious motives, repression, and symbols in dream interpretation. For instance, Freud proposed that a person's ego, in cooperation with the superego, censors repressed material that seeks to escape from the unconscious into the conscious. But he also asserted that repressed wishes can sneak past the censor in disguise—that is, in symbolic form. Thus, if a son dreams of driving his car into his mother's garage, an analyst will typically interpret this as the son's repressed yearning for sexual intercourse with his mother. Such notions in psychoanalytic theory have caused critics to harbor "the suspicion that Freudian theory can always be so manipulated that it escapes refutation no matter what the well-established facts may be" (Nagel, 1959, p. 44). Because I share this suspicion, I have rated traditional psychoanalysis low on its ability to accommodate new, conflicting evidence (item 5). In effect, the validity of a psychoanalyst's interpretation of a client's moral development depends almost entirely on one's faith in the analyst's opinions rather than on publicly testable evidence. Such one-time close associates of Freud as Alfred Adler (1930) and Carl Jung (1953) broke with the master and launched their own theoretical interpretations largely because Freud's scheme appeared to them ill suited to explaining features of human behavior that they considered important.

As a source of suggestions about how to cope with issues of moral develop-ment (item 3), psychoanalysis deserves a high rating. Freudian theory, and revisions offered by such followers as Erikson and Fromm, has exerted marked influence on child-rearing views of child psychologists, pediatricians, social workers, teachers, and informed parents. Of particular note are psycho-analytic suggestions about children's emotional needs, especially in the areas of sex and aggression, and on such concepts as unconscious motivation. Nursery-school and kindergarten practices have been influenced by Freudian beliefs about sexual curiosity, nontraumatic toilet training, and the symbolic meaning of children's play with water and such messy substances as mud and finger paints; children's needs for physical contact, as in hugging and stroking; and the importance of teachers as role models with whom children are likely to identify. Freudian proposals about children's sexual needs have apparently been influential in convincing parents that children's interest in matters of sex are natural and not evidence of innate wickedness.

Freud's Psychoanalytic Theory

How well do I think the theory meets the standards?

The Standards	Very Well	Moderately Well	Very Poorly
1. Is clearly understandable		X	
2. Explains past and predicts future moral behavior	specificity X		accuracy ?
3. Offers practical guidance in coping with moral matters		X	
4. Is readily verifiable and falsifiable			X
5. Accommodates new evidence			X
6. Stimulates new discoveries	X		
7. Is durable		X	
8. Is self-satisfying		X	

Psychoanalytic theory has an excellent record as a source of new discoveries (item 6), particularly of expanded applications of the model. The model has been the basis for hundreds of clinical studies focusing on human development and has motivated investigators to launch new journals dedicated entirely to Freudian topics—*Psychoanalytic Study of the Child, Contemporary Psychoanalysis, International Journal of Psycho-Analysis*, and more.

For its durability (item 7), I have rated psychoanalysis in the "moderately well" range. Freud's scheme is now about one century old. Although its popularity with both the professional community and the informed public has markedly diminished over the past three decades, numbers of Freud's concepts have entered the realm of general psychology and even of common sense (unconscious motives, the importance of sexual drives, infantile sexuality, ego defense mechanisms). These are lasting influences. Freud has ensured himself a place in the history of psychology in future years, even though his theory is not likely to serve as people's dominant view of moral development.

The last standard (item 8, self-satisfying) is particularly important for one's acceptance of Freudian views, since psychoanalysis depends so heavily on *personal affirmation*, that is, on the "feeling" that the theory does indeed explain much about moral development. As Sidney Hook (1959, p. 213) observed, some Freudians respond to criticism with the comment that "psychoanalysis may be unscientific, but it is true." To a degree, I must admit to sharing such a feeling. Despite the shortcomings of Freudian theory when judged against such scientific criteria as those in our chart of standards, important aspects of the theory make a kind of existential sense to me. I believe in the unconscious, in repression, in the superego, in guilt and shame as motivators of moral action, and in people's use of ego-defense mechanisms in moral situations. However, I remain skeptical about other aspects of the model—symbols in dream interpretation, libido as the principal motivating force behind human behavior, psychoanalytic therapy as the best method for correcting deviant behavior. For these reasons, I have rated psychoanalytic theory in the middle of the scale on item 8.

7

Marxist Conceptions

The theory of societal development published in 1848 as *The Communist Manifesto* by two German political philosophers, Karl Marx (1818-1883) and Friedrich Engels (1820-1895), provided a worldview from which elements can be extracted to represent a Marxist theory of moral development. Or, because there came to be several variants of the theory, it is perhaps more accurate to cast such a perspective in the plural, calling it Marxist *conceptions* of moral development.

Karl Marx and his lifelong associate, Engels, were not practical politicians who applied their ideas directly to governing a state or nation. Rather, they were visionaries who created a view of humankind and social organization aimed at providing all individuals freedom and equality of opportunity. Their persuasive rhetoric enabled them to attract followers dedicated to bettering the lot of the common people through political action. However, neither Marx nor Engels held any sort of political position that would put them in charge of implementing their ideas, other than to support labor organizations of their day. Nevertheless, their ideas were considered by government authorities in Germany and France to be inflammatory and a threat to the social status quo. Thus, Marx was outlawed by those governments, destined to spend the latter decades of his life in England in a condition of near poverty. Engels also ended up in England, managing a factory in Manchester owned by his family.

In the late 19th century and early decades of the 20th century, it would be key adherents of Marxist theory who would cast the master's vision into practical political and economic acts. Principal among these interpreters of Marxism were Vladimir Ilyich Lenin (1870-1924) and Joseph V. Stalin (1879-1953) in the Soviet Union, Mao Zedong (1893-1976) in China, Josip Broz Tito (1892-1980) in Yugoslavia, Fidel Castro (born 1927) in Cuba, and a variety of others in Eastern Europe and Africa. As a result, a present-day Marxist theory of moral development can be seen as a collection of beliefs founded on Marx's worldview and embellished with details and practical applications by his disciples. The version offered in this chapter is a composite theory, drawing its substance from a variety of sources that are in concert with the basic theme of Marx's proposal.

The following description is organized under six topics: (1) Marxism's philosophical roots, (2) moral virtues and human nature, (3) stages of moral development, (4) variants of the theory, (5) additional moral-development matters, and (6) an assessment of Marxist models.

MARXISM'S PHILOSOPHICAL ROOTS

Karl Marx was born in Prussia in 1818, the son on a successful Jewish lawyer who had transferred his allegiance to the Protestant Evangelical Established Church shortly before Karl was born. As a result of his father' recent conversion, young Karl would be baptized a Christian. Nevertheless, "his Jewish background exposed him to prejudice and discrimination that may have led him to question the role of religion in society and contributed to his desire for social change" (Feuer & McLellen, 1994, p. 531).

As a university student in Bonn and Berlin, Marx intensely studied the works of the philosopher Georg Wilhelm Friedrich Hegel (1770-1831) and engaged in revolutionary student political activities. Eventually he transferred to the university of Jena, where he completed doctoral studies. Hegel's main contribution to Marx's beliefs was the concept of *dialectics*. The term *dialectic* refers to an interpretive method in which an assertable proposition (the *thesis*) is necessarily opposed by a second, equally reasonable but apparently contradictory, proposition (the *antithesis*), with their mutual contradiction subsequently resolved at a higher level of truth by a third proposition (the *synthesis*).

Marx adopted Hegel's notion as a way to explain the development of societies. He proposed that societies evolve through a process of resolving dialectic confrontations that are created by technological innovations in the production and distribution of material goods. This was a theory of *dialectical materialism.* For example, feudal agricultural societies, with their landlords and serfs, continued uninterrupted until the technological advances of the industrial revolution placed productive power in the hands of entrepreneurs (bourgeoisie)—inventors and factory owners—rather than feudal landowners. The resulting conflict between the rising class of entrepreneurs and the traditional aristocracy was resolved by the emergence of capitalistic economies to replace feudal systems. However, the capitalistic system itself would result in workers laboring for low wages while the owners of industries gained high profits by simply investing in production facilities rather than actually laboring to produce goods themselves. Consequently, members of the working class could afford to consume only a small proportion of the society's goods, while the "idle rich" enjoyed lives of leisure and luxury. Marx viewed the resulting conflict between these two social-classes—management and labor (bourgeoisie and proletariat)—as a dialectical confrontation that could be properly resolved only by a socialistic system replacing capitalism. Under socialism, the means of production would be held not by individual managers but collectively by the workers themselves. In such societies as the Soviet Union after World War I, public ownership of factories and farms would replace private ownership. Marx contended that each era in the history of societies' development was associated with a corresponding version of class struggle until, finally, the common people would come into control, creating a dictatorship of the proletariat that would produce the ultimate just and righteous classless society. No one would exploit anyone else. Everyone would contribute equally to the system of production, and everyone would receive an equitable reward.

In his 1859 *Contribution to the Critique of Political Economy*, Marx summarized his beliefs about the nature of human societies and of how the form of a society—and particularly the mode of production and consumption of goods and services—determined what and how people thought.

> In the social production that men carry on, they enter into definite relations that are indispensable and independent of their will; these relations of production correspond to a definite stage of development of their material powers of production. The sum total of these relations of production constitutes the economic structure of society, the real foundation on which rise legal and political superstructures and to which correspond definite forms of social consciousness. The mode of production in material life determines the general character of the social, political, and spiritual processes of life. It is not the consciousness of men which determines their existence; but, on the contrary, their social existence determines their consciousness. (Marx, 1859, p. 43)

Three important inferences can be drawn from this proposition.

First, people's environment, rather than their heredity, determines their ways of thought, including their ways of applying moral values. In other words, people do not have an innate sense of right and wrong. Instead, the activities in which they daily engage as participants in the society's system of producing and consuming goods and services dictate the values people apply in their social interactions. Thus, it should not be surprising that the moral thought and behavior of people in one type of society, such as a capitalistic form, might differ from that of people in another type, such as a state socialist form. A variety of capitalism that emphasizes competition among individuals and groups and places high value on personal profits can be expected to encourage different moral precepts than a type of socialism that stresses cooperation among individuals for the sake of the general welfare rather than for personal profit.

Second, the moral values encouraged within a society will be ones in keeping with that society's cultural history, a history resulting from the dialectical confrontations typically experienced within the modes of producing and distributing goods and services. Thus, to understand why members of a given culture develop morally the way they do, it is necessary to understand their society's history.

Third, people who are caught in the midst of a change from one social system to another can be expected to experience some difficulty replacing their existing set of values with a new set suited to the requirements of the new social order. Thus, people growing up in a capitalistic system that emphasizes competition for personal gain must necessarily undergo a period of retraining if they are to adopt the moral values suitable for a socialistic system that emphasizes cooperation and the common good. In effect, a period of some confusion and discomfort will be felt by established members of a society until they adjust their modes of action and thought to the new order.

Practical implications of these inferences can be recognized when we consider in greater detail the sorts of moral values given primary emphasis in Marxist theory, which is the matter to which we now turn.

MORAL VIRTUES AND HUMAN NATURE

Two questions about moral virtues are of key significance for Marxist theory: What moral principles must guide people's behavior if they are to produce the ideal communist society? What must we assume about human nature if such virtues are to be realized?

Implied Moral Values

Moral values embedded in communist doctrine can be extracted from Marxist writings in the form of rights, obligations, and rejected policies. In the following review of representative Marxist values, the description of each moral principle is accompanied by the rationale educed in support of that principle.

People's Rights

Rights are opportunities and privileges to which people are automatically entitled by virtue of their membership in the society. Rights to which Marxist belief is dedicated involve income, jobs, and education.

1. The right to an adequate income, no matter what position the person fills in the society.

The supporting rationale: A communistic society, as the collectivity of workers (proletariat) devoid of social-class distinctions, is responsible for ensuring everyone a living wage, an income that provides the necessities of life. There should be no marked distinctions among citizens in how much they receive from the economy—no one very rich, no one poor—because everyone labors for the common good. One version of this principle is reflected in the motto "From each according to his ability, to each according to his need." In the People's Republic of China, this policy was called "the iron rice bowl"—an unbreakable guarantee on the part of society (in the form of the government) that everyone is entitled to an adequate income.

2. The right to a job—constructive work that contributes to the general welfare.

The supporting rationale: All land and other production facilities, including factories and farms, are to be owned by the general populace in the form of a centralized government rather than owned privately by individuals or groups. The state is to control credit by means of a national bank, to control all modes of communication and transportation, and to control both factory and agricultural production (Marx & Engels, 1848). Thus, economic planning must be centralized, including decisions about what sorts of workers are required in what places at what times. The state, therefore, is in charge of providing work opportunities for every citizen so that each person contributes in a coordinated way to the common welfare. The state, rather than the individual worker, is responsible for job assignments.

3. The right to a free education.

The supporting rationale: A progressive industrialized society requires that all citizens be educated. If education is to be distributed equitably throughout the populace, the state must provide it at no cost to the learners or their parents. Hence, there must be "free education for all children in public schools" (Marx & Engels, 1848). In order to prepare children for their work role in the economic system, academic studies need to be combined with training in industrial and agricultural production.

4. The right to lead a constructive, respected, satisfying life, free from oppression and exploitation.

The supporting rationale: Communism, like democracy and socialism, has been founded on the assumption that all people are created equal in terms of social rights and privileges. No one is inherently superior to anyone else in social status and personal worth (Park, 1976). This egalitarian conviction was reflected in Marx's ambition to create a classless society, a social order in which people necessarily performed different roles but in which one role deserved no more respect or material benefit than another.

People's Obligations

Obligations are responsibilities people incur by virtue of their membership in the society. Obligations in Marxist social systems relate to doing work, advancing social revolution, and paying taxes.

1. An obligation to do constructive work.

The supporting rationale: In their *Communist Manifesto*, Marx and Engels (1848) asserted that a communist society required "Equal liability of all to labor." Optimum productivity and, therefore, optimum economic output toward the general welfare depended on no one remaining idle.

2. An obligation to actively support the overthrow of capitalism and the establishment of a communist state.

The supporting rationale: In Marx's view, reforms instituted in a capitalist economic system will not suffice to end the exploitation of the common people. Only with the complete elimination of capitalist political economies can justice and equality prevail.

> Communists everywhere support every revolutionary movement against the existing social and political order of things. They openly declare that their ends can be attained only by the forcible overthrow of all existing social conditions. Let the ruling classes tremble at a Communistic revolution. The proletarians have nothing to lose but their chains. They have a world to win. Working men of all countries, unite! (Marx & Engels, 1848, p. 41).

By making the violent overthrow of capitalism their central aim, Marxists subordinate a variety of traditional moral values to the goals of the proletariat revolution. Killing, lying, stealing, and intimidation are advocated if they promote the establishment and safety of a monolithic communist state. To ensure that Marxist ideology is not threatened by competing ideologies, a number of freedoms cherished as moral values in typical democratic systems are abolished—freedom of speech, the press, religion, and political affiliation.

3. An obligation to pay taxes in proportion to one's income.

The supporting rationale: In keeping with the principle "From each according to his ability," Marx and Engels (1848), in the *Communist Manifesto*, recommended "a heavy progressive or graduated income tax." The higher a person's income, the larger the percentage of the income that should be given to the state to promote the common good.

Rejected Policies

Because a communist social order is designed to replace feudal and capitalist systems, being a good communist means actively rejecting unsuitable convictions and habits associated with feudalism and capitalism. Among the values of antiquated feudal and capitalist systems that must be repudiated are commitments to amassing wealth, receiving unearned income, acquiring private property, inheriting property, and permitting child labor. These values, which Marx and Engels contended are morally acceptable under a capitalistic economy, are considered immoral under communism.

1. Reject the amassing of wealth.

The supporting rationale: According to Marx's analysis, in a capitalist economy the price paid by consumers for any item is made up of two components: (1) the actual labor that workers (proletariat) have invested in producing the item and (2) profit taken by the owners (bourgeoisie) of the business that offers the item for sale. In such an economy, the owners try to keep workers' wages as low as possible and to raise their own profits as high as possible. These profits represent *surplus value* that is actually a contribution made to the selling price by the workers but for which they do not get paid.

Rather, the owners are getting profits that they themselves did nothing to earn. Such a system, in Marx's view, is unfair, because each person should be compensated in proportion to that person's direct contribution to the products or services sold. The bourgeoisie should not profit at the expense of the workers. Capitalism, therefore, permits nonproductive members of society to amass wealth and to privately control property that enables them to exploit the society's productive workers at an increasing rate. The bourgeoisie grow richer as the proletariat grow poorer (Marx, 1898).

2. Reject the inheritance of property.

The supporting rationale: Marx advocated the "abolition of all right of inheritance" because the inheritance of property concentrates wealth and the means of production in the hands of private individuals who have done no work to earn what they receive. They are merely profiting from the labor of others (Marx & Engels, 1848).

3. Reject private property in the form of land, natural resources, production facilities, and the like.

The supporting rationale: The earth and its resources are not inherently the possessions of any one person or group. People simply make claim to the land, either by settling on it first or wresting it from its present settlers by force or by payment. There is no reason for private ownership of land other than selfishness and the power to take the land either by force or by legal measures that favor land-holders. The earth's resources should be shared by everyone to promote the general welfare.

4. Reject child labor.

The supporting rationale: In the mid-19th century, there was widespread use of children in factories and on farms. Children's conditions of servitude were deplorable—long hours of labor, dangerous working conditions, malnutrition, disease, harsh punishment. In the *Communist Manifesto*, Marx and Engels (1848) urged the abolition of such labor and the substitution of free education that included training for work under safe and humane conditions.

Assumptions About Human Nature

The ideal social order that Marx envisioned required that people's behavior be motivated by a kind of altruism—or at least by a kind of enlightened self-interest—that causes them to (a) work hard for the good of the group rather than merely for their own personal gain, (b) be willing to accept benefits equal to, rather than superior to, the benefits received by other members of the society, and (c) pursue a vocation assigned by a central authority as a type of work needed for the common welfare.

The leaders who sought to establish communist societies recognized that self-sacrifice was not typically fostered in either feudal or capitalistic systems, which valued competition more than cooperation and encouraged people to work hard to increase their personal profit and to receive greater rewards than would be enjoyed by others who were neither so clever nor so diligent as they, or else who were not fortunate enough to be born into an upper-social-class family. Thus, the transition from a capitalistic to a communistic social order required not only a revolution in the system of producing and consuming goods, but also a revolution in people's motives and thought processes. This change in people's values is the most crucial educational task faced by the promoters of communism.

A key Marxist assumption about human nature is that selfishness is not an immutable, innate human trait. Although selfishness is encouraged by such social systems as feudalism and capitalism, communism does quite the opposite. It nourishes altruism, emphasizing the good of the many rather than individualism and self-indulgence. Thus, to change people's mental set from selfishness to altruism, it is necessary for the leaders of the communist order to impose unselfish behavior by means of education and strong punitive measures until the people willingly embrace the principle of self sacrifice for the welfare of all. In other words, during the period of transition from capitalism to communism, force may be necessary to ensure that everyone wholeheartedly subscribes to the values on which communism is based.

In summary, the foregoing values have been essential to the establishment of Marxist societies and provide the central aims of Marxist theories of moral development.

STAGES OF MORAL DEVELOPMENT

Marx and Engels were theorists who could analyze the structure of societies and identify the goals and general outlines of a just and egalitarian social order in which everyone has a voice and receives equal benefits. But neither of them was equipped to carry out the practical implementation of their vision. The task of implementation fell to such political leaders as Lenin and Stalin in the Soviet Union, Mao in China, and Tito in Yugoslavia. Furthermore, within the new communist societies that developed out of World War I, it was the job of social scientists to create a view of human development that suited Marx's vision of the good society. This job was performed most successfully in the Soviet Union from the early 1920s through the 1980s, with the Soviet conceptions of development subsequently refined and supplemented by additional proposals in such derivative communist systems as Mao Zedong's People's Republic of China and Kim Il Sung's Democratic People's Republic of Korea (North Korea).

The principal architect of the Soviet version of human development was Lev Semenovich Vygotsky (1896-1934), who charted the course of theorizing that would be pursued over the decades by such behavioral scientists as Alexander R. Luria, D. B. Elkonin, and V. V. Davidov. In the 1970s, Luria wrote:

Vygotsky was a genius. After more than half a century in science I am unable to name another person who even approaches his incredible analytic ability and foresight. All of my work has been no more than the working out of the psychological theory which he constructed. (Vygotsky, 1978, dust jacket)

Vygotsky necessarily began with Marx's contention that the contents of people's minds and their modes of thinking are constructed from the activities in which they engage. Hence, if people's daily acts determine how they think, then the way to fashion their mentalities—including their moral convictions—is to engage them in desirable activities. Operating from this assumption, Vygotsky and Elkonin created a six-stage description of mental development extending over the first two decades of life. Each stage featured a *leading activity*, which is the dominant focus of behavior during that stage. The change from one leading activity to another brings about a change in the person's perception of life and signals the transition from one stage to the next. A leading activity is marked by three characteristics: (1) it is the chief factor establishing a given period in the child's psychological development, (2) it is within the field of this activity that particular psychic functions emerge, and (3) the climax of the activity forms the foundation for the next leading activity. The best-known version of the stages contains the following six levels (Davidov, 1985; Elkonin in Cole, 1977, pp. 538-563).

1. *The activity of intuitive and emotional contact between the child and adults (birth to age 1):* The basic types of development deriving from this contact are a feeling for the need to interact with other people, the expression of emotional attitudes toward them, an ability to grasp things, and a display of a variety of perceptual actions. This early communication with others becomes a foundation for the later development of moral values that respected others exhibit.

2. *Object-manipulation activity (early preschool years, ages 1 to 3):* Children adopt socially accepted ways of handling things, and through interaction with adults they develop speech and visual-perception thinking (memory images). Acquiring basic language skills is an essential step toward understanding and mentally manipulating moral issues.

3. *Game-playing activity (later preschool years, ages 3 to 7):* Children engage in symbolic activities and creative play. They now have some comprehension of how to cooperate together in group endeavors. They discover rules, the consequences of violating rules, and notions of fair play.

4. *Learning activity (elementary-school years, ages 7 to 11):* Children develop theoretical approaches to the world of things, a function that involves their considering laws of reality and beginning to comprehend psychological preconditions for abstract theoretical thought (intentional mental operations, schemes for problem solving, reflective thinking).

5. *Social-communication activity (early adolescence, ages 11 to 15):* Adolescents gain skills in initiating types of communication needed for solving life's problems, including moral dilemmas. They progress in understanding other people's motives and in submitting to group norms.

6. *Vocational-learning activity (later adolescence, ages 15 to 17):* Older adolescents develop new cognitive and vocational interests, grasp elements of

research work, and attempt life projects, including ones that concern resolving moral conflicts.

The transition from one stage of development to another disrupts the stability of the child's ways of thinking and of interacting with the world, thereby producing crises as the child struggles to comprehend the next activity that is to occupy the leading role. Thus, moral development in the Soviet mode is composed of cycles of stability interspersed with crises at the point of transition to a successive stage.

In summary, the key to fostering proper moral development lies in providing suitable activities at each stage of child growth, activities that equip the young with the types of moral values required for the proper operation of a Marxist society.

VARIANTS OF MARXIST THEORY

Variants of Marxist theory outside the Soviet Union can be illustrated with examples from China and North Korea.

The Chinese Version

In China, the original form of communist moral-development theory under the direction of Premier Mao Zedong adhered closely to Marx's basic assumptions about human nature and to the practical features of communism that had been provided by Lenin in the Soviet Union. However, Mao and his fellow members of the Chinese Communist Party added a strong nationalist goal to the aims of international communism. China in the 1920s and 1930s was not a well-knit national state. Feudal warlords controlled important regions as fiefdoms, European powers maintained favored trading rights in selected territories, the country's Nationalist Party (Kuomintang) held sway in certain areas, and the Japanese in the 1930s and early 1940s maintained a tenuous hold over Manchuria and the seacoast provinces. Thus it became the ambition of the Communist Party to establish a strong central government that could consolidate the entire populace into a cohesive nation. That goal would be substantially achieved in the decades following World War II. Hence, in China the moral principle of patriotism—of loyalty to one's country—was added to the traditional Marxist values.

In the mid-1960s Mao expressed alarm at what he considered to be deviations from the true communist path. To thwart the putative deviationists (including intellectuals) and guide the populace back onto the Marxist track, he launched the Great Proletarian Cultural Revolution, designed to implement two of Mao's fundamental beliefs: (a) that the proper goal of moral development is to produce a classless society of the proletariat and (b) that human consciousness and knowledge derive from work, with *work* defined as the activity of producing and exchanging goods in the real world.

Whoever wants to know a thing has no way of doing so except by coming into contact with it, that is, by living (practicing) in its environment. . . . If you want knowledge, you must take part in the practice of changing reality. . . . All genuine knowledge originates in direct experience. (Mao, 1973, p. vii)

Nowadays, first, there are too many [school] classes; second, there are too many books. . . . Real understanding must be acquired gradually through experience at work. . . . We shouldn't read too many books. We should read Marxist books, but not too many of them either. . . . If you read too may books, they petrify your mind in the end. (Mao, 1974, pp. 195-211)

The ten-year period of the Cultural Revolution, 1966-1976, proved to be disastrous for both the economy and the social order. Two principal Marxist criteria for judging the success of a political-economic system are that (a) the production of material goods expands and (b) the distribution of goods reaches the populace in even measure—everyone benefits equally so that people become increasingly satisfied with their lot. On each of these measures the Cultural Revolution was an immense failure.

Following Mao's death in 1976, a radically new departure in economic, educational, and social policy was launched. Jiaying Zhuang, in a study of speeches and policy statements in official Communist Party periodicals for the period 1980-1985, concluded that, in contrast to Mao Zedong, China's current leaders (a) subscribed to a broader definition of *work* and *activity* that included scholarly pursuits. Confucian beliefs in the importance of self-discipline and dedication were revived, and the goal of human development was not only to contribute selflessly to a Marxist society but also to fulfill one's own personal ambitions (Zhuang, 1986).

The 1978 revision of the nation's constitution not only reiterated that Chinese society is founded on Marxist-Leninist-Maoist doctrine, but also added that "the state applies the socialist principles: 'He who does not work, neither shall he eat'" (Cheung, 1982, p. 24). Beginning in the latter 1970s, the government instituted the "responsibility system" as a way of stimulating economic growth. The system has offered people the chance to sell for their own personal gain whatever goods or services they produce beyond a basic level of contribution to the society. The system has also involved the government's contracting production tasks out to individuals. Undergirding this approach is the conviction that people are naturally motivated to work hard for self-gain, but they also can be convinced to contribute to the common good. In short, promoting one's own self-interest has become officially viewed as an acceptable moral value in communist China.

The North Korean Version

As in China, conceptions of moral values in the Democratic People's Republic of Korea have been true to basic Marxist doctrine, as reflected in such official statements of educational goals as the following:

We must make sure that all students fight selflessly for the interests of the working class. . . . It is particularly important to educate them to hate the enemy of the revolution. . . . By infusing students with hatred for imperialism and the landlord and capitalist classes, we should make certain that they fight resolutely against the class enemies. . . . We should educate all students to rid themselves of individualism and selfishness, and work, study, and live on the collectivist principle of "One for all and all for one." ("Theses on Socialist Education," 1980, no. 1, p. 17)

However, in addition to the values reflected in the doctrine of international communism, the North Korean variant has included a strong theme of Korean-culture nationalism. Patriotism has been stressed throughout the school curriculum and in the mass-communication media. Korean leaders have contended that Marxist educational theories "are enhanced and become particularly potent motivational devices when an emotional appeal to national pride and national identity becomes a stimulating force within a society" (Yang & Chee, 1963, p. 129).

Methods of instruction in the nation's extensive formal and nonformal education systems have reflected Marx's emphasis on the importance of practical activities as the formulators of people's minds. Teaching methods have required students to "see and hear directly with their own eyes and ears, touch and make things with their hands, 'think and grasp truth themselves', and put knowledge to practical application" (Shinn et al., 1969, p. 150).

The school system incorporates a theory-practice concept of education in which the theories of the classroom are translated into active participation in government-directed labor units designed to consolidate the student's learning and also to assist the government in its effort to industrialize the country. This segment of Korean society probably would not have developed to such an intense degree if it had been offered only the abstract concepts of international communism. The educational system's life-oriented, purposeful theories of learning are supported basically by the Marxist ideology of the dignity of labor as the origin of all value and wealth. (Yang & Chee, 1963, p. 129)

ADDITIONAL MORAL-DEVELOPMENT MATTERS

So far, this chapter has directly addressed four of the topics from Chapter 1 that concern the content of theories. Those four have included (a) stages of moral development, (b-c) guidelines—in the form of moral values—for distinguishing moral from immoral acts and for judging good from bad development, and (d) nomenclature particularly important for Marxist theory— such as *dialectical materialism, capitalism, bourgeoisie, proletariat, leading activity, social-class conflict,* and *classless society.* The purpose of the following section is to consider how the remaining topics from Chapter 1 can be viewed from the vantage point of Marxism.

The moral domain in Marxist theory encompasses people's interactions within the particular society's system of producing and exchanging material goods. All social life—government, education, religion, artistic endeavors, moral values—derives from the economic system. Therefore, the reality of moral development is found in the society's production and consumption of goods, that is, in the social order's dialectical materialism. The notion that morality involves obedience to a supernatural being, such as a God, has no place in Marxist belief.

Two convictions about human nature are of special import in Marxism. First is the belief that children are born amoral—with no knowledge of good or bad and no innate tendency to promoral or immoral behavior. Moral values are all acquired from the environment during the process of the child's growing up. Second is the belief that people are not innately selfish. Or at least if, by their original nature, they do tend to favor their own welfare over the welfare of others, this tendency can be overcome by means of education. People can learn to be altruistic and incorporate this trait into their personalities as a key moral virtue that guides their social interactions.

Questions about personality structure in Marxist theory must go unanswered, because Marx focused almost exclusively on how social experiences influence moral development instead of on the internal operation of the mind. In essence, he produced a sociological rather than a psychological theory.

In the heredity-environment controversy over the causes of people's moral condition, Marxism falls heavily on the environment side. It is true that Marxism does not deny some involvement of heredity in effecting people's moral judgments, such as in recognizing differences in moral-reasoning ability between the mentally retarded and the intellectually normal or gifted. However, in the main, the environment individuals inhabit while carrying out daily activities is believed to exert the principal effect on moral values and behavior. In keeping with this belief, individual differences among people in their moral development are accounted for by the social settings in which they are reared rather than by their genetic endowment. A capitalistic social setting is thought to produce a very different type of moral character than a communistic setting.

The length of moral development extends from infancy until physical death, with the first two decades of the life span regarded as especially influential. In such societies as the Democratic People's Republic of Korea, education is viewed as a life long process. People of all ages are expected to continue learning, with their moral education, according to Marxist political doctrine, regarded as an important feature of the curriculum (Thomas, 1983).

There are two sources of evidence on which Marxist theory is constructed. First is the careful observation of events of everyday life. Empirical science is thus accorded a central role in Marxism. Second is the logical analysis of the data gathered from observation, with the analysis featuring a dialectical approach. An event (thesis) is noted, along with contrary events (antithesis) that produce a dilemma or problem, which is then resolved by the creation of a new approach (synthesis) that accommodates both the original event and the contradictory ones.

There is no room in Marxism for divine inspiration or intervention, for intuition, or for unexplainable good or bad fortune.

Finally, the popularity of Marxist theory can be grossly estimated by the number of people living in countries that had communist governments prior to the 1990s. The total number of people who would have been acquainted with at least some aspects of a Marxist model would thus approach 2 billion. However, within that total, the individuals who would have sincerely subscribed to a Marxist version of moral development would obviously be far smaller, since so many people living in communist political systems would have had strong religious beliefs incompatible with Marxist precepts. Such competing belief systems would include Confucianism and Taoism in China, Judaism and Christianity in Eastern Europe, and Islam in the southern provinces of the Soviet Union. Furthermore, the commonsense-attribution convictions with which such peoples had grown up could also conflict with Marxist theory. Thus, while it is not possible to offer a convincing estimate of the number of people who have seriously interpreted moral development from a Marxist perspective, it still seems likely that the theory was widely accepted from the 1920s through the 1980s in communist regions, and that many people in those regions continue to embrace the central tenets of that theory today.

AN ASSESSMENT OF MARXIST THEORY

As has been the case throughout Part II, the criteria described in Chapter 2 are adopted in the present chapter as the standards against which Marxism is appraised.

I have rated the theory high for how readily it can be understood (item 1). Marx himself made clear the basic assumptions about society and people's mental development on which his proposal was founded. And the Soviet psychologists who devised a detailed Marxist theory of child development have likewise presented their version in a comprehensible form, supported by real-life examples and research evidence.

At least on the theoretical level, Marxist theory explains how people's moral values depend on their society's dominant mode of producing and consuming material goods and services. Whereas selfishness and competition are seen as values encouraged by capitalistic societies, altruism and cooperation for everyone's benefit are considered key virtues fostered by a communist form of social organization. However, in the practical operation of such socialistic societies as those of the Soviet Union, the People's Republic of China, and numbers of countries of Eastern Europe over the past few decades, many people's behavior on many occasions failed to reflect the ideal moral values. Production schedules often fell short of expectations because many workers did not fulfill their assignments to the extent of their abilities. Political and military leaders provided themselves with favors not available to the masses, so it was clear that none of the communist countries had produced the desired classless society. In communist China, a study by Zhuang (1989) of the social perspectives of residents of Shanghai showed that after decades of Marxist indoctrination, people still viewed the society as offering greater opportunity and privilege to some segments of the population than to others. Thus, on item 2 (explains past, predicts future), I have included two assessments—a high rating for theoretical prediction and a low rating for practical prediction. Marx's expectation about human nature appears to have been in error—that people in general will willingly work for the common good and be satisfied with everyone receiving identical benefits no matter how much or how little different members of the society contribute.

As a practical guide to moral development (item 3) Marxist theory deserves high marks. It offers three principal methods of fashioning an individual's moral thought and action—(a) intensive study of Marxist doctrine; (b) active engagement in daily activities involving moral matters, that is, learning by direct experience with one's social world; and (c) self-criticism in the presence of

---

Marxist Theory

How well do I think the theory meets the standards?

The Standards	*Very Well*	*Moderately Well*	*Very Poorly*
1. Is clearly understandable	X		
2. Explains past and predicts future moral behavior	theoretical T		practical P
3. Offers practical guidance in coping with moral matters	X		
4. Is readily verifiable and falsifiable	X		
5. Accommodates new evidence			X
6. Stimulates new discoveries		X	
7. Is durable			X
8. Is self-satisfying			X

others, with the criticism aimed at identifying one's faults and generating ways to correct the faults.

The theory also lends itself well to empirical tests of its validity (item 4, verifiable, falsifiable). Because Marxism predicts the ways people are expected to act in different types of societies, the process of assessing those predictions consists of observing people's behavior in moral-decision situations. Support for the theory takes the form of evidence that people in Marxist societies display more altruism, greater productivity for the sake of the group, and less self-interest than people living under other political-economic systems. During the 1980s, when it was apparent that many people in communist countries did not behave in the desired manner, some apologists for the system asserted that transforming attitudes from a self-centered to a group-centered focus was necessarily a long process, but one that could eventually succeed. The desired evidence, not yet available, would ultimately appear. In China in the mid-1980s, this hope was expressed by one writer in the following fashion.

> Under the socialist system, only a small number of advanced [people] can truly be selfless at the outset, but more and more people will attain such a level gradually. Those who are utterly selfish and benefit themselves at the expense of others are also in the minority. At first most people can only reach the level of integrating collective and personal interests and [then] submitting to the interests of the state and collective when contradictions arise. Socialism will eventually pass on to communism, and this requires ideology to go ahead of [people's actual behavior]. . . . Hence, we should energetically conduct education in communist morals and encourage people to carry forward the communist quality of selflessness. (Yi, 1985, p. 61)

By the mid-1990s, changes in the political and economic policies of a majority of former communist societies suggested that influential political leaders and a substantial portion of the populace were not convinced that the desired evidence would ever be forthcoming. They appeared to think that it was unreasonable ever to expect most individuals to act out of the degree of altruism envisaged in the Marxist ideal. In effect, they believed that Marx's conception of the pliability of human nature had not been verified.

I marked the theory low on its ability to adapt to new and potentially conflicting data (item 5) because typical adherents of Marxism have been so strongly dedicated to maintaining Marx's basic views intact. The two principal ways that proponents of the theory respond to additional data have been (a) to interpret the evidence in terms of the theory without altering the theory significantly (as in the above example from China) or (2) to avoid or dismiss evidence that appears to cast doubt on the model's validity.

As a stimulator of new discoveries in the realm of moral development (item 6), Marxist theory—particularly in the former Soviet Union—has been moderately significant by focusing attention on the influence of environments on ethical thought and action.

In terms of durability (item 7), I have placed Marxist theory near the lower end of the scale. The theory lasted as the official view of moral development as long as the political systems of communist nations remained intact. However, within the present-day populations of those nations, Marx's views are currently being replaced by religious beliefs that lay dormant during the height of communist control. Within the former Soviet Union, Christianity is newly flourishing. There are also active proponents of Islamic traditions. In particular, the large populations of Muslims in former southern Soviet republics (Azerbaijan, Kazakhstan, Kyrgyzstan, Tajikistan, Turkmenistan, Uzbekistan) are likely turning away from the Marxist-based position on moral development. In China, a recent revival of interest in, and respect for, Confucian and Taoist beliefs, along with the rapid growth of competitive entrepreneurship, significantly weakens the nation's dedication to Marxist moral principles. Thus, I estimate that Marxist theory, in its original form, will continue to decline in popularity.

In reflecting how well satisfied I am with Marx's view of moral development, I have marked the theory rather low on item 8. I agree with the Marxist concern for the importance of environments in forming people's moral nature, and I appreciate the honored place that altruism is accorded in the Marxist scheme. However, I disagree that people will not continue to act out of self-interest. I believe that people act altruistically (a) when they are forced to do so by societal sanctions or else (b) when they recognize that helping other people is enlightened self-interest. I also disagree with the lack of freedom of thought permitted in a Marxist system that endorses the use of killing, lying, cheating, and stealing to sustain and disseminate a Marxist political-economic system.

8

A Composite Theory*

No theory of moral development can boast of being an entirely new creation, because every theory to some extent includes elements of earlier models. Thus, the novelty of any new proposal is found in the particular components selected from previous theories, in additional components contributed by the new theory's author, and in how these components are assembled. The purpose of Chapter 8 is to illustrate one way that elements of various theories can be joined to form a composite theory that takes advantage of the strengths of models that have gone before.

I devised this composite theory by drawing on features of seven other models of human development, including cognitive-structuralism, social-learning theory, behaviorism, psychoanalysis, contextualism, and humanistic conceptions of the *self*, all set within an information-processing framework. The components that I added on my own concern the composition of moral values, causal relations, mental processes, the nature of the moral self, development progressions, and significant characteristics of environments that seem necessary for explaining how people's moral values develop and are applied in decision situations.

Throughout the chapter, the term *moral development* refers to *changes in the system by which people make moral decisions.* The theory, in effect, intends to explain how and why the moral aspects of the mind change with the passing of time. The term *moral reasoning* means the way an individual thinks about moral matters. The term *moral behavior* refers to how a person acts when faced with moral decisions.

The chapter's topics are addressed in this order: (1) principal characteristics of the model, (2) foundational components, (3) long-term memory, (4) environments, (5) working memory, and (6) progressions and stages.

---

*A similar version of this chapter appears as Chapter 3 in R. M. Thomas, *An Integrated Theory of Moral Development,* (Westport, CT: Greenwood, 1997).

PRINCIPAL CHARACTERISTICS OF THE MODEL

Figure 8-1 offers a graphic representation of the theory. Influential characteristics of environments are listed on the left side and essential features of the person on the right. At the bottom of the person rectangle are foundational components that derive from the individual's genetic inheritance and current biological state. The main genetic factors are (a) ability capacities, such as intellectual and physical potentials, and (b) the rate at which these capacities mature during childhood and adolescence. Furthermore, a person's current biological state is influenced not only by these genetic factors but also by nutrition, disease, and accident.

The foundational components support an information-processing network composed of the senses, working memory, long-term memory, and the neuromuscular system that acts on the world. Among the most important features of this network are the components of long-term memory, where the results of moral development reside. A person's current moral state is represented by the patterning of long-term memory components at the moment.

The environmental structure at the left is conceived to serve the three functions of determining (a) the opportunities a person has to encounter moral-decision situations, (b) the environmental cues that the individual believes should influence moral decisions, and (c) the kinds of consequences the person will experience from his or her actions in moral situations. The role played by these three factors in the life of a growing child is determined chiefly by the people who control the child's experiences. Such people serve as agents of the environments that the child encounters.

The following description of the model begins with the foundational components, then continues with long-term memory, the nature of environments, working memory, and acting on the world.

FOUNDATIONAL COMPONENTS

Five widely accepted principles of human development are that:

1. Genetic inheritance establishes the basic human needs or drives that motivate thought and action.
2. Genetic endowment defines a range of potential intellectual ability (genotype) within which environmental influences can operate to produce the actual intellectual skills people display in their lives (phenotype).
3. Such endowment can differ from one person to another, so one individual's potential will differ from another's.
4. The flowering of genetic potential evolves gradually over the first two decades of life.
5. The maturation rate of this flowering can differ from one person to another.

Figure 8-1

A Composite Moral-Development Model

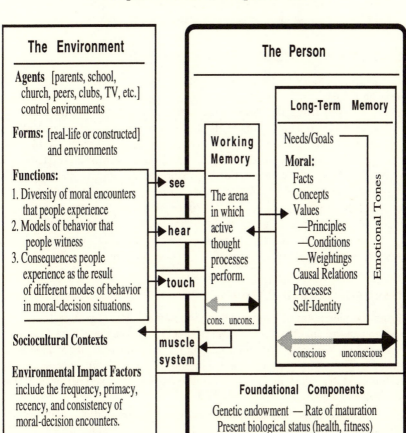

These principles reflect basic constraints that operate at any juncture of a person's life to influence what interests the person and how adequately the individual can understand moral issues and comprehend the consequences to be expected from different responses to moral situations.

Another foundational factor is the physiological state of the individual as a result of nutrition, illness, or accident. The term *nutrition* in this context refers to any substance that a person ingests. I am assuming that the growing child's nutritional state can influence how adequately the child derives moral "lessons" from the environment, stores those lessons in long-term memory, and uses them in making moral decisions. Furthermore, an individual under the influence of mind-altering drugs is not likely to respond to moral-decision situations in the same manner as one who is on a nutritionally balanced diet. In addition, any chemical imbalance or illness that alters the nervous system helps determine what the child is able to learn and how emotions alter moral decisions, particularly such emotions as depression, rage, guilt, and fear.

LONG-TERM MEMORY

Long-term memory performs two principal functions, those of directing the operation of the entire information-processing system and of storing coded material derived from the person's past experiences. For purposes of moral development, the principal components of long-term memory are conceived to be (1) needs/drives and goals, (2) facts and concepts, (3) causal relations, (4) moral values, (5) mental processes, and (6) the moral self. Each of these elements is presumed to be tinged with emotion—pleasure, pride, sorrow, shame, and the like. The components are also presumed to vary in terms of how readily available they are to conscious thought. In other words, they can range along a dimension that extends from the lucidly conscious to the deeply unconscious. Sometimes people are acutely aware of certain of the items stored in memory. Other times they cannot recall selected contents of their mind.

Needs/Drives and Goals

From the viewpoint of the present theory, humans are considered to be need-satisfying organisms that use the environment to meet their needs. In other words, people's actions are motivated by the twofold goal of (a) identifying objects and activities in the environment that will fulfill needs and (b) developing skills and strategies for obtaining those objects and performing those activities.

Some people prefer to call the forces that motivate human action *drives* rather than *needs*. The two terms are like the opposite sides of a coin—two facets of the same thing. Whereas *need* suggests a lack the person is attempting to satisfy, *drive* can suggest stored-up energy the individual is seeking to expend by investing the energy in particular objects and activities. Thus, the hunger drive represents a need for food, and the curiosity drive, a need to comprehend the environment.

Facts and Concepts

The term *facts* is used to mean mental records of either (a) discrete observations or measurements of people and their actions or (b) summaries of such observations and measurements. Thus, a fact can be the memory of a specific event, a person, an object, a place, or the like. Or a fact can be a summary report of the percentage of murderers apprehended by the police, the incidence of marijuana use by high-school students, or the amount of money contributed for the relief of famine victims. The fact portion of people's memories consists of past events in which they participated either as actors or as observers. Facts are what Tulving (1972) has called *episodic* memories. The events of significance are ones interpreted as involving moral matters—a teacher scolding a student for cheating on a test, a Sabbath-school lesson about forgiveness, an argument on the playground about breaking the rules, a TV program in which a woman is raped, a newspaper account of an army invading a neighboring country, and the like. Memories of facts are the raw materials used for constructing the other components of long-term memory—concepts, moral values, causal relations, mental processes, and the moral self.

In the present theory, a *concept* is a characteristic common to, and abstracted from, a variety of facts or other concepts, with a label attached to the concept so it can be consciously communicated in speech and writing and can be readily manipulated during thought. The label is typically a single word or short phrase. Examples of concepts significant in moral development are *lying, honesty, exploitation, altruism, felony, fair play, injustice, philanthropy, child abuse, compassion, hard-heartedness,* and *kindness.*

Causal Relations

A *causal relation* is an *if/then* belief a person has in mind. Such beliefs can be either *descriptive* or *prescriptive.* A descriptive or explanatory relation is an if/then conviction about what consequences actually will result in real-life situations if certain conditions obtain. For instance, "If the police catch that girl stealing jewelry from the store, she'll end up in jail." Or "If I give money to feed hungry people and then if sometime later I need help, some kind person will probably help me." Or "Give an embezzler counseling, and he might reform."

In contrast, a prescriptive causal relation represents a correlation that a person believes *should* obtain in life, whether or not it commonly does. Frequently a prescriptive relation begins with a proposal about a desirable way to act in moral situations. For example, the Chinese philosopher Confucius proposed: "If there are ways that you do not wish to be treated, then do not treat others in those ways" (Waley, 1938). This suggestion about how to behave is then linked to an assumed consequence. Thus, Confucius, as a social philosopher, suggested that if his precept was followed, the individual person would be happy, and the person's family, community, and nation would prosper. Prescriptive relations can also be cast in a negative form, with dire consequences predicted for people who disobey moral rules. According to Hindu lore, people who steal gold from a Brahmin priest will get diseased fingernails, those who steal cooked food will suffer dyspepsia, and adulterers will incur swollen limbs (Buhler, 1886, p. 440).

One important form of causal relations consists of linking (a) the way a person is treated to (b) an aim to be achieved. Parents take their daughter to Sunday school (treatment) in the hope that her experience there will help her become a "good person" (aim). A judge sentences a murderer to be executed (treatment) in order to prevent the felon from committing further misdeeds (aim).

Causal relations are crucial elements of moral behavior, for they represent what individuals expect will result from their actions. If people think the consequences of a given act will be contrary to their welfare, they will avoid that act and choose an alternative which they expect will bring more adequate need fulfillment Thus, causal relations link behaviors to consequences. Much of moral education involves teaching children about such relations.

Moral Values

The contents and applications of the *moral-values* component in Figure 8-1 are characterized by four key factors—principles, conditions, weightings, and emotional tones (Thomas, 1989; Thomas & Diver-Stamnes, 1993).

Moral Principles

At the core of each value is a moral principle in the form of an unembellished statement of what kind of behavior is right or, in its reciprocal form, what kind is wrong. Table 8-1 illustrates four principles found in many cultures.

Conditions

In any moral-decision situation, the application of a moral principle is affected by a series of conditions. The presumption here is that rarely if ever is any moral principle exercised unconditionally in every life situation to which that principle can apply. The way a principle is applied in moral decisions depends on selected circumstances of the particular case at hand. Here are three typical conditions:

1. *Age.* Whereas the age of the individuals involved in a moral situation is often a consideration in people's moral judgments, it is not really age itself but, rather, some other characteristic that is highly correlated with age, such as *knowledge of right and wrong* or *logical-reasoning ability.* A three-year-old who does not tell the truth is usually judged differently than a 19-year-old who is not truthful.

2. *Intention.* Whether an act is deemed moral or immoral can often depend on the answer to the question, "Why did he do it? Or what was she trying to accomplish?" Intention frequently is regarded as a defining characteristic of moral behavior, in that intention distinguishes acts involving morality from acts that result from mistakes, accidents, and chance.

3. *Seriousness of Consequences.* The severity of the consequences of a moral incident for recipients of the act as well as for the perpetrators can influence the

Table 8-1

A Sampling of Moral Principles

Virtues to Be Encouraged	Transgressions to Be Avoided
Regard for Human Life: Everyone should protect others from harm and should seek to enhance others' physical and mental well-being.	*Disregard for Human Life:* No one should exploit or harm others, either physically or psychologically.
Honesty: Everyone should tell the truth.	*Deceit:* No one should try to deceive others by lying or by deviously withholding the truth.
Contractual Integrity: People who have freely agreed, in either written or oral form, to perform an action should faithfully carry out that commitment.	*Contractual Unreliability:* People should never avoid performing actions that they have freely agreed to carry out.
Compassion, Altruism: Everyone should exhibit sympathy for, and offer aid to, people who suffer misfortune.	*Disdain, Coldheartedness:* No one should ignore or scorn people who suffer misfortune.

judgments about the moral status of the incident. For example, depending on the conditions, an incident of sexual intercourse may be judged in one case to be a mere peccadillo and in another case a felonious mortal sin.

In summary, conditions are contextual factors that qualify the application of moral principles in specific situations. A person discovers which conditions to apply by scanning the particular environment in which a decision is called for.

Weightings

A third distinguishing feature of moral values is a weighting factor. Certain principles are accorded more importance than others in people's moral judgments. To illustrate, in the case of a conflict between the principle "protecting human life" and the principle "telling the truth," an individual can regard the value of life more highly than the value of truthfulness and therefore arrive at a decision that gives greater weight to life than to truth-telling. Furthermore, conditions also can vary in their importance. In a decision that requires a choice between "intention" and "seriousness of consequences," a person may consider intention more important than seriousness of consequences in arriving at a moral judgment.

Emotional Tone

Moral values, and their application in specific situations, are assumed to be accompanied by affect, that is, by feelings reflected in such words as *guilt, pride, fear, confidence, hate, love, depression, joy,* and more. The emotional tone of a given moral incident is often complex, involving a combination or succession of different emotions. In addition, emotions can vary in intensity from weak to strong.

The emotional qualities of a moral event are significant in that they can influence a participant's willingness and ability to take particular actions. Emotions therefore have a motivating effect, inducing a person to adopt actions that will increase positive feelings and decrease negative ones. In the present theory, a person's *conscience* is represented as a linkage between a moral value and positive (rewarding) or negative (punishing) emotions. This linkage is presumed to result from the individual's past experiences with the world, so that over time people accrue a growing array of internalized rewarding and punishing emotions that influence how they feel and act when faced with moral decisions.

Emotions can also influence how rationally people will act and how well they can predict the consequences of their present actions. Furthermore, the emotional states of observers of moral incidents or of people who learn of past incidents (as in the case of a jury in a court trial) can also affect those individuals' moral judgments. As suggested by the diagram in Figure 8-1, an emotional tone is attached not only to moral values but to the other components of long-term memory as well.

Summary

The act of making moral decisions is assumed to involve a complex kind of mental algebra whose formulas are comprised of particular combinations of principles and conditions, their weightings, and accompanying emotions. The specific combination of variables that will be manipulated in carrying out such computations during a given moral encounter is determined by (a) the current patterning of the individual's moral-values contents (including emotions) and (b) that person's perception of which elements in the present environmental context are relevant to those contents.

Mental Processes in Moral Development

The term *processes* refers to patterns of mental operations that are involved in thinking about moral matters. There appear to be a number of major processes, with minor subprocesses or subroutines often embedded within them. One process, illustrated later under Working Memory, is composed of mental steps taken in arriving at a moral decision when the person is confronted with a moral event. Additional processes concern assigning blame for a misdeed, assigning rewards for a admirable act, comparing values, estimating the effectiveness of consequences in guiding behavior, predicting the outcome of moral encounters, and more. I am assuming that processes are stored in long-term memory and are drawn into working memory at the time they are needed.

In considering mental processes, we should recognize the significance of the *levels-of-consciousness* dimension in Figure 8-1, a dimension displayed as a double-pointed arrow at the base of the long-term-memory rectangle as well as at the bottom of the working-memory block. I propose that all of the contents of long-term memory can be at different levels of availability to consciousness. The individual, at the stage of working memory, may be quite aware of some contents and quite unaware of others; yet both the lucidly conscious and the hidden unconscious contents are presumed to affect moral thought and behavior. Processes are expected to function at different levels of awareness. I am also suggesting that as children grow up, their awareness of their needs and goals, past events, concepts, values, and processes increases in amount and complexity. This awareness of how one's moral-development processes operate might be dubbed *metaprocessing*, meaning "knowledge of how one's moral decisions are made." An implicit aim of moral education is to render moral components of the mind more conscious and thus more rational.

Moral Self-Identity

The central focus of humanistic psychology is the development of the *self*, which is a construct often defined in slightly different ways by different theorists. Combs and Snygg (1959, p. 124) described the self as "the individual as he seems from his own perspective." Rollo May called it "the organizing function within the individual . . . by means of which one human being can relate to another; consciousness of one's identity as a thinking-intuiting-feeling and acting unity" (in Reeves, 1977, pp. 286-287). Allport (1961, p. 110) described the self as a "kind of core in our being."

There are various aspects of one's overall self-concept. The physical aspect involves such matters as "how good-looking I am, how agile I am, how strong I am." The cognitive aspect concerns "how smart I am." The moral aspect represents answers to such questions as "Am I a good person or a bad person? What do I believe are right and wrong ways that people should be treated? What moral principles or ideals do I hold, and how faithfully will I abide by these principles under different life circumstances?" From the viewpoint of Freud's psychoanalytic theory, this moral self-identity is an individual's *superego*, as composed of two parts—the *ego ideal*, containing the person's convictions about proper ways to act (the "dos" of life), and the *conscience*, the person's convictions about the kinds of behavior that are immoral and should be avoided (the "don'ts" of life) (Freud, 1923, pp. 18-29).

The self is considered to be the unifying factor of the various components of personality, an integrator that binds all of the other aspects of mind into a coherent whole. The self also provides continuity of personality over time, furnishing a consistency of identity that extends unbroken from day to day. The "I" of today is experienced as being essentially the same as the "I" of yesteryear.

ENVIRONMENTS

As suggested on the left side of Figure 8-1, environments can profitably be analyzed in terms of four characteristics—their agents (including the contexts in which agents operate), forms, functions, and impact factors. I believe that when we identify various permutations of these factors, we go a long way toward accounting for the way people's encounters with different environments influence their moral development.

Agents

The word *agents* refers to the people and institutions in the society that establish which environmental events children will experience. It seems apparent that during the early years of the child's life the most important agents are parents. They determine the kinds of moral situations the young will face within the family, and they can control such outside influences as the child's companions, television programs, and story books. During middle childhood the school, neighborhood, and church serve to expand the range of people and media that determine children's exposure to moral events. For instance, the neighborhood incidents witnessed by boys and girls growing up in an inner-city ghetto can differ markedly from those seen by children in an affluent suburb or in a small farming community.

Agents not only affect the kinds of moral incidents children meet but also help shape the interpretations children draw about the incidents. In particular, an agent influences the values children assign to incidents when the agent proposes answers for such questions as: Was the behavior of the participants in that episode right or wrong? Should the participants be praised or condemned, rewarded or punished? And why?

In summary, people and institutions can control the kinds of moral situations a child meets and can influence the values the child applies when interpreting those situations. Because agents can differ markedly in the amount of control they maintain over the sorts of encounters and values children experience, children can be expected to differ in the resulting moral contents of their minds.

Sociocultural Contexts

Whereas *agents* means people and institutions that directly affect an individual's access to moral experiences, *contexts* is a more inclusive concept, embracing not only agents but also a complex of additional physical and societal factors that impinge on a person's moral beliefs and actions. More precisely, *context* refers to the broader physical-social milieu within which agents function. Context components include such diverse characteristics of a community as its population density, political conditions, information resources, occupational structure, incidence of crime, law enforcement, religious affiliations, economic health, ethnic composition, school curricula, patterns of property ownership, age ranges, attitudes toward sexual behavior, and far more. Contexts are expected to affect the types of environmental encounters people experience and the interpretations placed on those encounters.

Forms

The forms of environments in which children encounter moral matters can be divided into two general types—real-life and constructed. Real-life environments are ones met naturally in the routine of living. They have not been created by someone for either teaching children or assessing children's present moral status. Constructed environments, on the other hand, are ones devised to promote or to evaluate individuals' moral development.

Constructed environments can vary in the degree to which they approximate real-life settings. This point can be illustrated by our aligning examples of moral instruction along a scale ranging from *highly abstract* at one end to *highly realistic* at the other. An example at the highly abstract end would be a teacher's telling pupils to be honest, loyal, just, and compassionate, and then expecting the children to display such traits in daily life. Exhorting the young to memorize the biblical Ten Commandments or the Boy Scout Law provides a highly abstract environmental encounter.

A less abstract form is an anecdote that embodies a moral lesson. The parables of the Bible or Qur'an and incidents from the lives of mythical or actual heroes (Sir Galahad, Joan of Arc, Abraham Lincoln, Martin Luther King) are instances of this type of constructed environment. So also are the moral dilemmas posed by Piaget (1965) and Kohlberg (1984) for assessing the stage of children's moral development. Such anecdotes, in contrast to abstract concepts of honesty and justice, are able to perform three functions of environments— provide opportunities for children to meet an extended range of moral issues, offer models of behavior that children can imitate, and suggest consequences to expect from different types of behavior in moral situations.

At a point closer to the real-life end of the scale are the more detailed accounts of moral matters found in such reading matter as novels and biographies that picture people engaged in a series of moral decisions. Extended narratives can depict moral matters within more complex settings than can a brief anecdote.

Reality can be approached even closer when moral events are portrayed on the stage or in motion pictures and television programs. Unlike novels and biographies, which require considerable imagination on the part of readers, dramatic presentations can simulate the sights and sounds of real-life settings.

Implicit throughout the foregoing discussion is the conviction that the more closely a constructed environment approximates real-life conditions, (a) the more accurately children's mental maps (their moral development) will represent real-life moral decisions and (b) the more accurate will be the picture of children's moral development that researchers derive from constructed environments that are used as evaluation instruments.

Functions

For purposes of moral development, environments can be seen as serving the three principal functions noted earlier. Environments define the scope or range of moral events that children have a chance to witness, they furnish models of how people can act in moral-decision situations, and they suggest the consequences that will likely follow different kinds of moral behavior.

Impact Factors

The phrase *impact factors* refers to conditions that affect how, and to what degree, environmental encounters will affect the moral contents of a child's mind. Such factors are apparently quite numerous. Those described below have been chosen for purposes of illustration and are not intended to be definitive.

Perhaps the most obvious factors are ones found in traditional principles of learning as proposed by educational psychologists, such as *frequency, primacy, recency,* and *consistency.*

The frequency principle proposes that many repetitions of the same type of environmental encounter will exert a greater influence on moral development than will few repetitions. A child's witnessing 40 television programs involving sexual abuse will have a different effect on the contents of the child's mind than will two such programs.

In studies of certain forms of learning, the earliest items learned (primacy) as well as the latest ones (recency) are more readily recalled than are events in between. For moral development, we can propose that environmental encounters early in a child's life can have a particularly lasting effect on the contents of mind if, at the time of those encounters, the child is mature enough to assimilate the significance of those events. Likewise, we can postulate that recent events assume particular significance in affecting the moral contents, especially because they are still likely to be "fresh in mind," undiluted by intervening events and less subject to the fading of memory that so often occurs with passing time.

Consistency means the extent to which a person extracts the same moral message from a series of different episodes. Particularly important is the degree of uniformity of values and causal relations that the individual witnesses across a variety of moral environments.

WORKING MEMORY

Working memory is considered to be the arena of active thought, the stage on which the processes of interacting with the world and of manipulating contents of long-term memory are being performed at any given moment. Working memory puts moral decisions into action by issuing orders to the muscle system to take action—to speak over the phone, to write a letter, to run away, to strike an attacker, and the like.

The phrase *interacting with the world* means engaging in transactions with the environment. One example would be a girl deciding whether to tattle on her teenage brother whom she has seen sniffing cocaine. Another would be a student in a sociology class trying to understand the distinction between *misdemeanor* and *felony*.

The phrase *manipulating contents of long-term memory* refers to a person's thinking about matters that are drawn entirely from long-term memory rather than from the outside environment. The individual already has in long-term memory all the raw materials—events, concepts, causal relations, values— required for pondering moral matters. Much of people's creative thought and all of their dreaming are of this nature. Such thinking involves selecting materials from memory and rearranging them into new patterns. This type of manipulation takes place when a person tries to answer such questions as: If I had to choose between saving a classmate from a fire and, in the process, getting badly burned myself, what should I do? Or What are some of the consequences that could result from my writing anonymous threatening letters to a congressman?

An essential assumption held about working memory is that it can operate at more than one level of consciousness. In our earlier discussion, this matter of levels of consciousness (represented in Figure 8-1 by the double-pointed arrows at the base of long-term-memory and working memory) was given only passing mention. But because degrees of consciousness play such an important role in moral development, it is appropriate at this point to inspect the matter in greater detail. The phenomenon of consciousness, as intended here, is represented as a scale ranging from highly conscious to deeply unconscious. Operationally, a person is credited with recall whenever he or she expresses the retrieved material in verbal, graphic, or mathematical form. Although people may claim introspective recall ("I do remember it, but I can't quite put it into words"), they are not credited with retrieval unless they can express it in some public form, even if it takes the form of selecting the correct answer from an array of displayed options.

As already noted, I am presuming that much of the mental activity which bears on moral matters operates subliminally; that is, it occurs below the threshold of consciousness. Accepting this presumption can help explain why investigators have found the task of appraising people's moral development so troublesome. Individuals often cannot explain why they made a particular moral decision because they are not conscious of factors that produced the decision.

Next, we inspect the place of mental processes as functions of working memory. In our earlier description, I proposed that mental processes were stored in long-term memory, then brought to play in working memory when they were needed. As an illustration of one mental process operating at the level of working memory, consider the following postulated circuit of eight steps representing the process of making a decision when confronted by a moral event (Figure 8-2). Such an operation includes not only the manner of arriving at a decision but also the way the consequences of the decision can affect the contents of long-term memory.

Step 1. By means of the senses of sight and hearing, a high-school girl's working memory encounters an event in the environment that she interprets as a moral matter, because the incident fits the definition of *moral* in the moral-values component of her long-term memory. (The event consists of the girl's visiting a video store and, while she is inspecting the merchandise, noticing a boy—a schoolmate—slip two video cassettes under his jacket and begin to leave the store without paying for the items.)

Step 2. The girl's working memory extracts events and concepts from long-term memory that inform her of what actions she might take in this situation. (Before the boy can leave the store, she could shout to the clerk at the check out counter that the boy was stealing the cassettes. Or, after the boy leaves, she could report the incident to the clerk and tell him the boy's name. On the other hand, she could keep quiet about the whole affair. Or, later at school she could tell her classmates about the episode. In addition, she could accuse the boy in front of their classmates. Finally, by means of an anonymous phone call, she could describe the incident to the boy's parents.)

Step 3. From long-term memory's causal relations that seem pertinent to such events, the girl predicts what consequences will likely result from the alternative actions she could take.

Step 4. Weighing (in working memory) the advantages against the disadvantages of the various expected consequences, she decides how to act in order to maximize (in terms of need fulfillment) the advantages and minimize the disadvantages.

Step 5. She acts on her decision. (She chooses to report the incident to the clerk after the boy leaves the store and, later at school, to describe the event to a number of classmates.)

Step 6. Following her actions, consequences occur. (The store clerk learns the boy's address and phones the parents, asking whether the boy has two new cassettes that he neglected to pay for. At school, several classmates tease the boy, calling him "Lightfinger Louie," and tell students from other classes about

Figure 8-2

A Moral Decision-Making Process

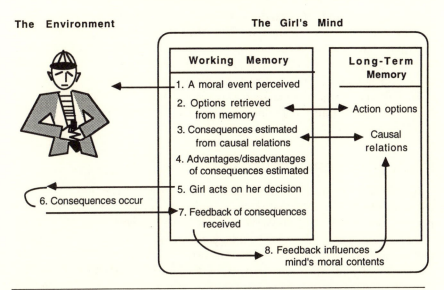

the incident. The boy discovers from the classmates that it was the girl who had seen him at the video store, and he threatens her: "I'll get you for this.")

Step 7. The girl receives feedback regarding the consequences. The feedback informs her about how accurately she had predicted the consequences at Step 3. (She receives three kinds of feedback: [1] She hears her classmates tease the boy. [2] She learns that the clerk phoned the parents. [3] The boy threatens her. In terms of her expectations at Step 3, she is not surprised that the classmates teased the boy, but she is astonished that the clerk phoned the boy's parents, and she did not expect the boy to threaten her.)

Step 8. The feedback influences the contents of long-term memory. To the extent that the actual consequences confirm her prediction at Step 3, the feedback strengthens the patterning of the original contents, that is, it strengthens the existing convictions about events and causal relations. But to the extent that the prediction of consequences proves to be in error, the feedback alters the original contents by generating changes in the mind's pattern of events and causal relations. In the girl's case, learning of the clerk's unexpected phone call and receiving the boy's threat will alter her conception of causal relations.

In summary, this hypothesized decision-making process, when carried through in overt action, serves moral development by strengthening the existing contents

of long-term memory whenever expectations are confirmed by ~~
But whenever expectations are not confirmed, the process
development by "changing the person's mind" in the sense of re
contents to render them more accurate, complex, and sophisticated
reality.

As the foregoing illustration implies, in this theory the
development refers to *changes in the system by which people*
decisions. That system is composed of the structure and contents o
memory as described earlier. *Development* means changes in the system
through interactions between internal neural maturation (determined chiefly by a
genetic timing mechanism) and working memory's environmental encounters
(which furnish learning opportunities that either strengthen or alter existing
contents of the mind)

STAGES OF MORAL DEVELOPMENT

Having now inspected the components of the model portrayed in Figure 8-1,
we turn finally to an additional aspect of moral development not pictured in the
diagram—the matter of progressions or stages of development.

In Piaget's, Kohlberg's, and Freud's conceptions of development, children
periodically advance from one stage to another. Each advance involves adopting
a new way of perceiving moral matters, of donning a new set of spectacles that
cast moral events in an new light so that henceforth the child abandons the
previous stage's way of interpreting moral encounters. However, in the present
theory I am proposing that although children do, indeed, progress to new levels
of cognitive skill, they do not abandon modes of interpretation used previously.
Instead, they retain the earlier modes in their perceptual repertoire for use on
suitable occasions. Thus a *stage* in this sense means the acquisition of a
significantly different ability to interpret events, but without the loss of existing
tendencies or abilities. Stagewise development is therefore defined as *the*
progressive accumulation of options—adding new arrows to the mental-
processes quiver.

From this progressive-accumulation viewpoint, children are not expected to act
on the basis of their latest acquired concept (stage) of moral values. Rather, they
can be expected to act on the basis of their decision about which of their accumulated concepts will likely bring the greatest satisfaction in the case at hand. In
other words, I am assuming that people estimate the likely consequences of
acting on various value positions, then choose the position that will yield the
greatest benefits in the present situation. Thus, on one occasion an individual
may behave in ways that appear very self serving, whereas on another this same
person may act in a seemingly altruistic manner. On a third occasion the
individual may obey the letter of the law (Kohlberg's stage 4 law-and-order

orientation) and on a fourth may act contrary to the formal law system as dictated by compassion (Gilligan's moral principal in Chapter 9).

CONCLUSION

Moral development, as conceived in this composite theory, has been defined as *changes in the system by which people make moral decisions.* Those changes, and the person's present state of development, are reflected in the moral content of the person's mind. As this chapter's description has indicated, the composite model focuses on two aspects of development: (a) components of the person and of the environment that are assumed to interact to produce changes in long-term memory and (b) the processes by which those changes occur. In contrast to Kohlberg's scheme, the Marxist approach, and the religious theories in Part III, the composite model does not identify which moral values are more desirable than others. The composite theory, in effect, emphasizes the process by which mental contents develop rather than prescribing what those contents should be in terms of concepts, values, causal relations, and the moral self.

In terms of the guide questions from Chapter 1, the foregoing description has addressed matters of personality structure, cause, development processes, individual differences, stages, and nomenclature. Answers to the remaining questions are as follows.

The moral domain concerns issues of constructive and destructive thought and action in relationships among people and in relationships between people and their environments. People are assumed to be born amoral, so that all of their values are acquired through learning across the life span, from birth until death. Evidence about moral development derives from empirical observations and the logical analysis of those observations, so that no supernatural forces are assumed to be sources of information about moral values or about the process of development. In other words, *reality* is defined in terms of the tangible, observable world of social relations rather than in terms of a world that includes unseen spirits which affect moral matters.

With this sketch of the composite theory now complete, we move to an evaluation of the model in terms of the standards introduced in Chapter 2.

AN ASSESSMENT OF THE COMPOSITE THEORY

Because I am the one who assembled this theory, I hardly qualify as an unbiased judge of the model. Thus, I trust that readers will feel free to correct any of the ratings that appear unduly self-serving. Two symbols, *P* and *X*, have been employed in the appraisal: P = potential and X = actual. Those items whose status seems to require a history of empirical research for judging the *actual* condition of the theory have been rated only on *potential* because the needed empirical evidence is not yet available. Items that can be judged on the basis of a line of logic without the need for empirical results have been given an *actual* rating.

I located the theory at the *moderately well* position for its clarity (item 1) on the basis of the reactions of university students who have read this chapter and discussed it in class. The model does not deserve a top rating because the students and I have been dissatisfied with the imprecision of certain aspects. In particular, we are not comfortable with the lack of detail about the way working memory interacts with long-term memory, about the role of unconscious factors in moral decisions, and about how different memories achieve their particular levels of consciousness. Furthermore, ways that needs or drives from long-term memory guide children's search of the environment are not explained satisfactorily.

A Composite Theory

How well do I think the theory meets the standards?

The Standards	Very Well	Moderately Well	Very Poorly
1. Is clearly understandable		X§	
2. Explains past and predicts future moral behavior	P*		
3. Offers practical guidance in coping with moral matters	P		
4. Is readily verifiable and falsifiable		P	
5. Accommodates new evidence	P		
6. Stimulates new discoveries	P		
7. Is durable			?
8. Is self-satisfying		X	

*P=Potential   §X=Actual

I marked the theory potentially high on explaining the past and predicting the future (item 2) because I think its components more adequately provide for the factors that affect children's moral development than do such proposals as Piaget's and Kohlberg's that have not been very successful (a) in accounting for why a child may make one level of moral decision in one situation and a different level in another, and (b) in explaining why children's moral behavior is often at odds with their moral reasoning. This composite theory can, I believe, go a long way toward explaining such matters.

Item 3—practical guidance in moral matters—is marked moderately high because the theory (a) identifies significant environmental variables that can be manipulated to influence children's morality and (b) alerts adults to the complex patterns that children's moral-values systems can assume.

I believe that a large portion of the model's proposals are empirically falsifiable. For example, evidence can be collected to test the effect of different features of environments on moral development, the values and causal relations in long-term memory can be at least partially assessed, and individuals' mental processes can be appraised to some degree. However, a major problem for verifying the theory is posed by the levels of consciousness. People's thinking processes at the unconscious level are very elusive, perhaps impossible to evaluate with any accuracy.

The theory potentially ranks high on adaptability (item 5). Conceived as a composite of elements from a variety of other theories, it is by its nature amenable to alterations that new evidence or theoretical suggestions might offer to render it more precise in explaining moral thought and action. It is thus a theory still evolving.

Since the model offers the possibility for generating a host of testable hypotheses, I judge that it has rather high potential for stimulating new discoveries. So far, two major investigations focusing on elements of the theory have already been published, with more in the offing (Thomas & Diver-Stamnes, 1993; Diver-Stamnes & Thomas, 1995).

The durability (item 7) of the theory is uncertain, since this particular model is of such recent vintage. However, I suspect that in its present form, at least, it will not last long but will be superseded by more adequate formulations.

Finally, I regard this scheme as fairly self-satisfying. It has helped me answer questions that I felt were not explained adequately by other theories described in this book. However, the composite model leaves vital issues unresolved, so more thought and experimentation are called for.

9

Specialized Theories

The phrase *specialized theories* identifies explanations of moral development that apply exclusively, or primarily, to selected aspects of moral thought and action or to certain types of people. Or, in some cases, moral development is only one portion of a broader theory that embraces other types of development as well (cognitive, emotional, social).

Although a great number of specialized theories can be found in the professional literature, the limited space available in this chapter permits the inclusion of only five. These few have been chosen because each is an exemplar of a particular kind of specialized theory. The aspects addressed in the first two illustrative models are (a) empathy and (b) unfairness and blame as viewed from an information-integration position. The next pair concern particular kinds of people, (c) females and their moral attribute of compassion and (d) juvenile delinquents. The fifth theory embeds moral development in ego development.

HOFFMAN'S EMPATHY

The theory devised by Martin L. Hoffman features the psychological process of empathy as the central concern in moral growth. Empathic reactions are mainly emotional responses to someone else's distress.

> I define a moral act in motivational rather than cognitive terms, that is, an act prompted by a disposition to do something on behalf of a person or group, or to behave in accord with a moral norm or standard bearing on human welfare or justice. Moral reasoning or judgment *may* be involved, but not necessarily. (Hoffman, 1991, p. 276)

In support of his assigning empathy a key role in explaining moral character, Hoffman has declared that

Empathic affects are congruent with two of Western Society's major moral principles—caring and justice—both of which pertain to victims and beneficiaries of human actions. Empathic affects may therefore provide motivation for the operation of these principles in moral judgment, decision-making, and behavior. The integration of empathy and moral principles may thus provide the heart of a comprehensive moral theory. (Hoffman, 1991, p. 275)

Hoffman's scheme involves five modes of empathic arousal that produce four stages of empathic distress over the first decade or so of life.

The first three modes of stimulating empathy are principally automatic and involuntary. The initial mode consists of an infant's crying at the sound of someone else crying. The second mode involves conditioning—another person is witnessed in a situation that has caused oneself distress in the past, so the other's situation automatically evokes feelings that one has experienced on such occasions. The third mode involves mimicry—emotionally copying the apparent grief or woe of people that one observes. Whereas the first mode—crying when someone else cries—largely drops out of children's repertoire early in life because of social disapproval, conditioning and mimicry can continue through the adult years.

The fourth and fifth modes of empathic arousal arrive only after the child gains language skills and more advanced thought processes, since the modes involve verbal communication and the ability to put oneself imaginatively in the place of another, in other words, to mentally assume another's role. Whereas the first three modes tend to occur automatically, individuals have more intentional control over the fourth and fifth (Hoffman, 1984).

Hoffman's hypothesized four stages of empathic distress, which result from the evolution of the modes of arousal, are assigned the titles (a) global empathy, (b) "egocentric" empathy, (c) empathy for another's feelings, and (d) empathy for another's life condition.

Global empathy is typical of infants' reactions during the first year following birth. "Distress cues from the dimly perceived other person are confounded with unpleasant feelings empathically aroused in the self" (Hoffman, 1991, p. 278).

"Egocentric" empathy begins to occur around the end of infancy when children become aware that other people are physical beings separate from themselves. However, the young do not yet perceive that others' feelings can differ from their own. They assume that another person who seems disturbed feels precisely the way they themselves would feel in that situation.

Empathy for another's feelings begins to appear around age 2 or 3, when children start to recognize that others' feelings may differ from their own because those feelings arise from the others' needs and from the particular way other people interpret their experiences. With this growth in maturity, a child looks for additional clues to what the others are actually feeling—what the person says, the sorts of events that precipitated the victim's discomfort or torment, and whether the person quickly recovers or continues to act despondent. The stage is also accompanied by a greater differentiation among feelings, with the child now better able to distinguish nuances of affect—deep sorrow, regret, embarrassment, shame, fear, and the like.

Empathy for another's life condition appears by the years of late childhood. Whereas at earlier stages children responded to another's immediate appearance of grief, worry, or embarrassment, by the latter years of childhood they are able to look beyond the present setting and envision the kind of life the other person faces. Deep empathy, therefore, can be felt for someone who at the moment exhibits a placid demeanor, yet who bears burdens of pain and care of which casual observers are unaware. In contrast, slight empathy may be felt for someone who presently seems highly distraught but whose general life condition is recognized as one of privilege and contentment. "This empathic level can provide a motive base, especially in adolescence, for the development of certain moral and political ideologies that are centered about alleviation of the plight of unfortunate groups" (Hoffman, 1991, p. 279).

Hoffman's theory distinguishes between *empathy* and *sympathy*. Empathy consists of a person's feeling the same distress that someone else apparently feels. Sympathy is the extension of the empathic reaction to include a desire to help alleviate the other's distress. Sympathy in this sense evolves in parallel to the second and third stages of empathic development as the growing child departs from an exclusive concern for self and becomes inclined to express compassion for the plight of others.

With the passing years, children not only advance in their capacity for empathy and sympathy, but they also compile a growing complex of moral values. In Hoffman's view, the moral decisions people make result from a combination of their empathic/sympathetic proclivities and their accumulated stock of values. In effect, as the young grow to adulthood, they acquire from their environment a selection of moral principles to guide their behavior in moral encounters. However, moral action is not controlled entirely by pure objective reasoning from those principles. Action is also influenced by feelings of empathy/sympathy for certain of the people involved in a moral event, feelings that bias the way the principles are applied in the case at hand.

Hoffman's model enables him not only to account for empathic responses to others' distress, but also to explain how empathy may result in (a) anger toward the estimated cause of the distress, (b) guilt for one's failing to alleviate the victim's plight, and (c) a sense of injustice at recognizing the unfairness of the way the victim has been treated.

ANDERSON'S INFORMATION-INTEGRATION THEORY

The interpretation of moral development proposed by Norman H. Anderson and his colleagues focuses on how people integrate information in their attempts to derive meaning from their experiences. Integration theory is founded on the conviction that "thought and action typically arise from multiple causes acting together" (Anderson, 1991a, p. 2).

Theorists operating from this perspective do not view moral development as a self-contained operation, separate from the development of other aspects of personality. Instead, "the processes involved in moral development are not essentially different from those involved in other social and cognitive judgment, [so] integration theory seeks a unified treatment of moral development within a general theory of judgment and action" (Anderson, 1991b, p. 137). Moral matters that advocates of this position have sought to explain include people's reasoning about blame, equity, unfairness, excuses, harm, and recompense (Anderson, 1991b; Farkas, 1991; Hommers & Anderson, 1991).

Foundational assumptions supporting the theory are that:

1. Every moral encounter involves a person's weighing multiple considerations in the effort to produce a satisfactory response to the moral event at hand. Hence, the challenge anyone faces in moral decision-making is that of identifying and integrating the significant multiple factors which affect that particular case.

2. The decision about what constitutes a "satisfactory response" depends on the goal—or the multiple goals—that the particular individual is seeking to reach. That is, the aim people hope to achieve in a moral situation becomes the force determining which factors they select and how they weight those factors. Thus, learning the person's goals in that situation is essential to understanding the individual's moral judgments and actions. It is also the case that goals are not static, but can shift during a moral episode as the person considers additional aspects of the incident. Information-integration theory, in contrast to Piaget's and Kohlberg's schemes, is therefore a functional approach "less concerned with structure of cognition [and] more with its operation in achieving goals" (Anderson, 1991b, p. 138).

3. The multiple factors that people weigh in generating their judgments and actions include values, attitudes, moral knowledge, their own and others' motivations, and features of the particular persons and conditions in the present episode.

4. The process of integrating the multiple factors consists of assigning positive and negative weights to each factor (in terms of the goal or goals being pursued), then applying a kind of moral algebra to the collection of factors so as to produce a decision about the event at hand. Although people perform the computation automatically, as their intellectual maturity advances they can become at least partially aware of their decision-making process and thereby bring it under greater intentional control.

Academics who till this field of information-integration theory have sought to devise and test formulas that reflect the manner in which people weigh and combine typical factors when arriving at moral judgments. Because factors influencing judgment in moral situations can be highly complex, theorists face a daunting challenge in trying to discover with any precision the moral algebra involved. This means that as yet the work in this realm is still in its infancy. It has consisted chiefly of experimenters posing hypothetical moral dilemmas for respondents to judge, with the judgments then analyzed to estimate how the respondents manipulated a limited selection of factors in arriving at their decisions.

For example, Hommers and Anderson (1991) confronted respondents with the case of a stamp collector who ruined an acquaintance's valuable stamp collection. The experimenters then asked the respondents to imagine they were the victim in this case and were to decide how much the offender should be punished. The case was altered somewhat in three of its details when presented to three different sets of respondents. The versions varied in the number of stamps damaged, whether the damage was caused by accident or on purpose, and the quantity and quality of the offender's stamps that should be given to the victim as compensation. By comparing the way the three sets of respondents weighed the three conditions, the experimenters were able to estimate the form of the moral algebra respondents applied when the factors under review were those of *intent, amount of damage,* and *type of recompense.*

Farkas (1991) pursued a similar aim in experiments involving people's judgments of what constitutes equity (fairness/unfairness) in the compensation different workers receive for the contributions they make in a business organization.

Leon (1982) studied children's decisions about how much blame to assign in a case of wrongdoing in which the three variables in the alternate versions of the transgression were (a) the motive (intentional or unintentional), (b) the amount of damage (much, little), and (c) the rationale of the harmdoer (apologized, admitted doing harm, was belligerently defiant). Most of the respondents (ages 6 and 7) determined the amount of blame by averaging the three variables (Blame = Motive + Damage + Rationale). However, a noteworthy number ignored the amount of damage and assigned blame solely by applying a Motive + Rationale rule. A few judged mainly on the amount of damage.

In summary, information-integration theorists work in the hope of establishing systematic ways of charting the cognitive rules by which people integrate factors to arrive at their conclusions about moral events.

GILLIGAN'S COMPASSIONATE CARING

Carol Gilligan, a colleague of Lawrence Kohlberg at Harvard University, objected to Kohlberg's contention that mature moral judgments are founded on (a) people reaching an agreement about rules of justice and (b) the even handed application of those rules to all members of society. She declared that Kohlberg's proposal might account for some people's behavior—such as typical male judgments—but it failed to account for the moral decisions of others—particularly of mature women. For these others, Gilligan held that compassionate caring, as associated with traditional female social roles and the act of mothering, was the guide to moral decision-making (Gilligan, 1982).

Gilligan described caring as a "different voice" from that of Kohlberg's contractual, even handed justice. In doing so, she did not admit to pitting women's viewpoints against those of men. Instead, she explained:

> The different voice I describe is characterized not by gender but theme. Its association with women is an empirical observation, and it is primarily through women's voices that I trace its development. But this association is not absolute, and the contrasts between male and female voices are presented here to highlight a distinction between two modes of thought and to focus a problem of interpretation rather than to represent a generalization about either sex. . . . Clearly these differences [between males' and females' perceptions] arise in a social context where factors of social status and power combined with reproductive biology to shape the experiences of males and females and the relations between the sexes. (Gilligan, 1982, p. 2)

Despite this disclaimer that only *theme* and not *sex* is the target of attention, the "empirical observations" and the general tenor of both professional and popular literature about justice and caring clearly feature putative differences between females and males. A case in point is Noddings' book entitled *Caring*, a volume devoid of empirical data but replete with generalizations designed to:

> strike many contrasts between masculine and feminine approaches to ethics and education and, indeed, to living. These are not intended to divide men and women into opposing camps. They are meant, rather, to show how great the chasm is that already divides the masculine and feminine in each of us and to suggest that we enter a dialogue of genuine dialectical nature in order to achieve an ultimate transcendence of the masculine and feminine in moral matters. (Noddings, 1984, p. 6)

In the 1982 version of her theory, Gilligan traced the moral development of girls and boys from infancy through adolescence, highlighting the increasing divergence of the two sexes' central values at each successive stage of growth. In Gilligan's opinion, the process of value differentiation is well established during the first three years of life when children's primary caregiver is typically their mother. At this early stage, mothers do not perceive girls and boys in the same way. They see girls as extensions of themselves, and the girls correspondingly identify with their mothers and adopt their female penchant for attachment and caring. In contrast, mothers see their sons as male opposites, so that boys come to define themselves as masculine and "separate their mothers from themselves, thus 'curtailing their primary love and sense of empathic tie'" (Gilligan, 1982, p. 8). In her analysis, Gilligan agreed with Chodorow's (1974) assertion that such a process results in children's gender identity being solidly established by the age of three. Consequently, "girls emerge from this period with a basis for 'empathy' built into their primary definition of self in a way that boys do not" (Chodorow, 1978, p. 167).

To illustrate gender identity and core values in the years of middle childhood, Gilligan focused on differences between girls' and boys' attitudes toward play and games, which she portrayed as "the crucible of social development during the school years" (Gilligan, 1982, p. 9). Drawing on studies of children's play by Lever (1976) and Piaget (1965), Gilligan concluded that as boys grow up, they become increasingly concerned about rules and of how to apply them fairly to solve conflicts. In contrast, girls are more tolerant of altering rules and making exceptions in order to accommodate people's feelings and interests.

Gilligan declared that adolescence and young adulthood further emphasize females' concern for caring and responsibility and males' concern for rights and rules as males increasingly engage in competitive activities and females' concentrate more on the quality of personal relationships.

In a 1988 version of her theory, Gilligan adopted a somewhat different tack, apparently influenced by recent empirical studies in which no differences were found between the sexes in the expression of empathy and in moral reasoning (Gilligan & Wiggins, 1988, p. 111). In this later interpretation of moral development, Gilligan featured a dialectical struggle faced by both girls and boys—the struggle to reconcile justice (equal rights, objective fairness) with compassion and caring (empathizing with the plight of others) (Gilligan & Wiggins, 1988). The struggle often ends up with a person resolving the conflict by adopting one perspective and discarding the other.

> This ability to see relationships in two ways or to tell a story from two different angles underlies what may well be among the most searing experiences of moral dilemma, creating an irreducible sense of ethical ambiguity and also perhaps a temptation to eliminate one version or one perspective and, thus, make the incongruity disappear. (Gilligan & Wiggins, 1988, p. 128)

Although it is not considered inevitable that females assume a caring orientation and males a justice position, it has been Gilligan's opinion that such is usually the case, given the traditional nature of social structure, a nature that perhaps is in transition toward less division between the sexes.

> While it is true that either we are men or we are women and certain experiences may accrue more readily to one or the other sex, it is also true that the capacity for love and the appreciation of justice is not limited to either sex. (Gilligan & Wiggins, 1988, p. 137)

In both the academic literature and the popular press, Gilligan's theory has met with mixed reviews. She has been acclaimed for drawing attention to the importance of compassion as a significant moral virtue that had been neglected by writers who defined morality exclusively in terms of justice and equal rights (Haste & Baddeley, 1991). On the other hand, critics have charged that moral development depends on far more variables than sex differences, so that Gilligan unduly emphasized gender and thereby offered a simplistic and misleading interpretation of moral matters (Thomas & Diver-Stamnes, 1993, pp. 123-128; Diver-Stamnes & Thomas, 1995, pp. 150-152, 177). And there are those who have sought to resolve the ostensible conflict between Gilligan's and Kohlberg's positions by locating the virtues of care and justice at different points in the individual's development (Brabeck, 1986). However, whichever position people adopt regarding the validity of Gilligan's theory, few would deny that she has made an important contribution to discourse about moral development.

SUTHERLAND AND CRESSEY ON DELINQUENCY

In the context of the present volume, delinquency can be defined as a serious breach of moral rules. The term *delinquency* is more often applied to law-breaking by children and youths than to the misconduct of adults.

Over the years, a host of theories have been proposed to account for delinquent behavior (Shoemaker, 1990). One variety has featured biological causes, that is, internal conditions that predispose a person to commit antisocial acts. When a condition is assumed to result from the individual's inherited genetic composition, the explanation has sometimes been referred to as a "bad blood" interpretation. Other biological theories have not blamed genes but, rather, declare that chemical imbalances—perhaps due to drugs or a brain tumor—alter the operation of the brain in ways that lead to misconduct (Hippchen, 1978). In contrast to biological explanations are social-psychological theories that locate the causes of delinquent acts in a person's interactions with the social environment. Illustrative of this approach is the differential-association theory espoused by Edwin H. Sutherland and Donald R. Cressey (1978).

The differential-association model can be seen as a limited version of social-learning theory, a version confined to explaining criminal behavior. The essence of the Sutherland-Cressey position is found in a series of propositions about how delinquency develops. The first proposition is that criminal behavior is neither inherited nor the result of a person's biochemical nature. Rather, people learn antisocial acts through communication with other individuals and groups who engage in those acts. This learning can be either direct (explained or demonstrated by the others) or indirect (observed secondhand, as in reading about the behavior or seeing it on television or in movies). The major part of the learning occurs in intimate personal groups, such as in a gang or with friends watching movies together.

The two sorts of things that potential delinquents learn through their personal associations are (a) motives and attitudes (reasons for committing antisocial acts) and (b) specific techniques of committing crimes (exactly how to steal a car, to rob pedestrians, to sexually assault a partner on a date, to forge a check). The motives and attitudes that juveniles learn about the law from their associates are usually of a mixed variety, some of them conducive to abiding by the law and others conducive to breaking or skirting the law. In other words, "exposure to delinquent norms and behavior is likely to be inconsistent and mixed, with simultaneous exposure to nondelinquent norms and behavior," so that the young receive conflicting messages about lawbreaking (Shoemaker, 1990, p. 153). Youths become delinquent when they acquire an excess of attitudes favorable to violating the law over attitudes favorable to obeying the law.

Individual differences among juveniles in their moral behavior can be accounted for by differences in the frequency, duration, priority, and intensity of their social contacts. More frequent associations with companions or role models and associations of longer duration exert greater influence on a juvenile's beliefs about lawbreaking than do less frequent and briefer contacts.

> Priority indicates that associations (whether delinquent or nondelinquent) formed in early childhood may take precedence in influence over later associations. Intensity refers to the prestige of an association or, actually, to the power of influence one person or group may have over another. (Shoemaker, 1990, p. 153)

A final proposition is that the general needs and drives of delinquents are quite the same as those of nondelinquents. What differentiates the two groups are the methods they use to meet their needs. Theft and honest labor are typically motivated by the same intent—to obtain money to pay for things that will bring satisfaction. Rape and mutually agreed-upon love making are both aimed at fulfilling sexual desires. Thus, from the viewpoint of differential-association theory, the task of rearing law-abiding children consists of ensuring that the individuals and groups with whom children frequently interact over an extended period of time (directly or via mass-communication media) display a far higher proportion of law-abiding methods of meeting their needs than of antisocial methods.

Critics of differential-association theory have charged that it fails to account adequately for all delinquent acts. However, a body of research supports the theory by verifying that delinquency is more common among youth who report having friendships with other delinquent or unconventional youth, whereas associating "with more conformist, or conventional, peers is correlated with lower rates of delinquency" (Shoemaker, 1990, p. 160).

LOEVINGER ON EGO DEVELOPMENT

Jane Loevinger, a professor at Washington University in St. Louis, generated a theory of ego development from analyzing the answers respondents gave to a sentence-completion test consisting of 36 sentence stems. The stems were designed to reveal various aspects of an individual's personality, aspects that together might compose a picture of the person's stage of ego development

(Loevinger, 1976). The following illustrate typical sentence stems (Loevinger, 1987, pp. 230-232).

If my mother	A pregnant woman . . . .
When they avoided me	A woman's body . . . .
Most men think that women	

Loevinger declined to offer a "logical definition" of *ego* or *self,* preferring instead to "present impressionistic stages," then apparently let readers draw their own conclusions about what sort of concise definition might best reflect the essence of the stage structure. She did, however, suggest that "What changes during the course of ego development is a complexly interwoven fabric of impulse control, character, interpersonal relations, conscious preoccupations, and cognitive complexity, among other things." Ego development, from the Loevinger perspective, is thus a multifaceted yet "single coherent process. . . . Nothing less. than the *ego* encompasses so wide a scope, [including] moral development, development of cognitive complexity, and development of capacity for interpersonal relations" (Loevinger, 1976, pp. 26-27).

In brief, then, moral development is imbedded in Loevinger's broader ego-development scheme, with her notion of ego development resembling "the conception of moral development (in the Piagetian and Kohlbergian tradition), though it is a broader concept and the methods of study have been different" (Loevinger, 1987, p. 222).

Loevinger originally extracted five stages of development from the results of her sentence-completion test. But with the compilation of more data from a more diverse sample of subjects, she extended the system to include nine stages, with the possibility of even more in the offing. "Additional intermediate stages may become evident with further experience; so the levels should be described by names rather than numbers. Numbers inevitably lock the conception into whatever set of stages are current when numbering takes place" (Loevinger, 1987, p. 226).

In contrast to Piaget's, Kohlberg's, and Freud's proposals, the stages in Loevinger's system do not form a single ladder that children ascend in regular sequence. Instead, Loevinger's stages are, as she explains, no more than roughly correlated with age.

> In principle, I seek to describe every stage in a way that applies to a wide range of ages (granted, of course, that the earliest stages are rare after childhood and that the highest stages are impossible in childhood and rare even in adolescence). (Loevinger, 1976, p. 14)

In the following brief description of the nine stages (Loevinger, 1976, pp. 15-26), I have taken the liberty of suggesting sorts of moral reasoning or moral behavior that might be expected at each level of Loevinger's system.

Presocial Stage. Newborns have no ego, no sense of self that is differentiated from the surroundings. Distinguishing between *me* and objects that are *not me* is the infant's step toward establishing an ego. The neonate is amoral—without any moral awareness or status. Beginning to acquire passive and active language promotes the infant's sense of being a separate person.

Impulsive Stage. Children's impulsive assertions—"No," "Don't want to" and "Do it myself"—help establish their sense of separate identity. Their focus is chiefly on the present, rarely on the past or future. They tend to class people as good or bad, "not as a truly moral judgment but as a value judgment. Good and bad at times are confounded with 'nice to me' versus 'mean to me'" (Loevinger, 1976, p. 16). They are controlled in their behavior far more by constraint and punishment than by conscience. Children who stay at this stage a long time may be deemed uncontrollable or incorrigible.

Self-Protective Stage. Children begin to learn moral rules, but will manipulate the rules to suit their own desires, operating on the moral principle of not getting caught. They start to comprehend the concept of blame, but are prone to locate blame in others rather than in themselves. Therefore, the young are cautious and guarded. Those who continue in this vein into adolescence or adulthood function as opportunistic hedonists, avoiding work and expecting an easy life with all the good things readily at hand. They bend or break the rules to get their own way.

Conformist Stage. Children achieve a major advance in ego development when they identify their own welfare with the welfare of the group—with the welfare of the family for the young child, with the peer group for the older one. The reason conformists obey rules is because the rules are endorsed by the group and not simply for fear of punishment, though the group's disapproval is a strong impetus to conform. Rather, the individual's "moral code defines actions as right or wrong according to compliance with rules, rather than according to consequences, which are crucial at higher stages" (Loevinger, 1976, p. 18).

> While the Conformist likes and trusts other people within his own group, he may define that group narrowly and reject any or all outgroups. . . . The Conformist values niceness, helpfulness, and cooperation with others, as compared to the more competitive orientation of the Self-Protective person. However, he sees behavior in terms of its externals rather than in terms of feelings, in contrast to persons at higher levels. . . . His concern for the externals of life takes the form of interest in appearance, in social acceptance and reputation, and in material things. Belonging makes him feel secure. (Loevinger, 1976, pp. 18-19)

At the conformist stage, the nature of a person's reference group affects whether that individual will be law-abiding. Identifying oneself with a gang of delinquents can promote lawlessness. In contrast, identifying with a church's youth society, a scout troop, or an athletic team can encourage promoral behavior.

Self-Aware Level This is a transition phase between the conformist stage and the upcoming conscientious stage. Loevinger has suggested that the self-aware level is the typical status—the modal level—of adults in American society. Most adults who reach this level will not move beyond it, "for it appears to be a stable position in mature life" (Loevinger, 1976, p. 19). It is marked by an increase in self-awareness and an appreciation of numerous possibilities in situations that arise. In moral encounters, the individual is better equipped to envisage multiple ways to respond and to foresee multiple potential outcomes.

Conscientious Stage. At this point the principal features of adult conscience appear. The person does not simply feel guilty for breaking rules, but now selects long-term goals and ideals, engages in multifaceted self-criticism, and displays a sense of responsibility for others' welfare. In Loevinger's opinion, only a few people as young as age 13 or 14 reach the conscientious stage.

> Distinctions are made between, say, moral standards and social manners or between moral and esthetic standards. Things are not just classed as "right" or "wrong." The ability to see matters from other people's view is a connecting link between [a person's] deeper interpersonal relations and his more mature conscience. (Leovinger, 1976, pp. 21-22)

Individualistic Level. This is a transition phase linking the conscientious mode to the next stage, that of personal autonomy. The individualistic level is characterized by an increased awareness of individual differences among people and tolerance for oneself and others The rather strict moralism of the conscientious period is mitigated by greater recognition of the complexity of moral events. In their moral judgments, people take more factors into consideration and perceive matters from more than one person's perspective.

Autonomous Stage. At this stage, people are able to accept and consciously act to resolve conflicting needs and duties, to cope with complexity, and to display a high toleration for ambiguity. Moral issues are increasingly seen as multifaceted and not amenable to simple solutions. Autonomous individuals subscribe to wide-ranging social ideals, such as that of justice, and weigh these ideals in their moral judgments.

Integrated Stage. Loevinger writes that "We call the highest stage Integrated, implying some transcending of the conflicts of the Autonomous Stage." Because, in her opinion, people rarely reach this level, "one is hard put to find instances to study" (Loevinger, 1976, p. 26). A person reaching the integrated stage not only displays all of the features of the autonomous level, but also possesses a more secure sense of identity, a confident image of self beyond that of people at lower levels in the ego-development hierarchy. The moral judgments of an integrated ego represent a balanced consideration of the complexities of different people's needs and motives, of causes, of competing moral values, and of likely consequences of potential solutions.

Commenting on her development scheme, Loevinger wrote:

> To telescope the whole sequence of ego development in terms of describing the lowest and highest levels is to miss the spirit of the exposition. Growth does not proceed by a straight line from one low level to another higher level. There are many way stations, and they are all important as stages of life and as illuminations of the conception. In some sense, moreover, there is no highest stage but only an opening to new possibilities. (Loevinger, 1976, p. 26)

In summary, then, Loevinger has embedded a conception of moral development in her posited system of ego development. In assessing the validity of her system, we can profitably consider two questions. First, how generally applicable is a theory that is founded solely—or primarily—on responses to a 36-item sentence-completion test that was originally designed to measure women's attitudes? Second, does not the ordering of stages into a hierarchy of desirability involve a strong measure of subjective preference on the part of the theorist? Or do the locations of levels reflect a bias peculiar to the culture in which the theorist has been reared—"a rationalization of a society's scheme of values"? In response to these questions (which also have been asked about Kohlberg's moral-development hierarchy), Loevinger has contended that the "substantial agreement among authors" who have used other methods of investigation verifies the pattern of stages that she has proposed (Loevinger, 1976, pp. 27-28).

CONCLUSION

The purpose of Chapter 9 has been to provide a small sample of the numerous theories that are not designed to explain moral development as a general phenomenon but, instead, treat only selected aspects of such development (empathy, compassion, unfairness, blame) or only certain types of people (females, delinquents). In addition, as illustrated by Loevinger's theory of ego development, a conception of moral development is sometimes incorporated within a theory that encompasses a variety of aspects of personality.

The five schemes included in this chapter have been identified as special theories so as to differentiate them from the models reviewed in chapters 3 through 8.

Part III

Theories Implied in Religious Doctrine

Because not everyone defines the term *religion* in the same way, it is important at the outset to describe the meaning assigned to it throughout Part III.

Some writers conceptualize religion in a broadly inclusive way, defining it variously as "the collective expression of human values," as "the zealous and devout pursuit of an objective," or as "a system of values or preferences—an inferential value system." Such definitions are so broad that they encompass not only the belief systems of Judaism, Christianity, Islam, and Hinduism but also those of communism, democracy, and logical positivism.

Other writers place far greater limitations on the term *religion*, proposing that a conceptual scheme qualifying as religion must be an integrated system of specified components, including the nature of a supreme being or of gods (theology), the origin and condition of the universe (cosmology), the nature of being (ontology), the nature of knowledge and its proper sources (epistemology), rules governing social relations (ethics, morals), the proper behavior of people toward superhuman powers (rites, rituals, worship), and the goal of life (teleology). Under this sort of definition, Judaism, Christianity, Islam, and Hinduism are religions but communism, democracy, and logical positivism are not. This second way of defining religion is the one used for selecting the belief systems included in Part III

Whereas the secular models examined in Part II were created by their authors as formal theories of moral development, the theories inspected in Part III were not. Instead, the versions of religious theories offered in Part III are constructions that I prepared by extracting elements from religious doctrines, then organizing the elements within a framework dictated by the questions described in Chapter 1.

Although the world, past and present, has contained thousands of systems of religious belief, only three clusters of major traditions are analyzed in any detail in Part III. The trio represent separate patterns of historical development. As described in Chapter 10, Judaism was the principal forebear of Christianity, and

Islam subsequently grew out of both Judaism and Christianity. In Chapter 11, Hinduism is pictured as the ancestor of Buddhism and of such lesser variants as Jainism and Sikhism. Chapter 12 notes common elements of Shinto and Confucianism that resulted from transactions between those two persuasions.

Figure III-1 displays in graphic form developmental relationships among these nine traditions. However, the starting dates for several of the sects are admittedly only rough estimates, for when those faiths originated as orally conveyed beliefs is unknown. Such is the case with Judaism, Hinduism, Confucianism, Shinto, and perhaps Jainism.

Chapter 13 is designed to carry the description of religious theories beyond the foregoing major denominations in order to illustrate features of four other faiths (Navajo, Zulu, Vodou, Okinawan) that have attracted smaller numbers of adherents than have the major sects.

Finally, in keeping with recently developing usage, throughout Part III the symbol BCE (*before the common era* or *before the Christian era*) replaces the traditional BC (*before Christ*) to identify dates more than two millennia in the past. Dates within the past 2,000 years are either cited with no appended letters or are accompanied by the symbol CE (*common era*) instead of the traditional AD (Latin *anno Domini* that stands for *year of our Lord*).

Figure III-1

Patterns of Development of Religious Faiths

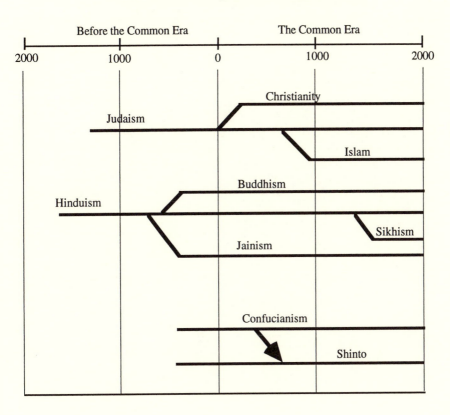

10

The Judaic-Christian-Islamic Line

The Jewish-Christian-Islamic sequence of religious ideologies consists of an initial tradition followed by two major reformation movements that today exist as separate doctrinal and organizational systems. The initial tradition was that of Judaism, founded well over 3,000 years ago. Today Judaism is credited with having 13.5 million adherents around the world. The first great reformation movement, intended to correct ostensible shortcomings of Judaism, was Christianity, established around 2,000 years ago. In the closing decades of the 20th century, an estimated 1.9 billion people have been identified as followers of Christianity. The second major reformation effort, Islam, was launched over 1,300 years ago to remedy putative doctrinal errors and improper practices of both the Judaism and the Christianity of that era. At present, there are an estimated 1.03 billion members of the international Islamic community (Barrett, 1995, p. 275). It is thus apparent that Judaism, Christianity, and Islam continue to be extremely popular as theories of moral behavior.

As explanations of moral development, these three philosophical persuasions share so much in common that it is convenient in the following pages to inspect them together.

At the outset it should be recognized that no Judaic, Christian, or Islamic doctrine was ever issued as a formal theory of moral development. However, components that can comprise such a theory are embedded in the three religions' basic literature and can be assembled in theory form. The task of discovering and assembling those components is what I attempt in the following pages. The principal documents used in this search have been (1) the Jewish Bible and the Talmud, (2) the Christian Bible, and (3) the two most basic Islamic books—the Qur'an and the Sunnah or Hadith. The Qur'an contains God's word as revealed to the Prophet Mohammed, whereas the Sunnah describes significant deeds and sayings from the life of the Prophet. These several documents are linked in a chronological sequence. The Jewish Bible appears as the Old Testament of the

Christian Bible (with the Christian New Testament then depicting the life and works of Jesus Christ); and the Qur'an frequently alludes to events from the Jewish Bible and occasionally to elements of Christian belief.

The following treatment opens with a review of convictions held by members of all three traditions, then turns to significant differences among the three faiths' conceptions of moral thought and action, and closes with an assessment of the Judaic-Christian-Islamic line of faith.

To put the discussion in proper perspective, I should note that none of the three religions comes in a single version. Judaism, Christianity, and Islam have each spawned a variety of sects that differ from each other in their practices, doctrines, or organizational structures. Judaism has its Orthodox, Conservative, and Reform branches. Christianity is divided between Catholicism and Protestantism, with the Protestant branch composed of Methodists, Presbyterians, Baptists, Seventh Day Adventists, and many more. Islam has Sunni, Shi'ah, Sufi, Druze, and other sects. In this chapter I do not pretend to describe the multiple variants of the three faiths. Instead, I have sought to identify elements of each of the three traditions that seem widely accepted by their constituent denominations, thereby producing a kind of generic version that is intended to represent the essence of the faiths' beliefs as they apply to moral matters.

BELIEFS HELD IN COMMON

Judaism, Christianity, and Islam are in basic agreement on the most fundamental questions about the source of truth, the nature of reality, origins of the universe, the purpose of human life, causes of moral and immoral behavior, the role of consequences in morality, and personality structure. These beliefs were first expressed in Jewish doctrine. Then Jesus Christ (himself a Jew) and his followers incorporated the main body of Jewish dogma into the Christian reformation movement. Six centuries later, the prophet Mohammed also included much of Judaic belief in the religious system he founded. As a result, adherents of the principal forms of all three traditions subscribe to the following beliefs:

1. *Sources of evidence.* The evidence on which followers base their convictions consists of the content of their holy books and of interpretations of those contents offered by recognized religious authorities. To believe that the scriptures of one's own religion represent the truth requires an investment of faith and trust in the assurances of religious leaders. In brief, the validity of the contents of holy books cannot be empirically tested. In each religion, people identified as *fundamentalists* accept the literal meanings of the scriptures. People identified as *modernists* and *relativists* accept some passages as literally true but interpret others as symbolic of the truth or as no more than estimates of the truth.

2. *A Supreme Being*. The universe and all its components were created by a single Supreme Being known by such titles as Yahweh (Jahweh), Jehovah, God, the Lord, and Allah. That Supreme Being, who continues to manage the universe today, is all-knowing (omniscient), all-powerful (omnipotent), and in all places at once (omnipresent, ubiquitous).

3. *Creation*. The creation of the universe and of humans occurred as described in the opening book of the Jewish Bible (the Old Testament of the Christian Bible). In the opinion of fundamentalists, God created the first man, Adam, in the same form as men are found today. The first woman, Eve, was then created from one of Adam's ribs in the same form as women appear today.

4. *Original sin*. Adam and Eve enjoyed an ecstatic life in a idyllic setting, the Garden of Eden, until enticed by one of Satan's emissaries (in the form of a snake) to disobey God's commandment about not eating a forbidden fruit, which symbolized "knowledge of good and evil." For this act of disobedience, Adam and Eve were expelled from the Garden. Since that time, the duty of each human has been to live an exemplary moral life, obeying the Lord's commandments and thereby atoning for that original sin.

5. *Reality*. Reality consists not only of the visible objects of the universe but also of unseen beings and places.

The invisible beings include not only the Lord but, in addition, his emissaries (angels) who carry out God's assignments. There are also evil unseen beings who act in opposition to the Lord's commandments. These evil operatives act on the orders of an archangel (known by such titles as the Devil, Satan, Beelzebub) who broke away from the Lord's flock some time before humans appeared on earth. Since that time Satan has conducted a continuing battle against God, seeking to enlist humans in a pernicious campaign to thwart the Lord's commandments and to produce universal chaos and suffering.

Reality's main unseen places are Heaven and Hell. Heaven is the celestial abode of God and of selected, favored humans after their earthly death. Hell—also known as the Underworld—is the abode of Satan and of evil humans following their death. Heaven is a setting of everlasting joy and bliss. Hell is a place of everlasting disappointment, anguish, hardship, and pain.

6. *Life's purpose*. The moral duty of all human beings—and indeed, the entire purpose of their life on earth—is to obey the commandments of the Supreme Being. The moral domain is defined primarily by God's commandments and secondarily by interpretations of those tenets by the clergy. Proper moral development consists of learning to abide by the commandments.

7. *Causality*. All moral development (values and behavior) results from the interaction of supernatural and natural forces. The supernatural forces are divided into two opposing camps, the good and the evil, with the good headed by God and the evil by Satan. God and His angels act to foster the right things to do. God is all powerful, able to accomplish anything. Satan and his cohorts (other angels who, like Satan, fell from the grace of God) are evil, acting to promote hate, disorder, and destruction. The power that the Satanic forces wield was originally derived from the omnipotent God, probably by fraud.

The natural forces are human beings. Humans are pawns in the cosmic struggle between good and evil, with God and Satan each striving to win over the greatest number of converts. Humans on God's side are of two major varieties, those with special gifts or training in religious matters (the clergy—rabbis, priests, ministers, imams) and the religion's followers who are not specialists (the laity—common church members). The humans in Satan's corps are people who try to entice others into evil ways (seducers, pimps, cheats, deceivers, law-breakers, promoters of false religions, and the like).

Members of the clergy serve as mediators between God and the common people by interpreting God's words and actions, soliciting God's aid, and strengthening parishioners' resolve to abide by the Lord's commandments. On God's behalf, angels perform a similar mediating function with humans, transmitting God's orders to people (presenting Moses the Ten Commandments, dictating the Qur'an to Mohammed) and helping protect people from harm, as suggested in the phrase *guardian angels*. Angels can infuse people's souls with the *Holy Spirit* as a means of stimulating moral thought and action.

Satan, either directly or through his emissaries (the fallen angels), infects people's souls with evil desires and intentions, impelling them into wrong-doing.

The belief that God is all-knowing and all-powerful suggests that He has predestined every human's moral development, leaving no room for individual choice of action. If such were the case, no one should be held responsible for his or her immoral actions, and thus no one should be blamed for misdeeds. However, Judaic-Christian-Islamic theory does not support such complete determinism. Instead, people are thought to be endowed with a *free will* that allows them—that, indeed, obliges them—to make moral decisions. Therefore, although an individual's fate may be partly the result of conditions that God preordained, each person is also partially free to make moral judgments. This means that everyone bears some responsibility for his or her actions and thereby deserves blame for wrongdoing (Farah, 1968, pp. 118-124; Haddad, 1980, p. 118; Ott, 1974, pp. 246-249).

By force of their free will, followers of the faith—Jewish, Christian, and Islamic alike—have a variety of ways of influencing their own moral development. They can learn the Lord's commandments. Through prayer, they can appeal to God or to God's earthly representatives (the clergy) for guidance in solving moral dilemmas. By means of prayer and good works, they can display their respect and love for the Lord. They can conduct their lives in keeping with the commandments.   And whenever they do happen to sin, they can confess their sins and do penance so to absolve themselves of guilt and blame.

8. *Individual differences.* Differences among people in moral development result from variations in the causal factors from one person to another. Satan may cast a spell on a particular person, effectively forcing that individual into sinful ways. God may test another's religious zeal by submitting the person to more severe trials of the flesh or mind than those faced by others. One youth may have extraordinary willpower and thus be able to resist temptations better than his age-mates. One child's parents may be more dedicated to their religious faith and thus serve as more effective conveyors of God's word than will another child's.   One individual may live in a neighborhood filled with habitual

wrongdoers, whereas another is reared in a community populated by faithful servants of the Lord.

All such variables, and many more, contribute to the differences observed among people in their moral thought and action.

9. *Effect of consequences.* Moral behavior is controlled to a great extent, if not entirely, by people's expectations of the consequences they will experience for their actions—reward for abiding by God's commandments and punishment for neglecting or violating them. The Jewish Bible asserts that "they that . . . sow wickedness shall reap the same" (Job 4:8).* The Christian New Testament contends that "whatsoever a man soweth, that shall he also reap" (Galatians 6:7). An Islamic hadith warns that "Verily your deeds will be brought back to you, as if you yourself were the creator of your own punishment" (Suhrawardy, 1941, p. 73).

Some rewards and punishments may be dispensed during people's lifetime on earth—good fortune for obedience (good health, occupational success, a happy marriage, admirable offspring, and the like) and misfortune for disobedience (illness, loss of loved ones, financial setbacks, mental distress, and more). But the most important and inevitable consequences occur in life after death, on Judgment Day, when God ensures that people experience the results of their lives on earth. Obeying God's commandments increases one's chances of enjoying eternal life in Heaven after earthly death. However, good behavior on earth does not guarantee a place in Heaven. An assignment to Heaven still depends on "the grace of God," a decision not necessarily based on the morality of the life a person led but, rather, on divine wisdom that is beyond human comprehension (Ott, 1974, pp. 242-244). In contrast, disobeying God's commandments— committing sins that are not subsequently forgiven or paid for by redemption and penance—can be expected to condemn a person to everlasting punishment in Hell. Judaism, Christianity, and Islam are alike in warning their followers to fear the wrath of the Lord.

How successfully people's moral behavior is influenced by threats of punishment and promises of rewards in an afterlife depends on the strength of their faith in the existence of an afterlife and of a vengeful but loving God.

10. *Personality structure.* Each human is a combination of an observable physical entity (the body) and an invisible moral essence (the soul). The life span of the body begins with biological conception nine months before birth, and the life span ends with corporeal death when the heart finally stops beating. The life span of the human essence (the soul) begins either with biological conception or soon afterward but does not end with physical death. Instead, the soul continues to exist eternally in one of reality's invisible locations—Heaven or Hell, or sometimes in a temporary holding area known as Purgatory or Limbo.

Whereas Judaism, Christianity, and Islam are bound together by the foregoing beliefs in common, they are separated by certain details of those beliefs as well

---

*Biblical citations are identified by the name of the book (such as *Job*), the chapter number (*4*), and—following a colon—the verse number (*8*) in the King James version, listed as *Holy Bible* among the references at the end of this book.

as by their views about (a) which scriptures are truly of divine origin; (b) the moral values, in the form of commandments, that deserve attention; and (c) the status of Jesus Christ as the divine Son of God. It is to these differences that we now turn.

JUDAIC DOCTRINE

The aspects of Jewish theory treated in the following discussion include (1) the source of evidence about moral values, (2) the will of God, (3) Jewish moral values, and (4) stages of development.

The Source of Evidence

As with all other religions born in ancient times, Judaism was originally an oral tradition, with theology, history, rites, and rules of behavior passed from one generation to the next by word of mouth until scribes eventually compiled the beliefs in written form.

The traditional Jewish Bible, which is also the Old Testament of Christian bibles, is organized as a series of books categorized into sections that generally reflect different time periods when the materials were created and when they were finally cononized, that is, finally decreed as the authentic precepts and history of the Jewish faith.

The first five books of the Bible (the Pentateuch—Genesis, Exodus, Leviticus, Numbers, and Deuteronomy) form the Torah, the oldest of the materials, dating to the time before the Jews escaped from captivity in Egypt. The Torah, which closed with the death of the great leader Moses, was long believed to have been written by Moses in the 13th century BCE. However, according to well-documented present-day accounts, the five books were actually a combination of the efforts of four authors who wrote in different styles and with different emphases and interests. Scholars assigned the code letters J, E, P, and D to the four ancient writers. J stands for the Hebrew kingdom of Judah and E for the adjacent kingdom of Israel. P stands for *priests* and D for Deuteronomy. Both J and E recount the same sorts of events in Jewish history, but each sometimes offers a slightly different version. The J and E sources may extend back to the 10th century BCE. The priestly material was embedded in E's account. D appears to have written the book of Deuteronomy on his own at a later time, perhaps around the 5th century BCE. Eventually some clever scribe took on the editorial task of combining the four versions into a single narrative that attempted to be true to the spirit of the four. In doing so, he included parallel versions of various key events—the creation of the world in Genesis, the story of Noah and the ark, the Hebrews' enslavement in Egypt, and more. The Torah assumed the final form of a single integrated version perhaps around 400 BCE.

Following the five books of the Torah (The Law), the Bible offers two categories of scripture—the Nevi'im (Prophets), consisting of 21 books, and the Ketuvim (Writings or Hagiographa), consisting of 13, making a total of 39. Certain of the writings were adopted as authoritative at a later time than others, so that the Jewish canon as found today was not complete until the 2nd century CE. Thus, it took nearly a thousand years for the Judaic Bible to reach its ultimate form (Friedman, 1987, p. 244).

Supplementing the Bible as an authoritative source of moral directives is the *Talmud* (meaning Teaching), a large body of writings that contain extensions and interpretations of biblical matter, many of them said to derive from a long oral tradition, including messages ostensibly whispered to Moses on Mount Sinai but not written in the Torah. The Talmud in its present-day version evolved over eight centuries (350 BCE to 500 CE) as a record of Jewish scholars' discussions of ecclesiastical matters.

Abiding by the Will of God

The foundation of moral virtue in Judaic tradition has been explained by Rabbi Charles B. Chavel in the following fashion.

> The basic concept in the Jewish religion relating to practice is undoubtedly the *Mitzvah*, or the Commandment of the Lord. The Torah being of Divine origin, and the primary object of man being to lead a life that will be fully consonant with His will as expressed in the Torah, the great concern of Jewish religious thought is to ascertain what precisely constitutes the will of God, and what are the details and conditions pertinent to its exact fulfillment. In brief, to lead the highest type of Jewish life is possible only through observance of the mitzvoth. Whatever is conducive to that observance is held to be intrinsically good, and whatever obstructs it is held to be sinful, or intrinsically bad. (Chavel, 1967c, p. vii)

Jewish Moral Values

The moral values in a Jewish theory of development derive from three sources—the Bible, the Talmud, and priests' additions. The following discussion offers examples from the first two of these sources.

Values from the Bible

Because in Judaism morality consists of obeying God's commandments, the most basic values of Judaic theory are to be found in the Bible or, more precisely, in the first five chapters that form the Torah. Many people apparently believe that the commandments are limited to the ten that Moses conveyed to the people of Israel on stone tablets when he descended from Mount Sinai. Those ten exhorted the Jewish populace not to have any gods other than Jehovah; not to carve idols of gods; never to use God's name lightly as in cursing; not to work on the Sabbath day; to honor their parents; and not to kill, steal, lie about others, commit adultery, or yearn for their neighbors' possessions (Exodus 20:3-17).

However, the ten fall far short of telling what the scriptures require of the faithful. A host of additional commandments are asserted or implied in the Torah. The standard catalogue of those dicta is the list of 613 rules extracted from the scriptures by a renowned 12th-century Jewish scholar, Maimonides (Moses ben Maimon, 1135-1204). Of the total, 248 are positive mandates (thou shalts) (Maimonides, 1967, Vol. 1) and 365 are negative admonitions (thou shalt nots) (Maimonides, 1967, Vol. 2).

Although the limited space available in this chapter does not permit an enumeration of the entire list of 613 principles, there is room for the following selection of commandments that reflect the diversity of precepts Maimonides discovered in the Torah.

Positive Values. These examples of positive commandments focus on people's attachment to God, human relations, behavior in a court, holy offerings, holy days, and formal laws.

According to Maimonides' list, proponents of Judaism are obligated to (Maimonides, 1967, Vol. 1):

- (*Attachment to God*) Believe in God; love, fear, and worship God; follow God's commandments; honor God's name; study the Torah; confess sins; heed the advice of the prophets; and destroy all idol worship.
- (*Human relations*) Honor parents, scholars, and the aged; fulfill oral commitments; show love for neighbors and strangers; lend money to the poor; pay wages on time; return lost property to its owner; rebuke sinners; and exact fines from idolaters.
- (*Behavior in court*) Abide by majority decisions, treat litigants equally before the law, testify truthfully in court, and condemn witnesses who testify falsely.
- (*Sexual conduct*) Engage in sexual intercourse only within the bonds of marriage.
- (*Holy offerings*) Correctly present sin offerings, guilt offerings, peace offerings, meal offerings, childbirth offerings, substituted offerings, and consecrated offerings.
- (*Holy days*) Rest on the Sabbath, on Rosh Hashanah, on Yom Kippur, and on Shemini Atzereth.
- (*Formal laws*) Abide by laws governing marriage, divorce, circumcision, seducers, captive women, suspected adulteresses, manslaughter, burial, Hebrew bondmen, theft, borrowing, litigants, and inheritance.

Negative Values. The illustrative proscribed acts concern human relations, objects of worship, holy offerings, holy days, forbidden foods, littering, and the conduct of priests.

Jews are prohibited from (Maimonides, 1967, Vol. 2):

(*Murder*) Killing a human being.

(*Ransom*) Accepting a ransom from one who has committed murder, either willfully or unwittingly.

(*Lying*) Bearing false witness.

(*Convicting*) Convicting on the testimony of a single witness.

(*Punishment*) Inflicting excessive corporal punishment.

(*Misguiding*) Giving misleading advice.

(*Gossip*) Bearing tales.

(*Enmity*) Bearing a grudge.

(*Sexual conduct*) Engaging in sexual intercourse with: a person of one's own sex, another man's wife, animals, a menstruant, one's mother, one's father's wife, one's son's daughter, a woman and her daughter, one's father's sister, any other kinswoman, and more.

(*Disrespect*) Hitting one's parents; cursing a Jew, a judge, or a ruler; worshiping idols or studying idolatrous practices.

(*Holy offerings*) Dashing the blood of blemished beasts upon the altar; offering a sacrifice without salt; mingling olive oil with the meal offering of a suspected adulteress; bringing frankincense with the meal offering of a sinner; allowing any of the meat of the Passover offering to remain until morning.

(*Diet*) Eating any unclean animal, fish, or fowl; eating any swarming creature or any creeping thing that breeds in decayed matter; eating blood, the fat of a clean animal, meat cooked in milk, the flesh of a stoned ox, fresh ears of grain, or other forbidden substances.

(*Respect for holy days*) Working, traveling, or punishing on the Sabbath, on Rosh Hashanah, or on Yom Kippur.

(*Littering*) Leaving obstacles on public or private domain.

(*Rules for priests*) Priests are forbidden to eat first fruits outside Jerusalem; to marry a divorced woman; or to have disheveled hair or torn garments when entering the sanctuary. High priests are forbidden either to marry or to have intercourse with a widow, or to be under one roof with a dead body.

Since the time that Maimonides published the 613 commandments, his list has been widely accepted as representing the moral values decreed in the Torah. However, some biblical scholars have criticized Maimonides' choices, so they have deleted certain commandments that he included and added a few others (Chavel, 1967b, Vol. 1, pp. 263-265; Chavel, 1967a, Vol. 2, pp. 335-337).

To render the commandments more easily applied by the common people, Maimonides extracted those items that bore solely on the priesthood, thereby leaving a list of 60 positive precepts (from the 248) for the use of Jews not in the clergy. This set, along with a similar list of 200 negative rules (out of the 365) selected by later scholars, has been judged suitable for modern-day followers of Judaism (Chavel, 1967d, Vol. 2, pp. 348-356).

Values from the Talmud

The Talmud comprises hundreds of items of various sorts—debates over ecclesiastical matters, legends, philosophical talks, parables in the form of fables, wise sayings, medical advice, fantasies, word analyses, witty puns, satires, and rules that have come to enjoy the status of laws (Cahn, 1962, pp. 187-188). Some of the Talmud's contents qualify as moral obligations and others as prudential advice (Cahn, 1962, pp. 275-301).

The following are examples of obligations:

A man must never say, "I need not work, for God will help me." Instead, man must work diligently, for only then will the Lord help him.

The glory of God rests only upon that home where there are children.

A man must protect and guard the honor of his wife.

A man can divorce his wife only if he has found out that she has sinned with another man.

He who hopes that his wife will die before him so that he may inherit her money will die himself and be survived by her.

It is incumbent upon every father to provide for the sustenance of his offspring while they are young.

He who accuses an innocent man of a crime will be punished for his false accusation.

Then there are suggestions about how to lead a prudent life:

Be on your guard against drinking. Too much drinking is bad, particularly when a woman drinks too much wine.

One must not criticize the food one eats.

A head long unwashed may be the cause of blindness; unwashed garments may lead to insanity; and an unbathed body may cause pocks.

He who marries for money will not have good children, and he will have no profit from the money.

Greet everyone with a smile.

Do not attempt to ask a friend's forgiveness while he is still in anger, do not try to comfort him while grief is still heavy in his house, and do not attempt to watch him while he does a foolish thing.

A home in which there is discord will gradually destroy itself.

Stages of Development

Development over the life span is identified with a number of ceremonies that mark major changes in the person's moral maturity. The initial ceremony, performed on the eighth day after birth, is circumcision, the removal of the foreskin of the male infant's penis as enjoined by God (Genesis 17:10-12). In biblical times "the presence of the foreskin was regarded as a [physical and moral] blemish, and 'perfection' was to be attained by its removal" (Werblowsky & Wigoder, 1966, p. 90).

At the time of puberty, each 13-year-old youth participates in the bar mitzvah rite that confers on him adult status in the religious community. He is thereupon judged a responsible person, morally liable for the results of his own actions. "The performance of all the duties of a Jew are now incumbent upon the youth" (Werblowsky & Wigoder, 1966, p. 57). A passage of the Talmud declares that:

> Children must be trained, because most of them are wild by nature. A father must devote himself to the training of his son until the boy reaches the age of 13. It is only then that he may thank God (at the bar mitzvah ceremony) for having relieved him of the direct responsibility for the actions of his son. A twig must be bent early in the direction in which it is to grow. The same is true of the child. (Cahn, 1962, p. 288)

The Talmud also describes duties the father has toward his son over the first few decades of life. Fathers are advised: After birth, circumcise the infant. As the boy grows older, tutor the child or send him to a school. During the youthful years, see that the son learns a trade. Later find the son a wife (Cahn, 1962, p. 288).

Marriage in Judaism has always been "a social, moral, and religious ideal, and as a necessary condition of spiritual perfection." According to the rabbis, "a wifeless man is a deficient man." The wife has been assigned by God "to fulfill the modest role of man's 'help-mate'." She is a "woman of valor" whose worth is far above that of rubies (Werblowsky & Wigoder, 1966, p. 252-253).

Conclusion

Over the centuries, Judaism's conception of moral development has continued to thrive, despite—or perhaps partially because of—the periodic persecution of the religion's followers in various parts of the world. However, the end of the 20th century still witnessed continued debate between traditionalists and modernists over moral-development issues.

With the foregoing sketch of Judaism as a background, we turn now to Christianity, the first of the two efforts to revise the practice of Judaism. Whereas Jesus Christ would proclaim himself the special Son of God and the long-awaited Messiah who would save the Jewish people, the Jewish clergy considered him a charlatan who sought to mislead the faithful from the traditional Judaic path.

CHRISTIAN DOCTRINE

Christianity appeared 2,000 years ago as a reform movement within the Jewish community, aimed at correcting the manner in which the priesthood was conducting religious affairs. At that time, the Jewish community was deeply divided along both political and doctrinal lines. The leader of the new movement was a Jew, Jesus, who as a youth acquired an intimate knowledge of Judaic tradition and of the religious issues of his day. At age 30 he launched an independent ministry, aided by a dozen disciples who accompanied him as he preached his new version of the faith. His ministry lasted three years, until he was executed for expressing views unacceptable to both Roman civil authorities and the established Jewish religious hierarchy.

Jesus' chief complaint was that the priests were unduly legalistic, focusing solely on the minutiae of religious law and thereby ignoring the true spirit of the faith. As al-Faruqi has explained, ultraconservative Pharisee priests

> conceived of the Torah, or the Law, as a body of statutes which command absolute and literal obedience and loyalty. For, by such absolute and literal obedience, they hoped to reproduce the life of the Jews under the great kings [David, Solomon], which they interpreted as being due to such obedience on the part of their forebears. (al-Faruqi, 1967, p. 59)

Not only did the priests require strict adherence to the Torah's hundreds of commandments, but they added a host of rules under many of those laws, rules that became part of an expanding oral tradition. For example, the commandment proscribing work on the Sabbath was rendered more precise by a detailed 39-item definition of forbidden labor. The 39 prohibited types of work included such activities as sowing grain, plowing, baking, washing, dyeing, writing two letters, and beating an object smooth with a hammer (Ramsey, 1950, p. 49).

Jesus saw his mission as that of redirecting the allegiance of the populace to the most fundamental moral principles that should guide human behavior rather than allowing people to be misled by a legalistic fixation on a multitude of specific acts.

The following account of Christian theory opens with (1) the principal sources of evidence, then continues with (2) Christian moral values, (3) the nature of personality, and (4) stages of moral development.

Sources of Evidence

The basic source of evidence on which a Christian theory of moral development is built is the Christian Bible. It consists of the Old Testament (essentially the Jewish Bible) and the far shorter New Testament of 27 books that recount events in the life of Jesus and address developments in the early Christian church movement. These books are the residue out of many first and second century CE writings that Christian groups considered sacred. By an ostensibly "self-evident" process of selection, church leaders by the end of the fourth century had established the set of 27 as the authoritative canon. The first four books (Matthew, Mark, Luke, John) mainly portray incidents in Jesus' three-year ministry, with the material in Matthew and Luke apparently derived from the contents of Mark, whereas John is a separate account. The fifth book, the Acts of the Apostles, portrays the activities of Jesus' principal supporters after his death. The remaining 22 books are letters written to Christian congregations in the eastern Mediterranean region, offering spiritual advice and guidance in the conduct of church affairs. Most of the letters were from Paul, the chief church organizer of early times. The final book, entitled Revelation, is a letter attributed to Saint John the Divine, sent to members of seven churches in Asia Minor, offering a host of symbolic, mystical predictions about the ultimate fate of the world.

Today there exist two major versions of the Christian Bible, one endorsed by the Roman Catholic church and the other by Protestant denominations. The principal difference between the versions occurs in the final books of the Old Testament, with the Catholic canon including materials considered by Protestants to be apocryphal—certain Hebrew writings not regarded as divinely inspired by the Protestant scholars who compiled renditions of the Bible after the Protestant break with Catholic authority in the 16th century.

Christian Moral Values

For convenience of analysis, moral values that Christians are expected to adopt can be divided into four classes: (1) two basic moral principles that Jesus declared, (2) more specific precepts derived from those principles, (3) values from the Jewish Bible (the Old Testament), and (4) directives issued by various church authorities.

Basic Commandments

When criticizing the Pharisee priesthood's preoccupation with a multitude of rules, Jesus is reported to have reduced the commandments to two: love for God and love for one's fellow human beings.

> And thou shalt love the Lord thy God with all thy heart, and with all thy soul, with all thy mind, and with all thy strength: this is the first commandment. And the second is like, namely, this: Thou shalt love they neighbor as thyself. There is no other commandment greater than these. (Mark 12:30-31)
>
> Therefore, all things whatsoever ye would that men should do to you, do ye even so to them. (Matthew 7:12)

Theologians have often interpreted such statements to mean that Christian morality does not consist of following a set of rules but, rather, they mean being guided by love for God and for humankind. This makes Christian morality a kind of situational or contextual ethics. Since no list of detailed rules can properly accommodate the conditions of every situation one meets in life, it is necessary for people to use general moral principles for responding wisely to the diverse moral episodes they encounter.

> Because God's rule is dynamic, forever making all things new, Christian morality is not a set of rules or a list of virtues. The single ethical quality of the Christian life is *agape*. Obedient and grateful love to God must issue in service to neighbor within the orders of society. The particular form such service will take cannot be specified exactly ahead of time. (Beach & Niebuhr, 1973, p. 533)

Derived Values

It is the case, however, that Jesus did provide more precise guides to behavior that were assumed to derive from his two basic commandments. For example, in his Sermon on the Mount (Matthew, Chapter 5), he included such virtues and admonitions as:

> Blessed are the meek, for they shall inherit the earth.
> Blessed are the peacemakers, for they shall be called the children of God.
> Whosoever shall kill shall be in danger of the judgment.
> Whosoever looketh on a woman to lust after her hath committed adultery with her already in his heart.
> Ye have heard that it hath been said, "An eye for an eye, and a tooth for a tooth." But I say . . . whosoever shall smite thee on thy right cheek, turn to him the other also. And if any man will sue thee at the law, and take away thy coat, let him have thy cloak also.

Old Testament Values

In addition to guiding their lives by precepts attributed to Jesus, Christians also have typically embraced commandments from the Jewish Bible, especially Moses' Ten Commandments and such directives as one related to tithing (contributing one-tenth of one's income to the support of the church).

Rules Issued by Church Authorities

Over the centuries, church authorities have been moved to distribute written and oral mandates regarding proper moral behavior. The authors of such material have been either individuals (a religious scholar or church official) or groups (an appointed ecclesiastical commission or a conference of pastors). The nature of such directives can be illustrated with examples from encyclicals issued periodically by the pope as head of the world wide Roman Catholic priesthood.

Conservatives and Modernists

Over the centuries, conflict has always arisen between conservative and modernist forces in the church regarding the moral precepts that should guide the lives of the faithful. Conservatives have tended to adhere strictly—usually literally—to the contents of the biblical canon of the early days. Modernists have sought to adjust precepts to the present day to accommodate currents of social change. Within the Catholic church such adjustments have usually assumed the form of encyclicals issued by the pope in Rome and of revisions of catechisms used in teaching Catholic dogma to church members. For example, as noted in Chapter 2, an edition of the official catechism published in 1994 added the following items as sins: driving a car or piloting a commercial jet airplane while intoxicated, cheating on taxes, peddling illicit drugs, and committing fraud in business transactions (Castro, 1992).

Editors of Christian Bibles may also alter the traditional contents to suit the editors' conceptions of current language usage and, in some instances, of political correctness. A case in point is Oxford University Press's 1995 "inclusive language version" of the New Testament and Psalms. To be gender fair, the term *Father* is no longer applied to God nor is Jesus referred to as *Son*, because the editors judged that such terms had a "blatantly androcentric and patriarchal character." The Lord's prayer begins: "Father-Mother, hallowed be your name." In the book of Matthew (11:27), Jesus' identifying himself as God's only son is recast as "No one knows the Child except the Father-Mother; and no one knows the Father-Mother except the Child" (Woodward, 1995, p. 76).

> Darkness has been banished in connection with evil because the editors fear it may remind some readers of "darkies" Even God's metaphorical "right hand" has been amputated out of deference to the left-handed. . . . Avoiding another traditional phrase, Son of Man, the Oxford text reads: "Then they will see 'the Human One' coming in clouds with great power and glory." [Mark 13:26]. The editors do not claim that Jesus spoke in gender-neutral language. But they obviously think he should have. The changes they have made are not merely cosmetic. They represent a fundamental reinterpretation of what the New Testament says—and how it says it. (Woodward, 1995, p. 76)

In effect, by implication at least, the editors have added to the Bible a new set of moral values that concern references to gender, potential ethnic connotations, and allusions to the physically handicapped.

The Nature of Personality

Since ancient times, controversy has continued over two aspects of human personality—the personality's components and the advent of the soul.

Personality Components

As mentioned earlier, the most basic components of human beings in Judaic-Christian-Islamic doctrine are the physical and the immaterial—the body and the soul. This bipartite division is initially described in Genesis (2:7) with the creation of the first man: "And Jehovah God formed man of the dust of the ground, and breathed into his nostrils the breath of life; and man became a living soul." The two aspects are recognized again at the time of death: "Then shall the dust return to the earth as it was, and the spirit shall return unto God who gave it" (Ecclesiastes 12:7).

However, Christian interpretations of human nature often go beyond this bipartite concept to propose additional components of the noncorporeal human being, the portion that can be called *personality*. One question theologians have long debated is whether soul and spirit are merely different words for the same thing. Or are soul and spirit separate components of the personality, as implied in the benediction "your whole spirit and soul and body be preserved" (1 Thessalonians 5:23)? A further problem has been that of determining if spirit and soul are identical to, or different from, heart or mind as in the passage "thou shalt love the Lord thy God with all thy heart, and with all thy soul, and with all thy mind" (Mark 12:30).

The controversy over the personality's composition has become even more complex through the years as Christian scholars have proposed further divisions of the nonphysical self. By the 20th century these divisions had emerged as faculties of the mind, with the term *faculty* meaning a power, capacity, function, or trait of personality. In recent centuries, this faculty psychology has provided the generally accepted view of personality for large numbers of Christian theologians, and it continues to do so today. Typical faculties within Christian conceptions are intellect, sensibility, will, and conscience.

> Intellect is the soul knowing; sensibility is the soul feeling (desires, affections); will is the soul choosing (end or means). . . . Man has intellect or reason, to discern the difference between right and wrong; sensibility, to be moved by each of these; free will, to do the one or the other. . . . But in connection with these faculties there is a sort of activity which involves them all, and without which there can be no moral action, namely, the activity of conscience. (Strong, 1907, pp. 497, 505)

The above four are not the only powers or divisions of mental activity. Theologians also speak of such faculties as judgment, intuition, memory, imagination, reverence, obedience, and compassion—all of which can contribute to a person's moral character. The greater the quantity of these capacities in an individual's personality, the more likely that person will behave in a moral manner.

Included in the dogma of most Christian sects is a belief that the primary distinction between humans and other living things is found in the soul, which only humans possess; it is the soul that gives people their God like character and makes them supreme among living beings. ("And God said, let us make man in our image, after our likeness. . . . [to] have dominion over the fish of the sea, and over the fowl of the air, and over the cattle, and over all the earth" [Genesis 1:26]). An alternative interpretation holds that plants and animals have an immaterial essence that can be called *soul*, but their souls are not identical to the human soul. From this perspective, the human soul is a unified object comprising a trinity of a vegetative soul, a sensible soul, and a rational soul. The vegetative type has the powers of nourishing and propagating, two characteristics that people share with plants. The sensible soul not only has those two features but also additional characteristics found in animals—external senses (sight, hearing, touch), musculature that makes locomotion possible, emotions, and faculties of memory and imagination. But it is the rational soul, the highest in the trinity, that contains all the powers of the other two, plus the faculties of reason and will and conscience that make humankind more Godly than the beasts (Miller, 1963, pp. 240-244). It is the rational soul that acquires moral values and exerts control over behavior in moral situations. The rational soul may be aided in these functions by divine support. As the American colonial Protestant theologian Jonathan Edwards explained:

> Conscience naturally gives men an apprehension of right and wrong, and suggests the relation there is between right and wrong and retribution; the Spirit of God assists men's consciences to do this in a greater degree, helps conscience against the stupefying influence of worldly objects and their lusts. (J. E. Smith, 1959, p. 207)

Whereas among Protestant denominations there may be somewhat varied conceptions of the composition of human personality, Ott (1974, p. 97) contends that in Catholic dogma the notion of multiple kinds of souls is rejected on the conviction that "man possesses only one single spiritual [rational] soul" that is "essentially the form of the body."

The Origin of the Soul

The matter of how and when the soul of the individual person originates is an issue not only of theoretical interest but of practical importance as well, for it bears on the matter of abortion. It can be argued that if a fetus is aborted before it has a soul, then it is not truly "human," and so the abortion does not qualify as murder. In medieval times, theologians asserted that God created a soul in each unborn male 40 days after conception and in each unborn female 80 days after she was first conceived (Goring, 1994, p. 124). Three traditional theories about the soul's origin continue under dispute today.

First is the preexistence theory as proposed by Plato—the belief that every person's soul existed in the mind of God prior to the creation of the individual's body. Such a theory is intended to account for what are presumed to be people's intuitive ideas—their sense of space, time, God, and right and wrong—with which they supposedly are born. It is reasoned that since these ideas are innate and not the result of experience in the world, they must have existed in a soul or mind prior to the individual's conception and birth.

Second is the creation theory, the proposal that at the moment of conception "each individual soul is created by God out of nothing at the moment of its unification with the body" (Ott, 1974, p. 100). Creationism has been advocated by most Roman Catholic and Reformed theologians who support the belief by "referring to God as the Creator of the human spirit, together with the fact that there is a marked individuality in the child, which cannot be explained as a mere reproduction of the qualities existing in the parents" (Strong, 1907, p. 491).

Third is traducian theory, a prevailing view of many followers of Martin Luther. From the traducian perspective, the human race began with God's producing Adam and Eve—creating them body and soul—and from that original pair all subsequent humans have inherited their characteristics, both corporeal and spiritual. Since that time, all individual bodies and souls have been transmitted from one generation to the next through the combining of the parents' sperm and ovum at the moment of conception. In this manner, the original sin of Adam and Eve is passed automatically from one generation to the next. From such a perspective, each child is born in sin—immoral, with a tendency to wrongdoing. Thus, the task of child rearing becomes one of combating the sinful nature of the young through instruction in God's commandments, punishment for disobedience, and reward for conforming to the Lord's dicta.

The dominant position of most Christian sects appears to be that children are naturally inclined to evil. Even Christians who do not subscribe literally to the inheritance of original sin still typically see humans as inclined toward immoral behavior.

> In the sight of God, man is a sinner. . . . This is not a condition to which God has fatally condemned mankind, but a perversion of the nature and destiny of man as God created him for which man himself is responsible. It is a misuse of the great powers with which God has endowed man, so that he oppresses his fellows instead of loving and serving them, is inwardly at war with himself, and becomes the slave of those natural and temporal forces he was meant to dominate. So long as man remains impenitently in this condition, he remains under the condemnation of God his Judge. (Dunstan 1961, p. 208)

Stages of Moral Development

As used here, the term *stages* refers to a period of life which is marked by characteristics that differ significantly from those of other periods. Passage from one stage to another is usually indicated by a society's assigning responsibilities and rights not expected at an earlier stage. Passage is often signified by a formal ceremony.

There appear to be at least five stages of moral development in Christian theory—the prebaptismal, the postbaptismal childhood stage, the age of reason, the years of marriage, and the postmortem period.

In most Christian denominations the prebaptismal stage consists of the nine-month prenatal period as well as the early days or months of infancy until the baby is baptized. In the baptism ceremony, the child is officially assigned the Christian name he or she will bear, and the event proclaims to the world that the parents dedicate the child to a Christian life. More important, however, baptism cleanses the infant of original sin, for in the prebaptismal period an infant bearing the taint of original sin is in danger of not entering heaven if it should die before being baptized. For people not baptized until adulthood, the rite not only disposes of original sin but also of all personal sins they committed. In short, baptism "effects the remission of all punishments of sin, both the eternal and the temporal" (Ott, 1974, p. 155).

During the postbaptismal period of childhood, which typically extends from infancy until around puberty, children are expected to gradually learn how to be good Christians. However, during this first decade of life, the young are regarded as too immature to fully understand Christian doctrine or the consequences of their behavior, so they are not held responsible for most moral decisions. But in early adolescence they are thought to reach the age of reason and thus become capable for comprehending more completely the significance of Christian commitment. They are now considered to be accountable for their moral judgments. This passing from the state of irresponsible childhood into the fellowship of responsible, mature Christians is signified by a formal ceremony conducted before the church congregation. The ceremony in the Catholic church is the confirmation rite, and in most Protestant denominations it is the ritual of accepting the youth as a full church member, qualified to partake of Holy Communion, which is the symbolic accepting the blood and flesh of Christ as a sign of religious dedication and of the soul's salvation. The youth has now entered the stage of truly enlightened Christian dedication.

Entrance to the next stage, which traditionally occurs in early adulthood, is signified by a marriage ceremony in which the bride and groom publicly pledge to respect, love, and protect each other, forsaking all other potential mates "until death do us part." An important aspect of marriage is that of achieving parent-hood and thereby incurring responsibility for the moral development of offspring.

In certain versions of Christian theory an additional stage or substage during the period of adulthood is that of the born-again Christian, a condition achieved when an adult experiences a spiritual reawakening accompanied by moral regeneration, and event that typically occurs during the conduct of a religious ceremony.

The final stage of moral development is initiated by death, when the physical self meets its end, and the soul passes on to the sort of eternal life after death determined by God's grace, with God's decision likely influenced by the individual's moral behavior while alive.

Conclusion

The modern Christian world is characterized by a multiplicity of denominations that subscribe in common to such basic precepts as Christ's commandments (love God and love humankind) and belief in life after death. However, the denominations often differ on a variety of matters bearing on moral values and moral behavior. For example, certain Christian sects are sharply divided over the morality of contraception, abortion, homosexuality, and women's roles in church affairs. With increased social change in the offing during the early 21st century, disagreements among denominations over moral issues will likely grow.

ISLAMIC DOCTRINE

In the following pages, features of Islamic dogma that differ from those of Judaism and Christianity are discussed under these headings: (1) Mohammed's mission, (2) sources of evidence, (3) personality structure and the life span, (4) moral values, and (5) stages of moral development.

Mohammed's Mission

Just as Christianity was a movement intended to reform the deviant practices into which Judaism supposedly had fallen, so also was Islam intended to correct ostensible errors Mohammed observed in both the Judaism and Christianity found in Arabia during the 5th and 6th centuries CE. Mohammed's dual mission was to advance Judeo-Christian belief to a final stage of perfection and to convert to Islam the majority of the peoples of Arabia who still worshiped idols, the stars, and sacred stones.

As passages of the Qur'an attest, Mohammed was considerably more distressed with the Judaism of his day, which he felt deviated badly from the religion of Moses and Abraham, than he was with Christianity. Jesus is mentioned 25 times in the Qur'an and today is typically viewed by Muslims as second only to Mohammed as an honored prophet. Mohammed himself revered the prophets of the Jewish Bible and considered Jesus a man of great character and good works. The main fault he found with Christians was their insisting that Jesus was the Son of God. Mohammed is quoted as saying:

> Do not exceed bounds in praising me, as the Christians do in praising Jesus, the son of Mary, by calling Him God and the Son of God; I am only the Lord's servant; call me God's servant and His messenger. (Suhrawardy, 1941, p. 60)

In effect, Mohammed not only denounced claims of Christ's divinity, but he made no such claims for himself. He portrayed himself simply as one of the holy men in the Judaic-Christian line and, more precisely, as the last and greatest of the prophets.

Sources of Evidence

Islamic belief is grounded in two sets of holy scripture, the Qur'an and the Sunnah. An Islamic theory of moral development can be found in their content.

The title *al-Qur'an* (or *Koran*) means the word of God as delivered in segments to Mohammed by the Angel Gabriel during Mohammed's periodic visits to Mount Hira, near the city of Mecca, in the region that is now Saudi Arabia. On each occasion, the Prophet immediately returned to his disciples to dictate the utterances from God so that scribes might cast the messages in written form. Under the Prophet's direction, the Qur'an's 114 chapters (*suras*) and their constituent verses (*ayats*) were arranged in the order of their length— from the longest to the shortest—rather than in chronological sequence. Within two years after the Prophet's death in 632 CE, the first caliph, Abu Bakr (successor to Mohammed), ordered the scattered written segments to be gathered, with this collection subsequently used for issuing the authoritative version of the Qur'an as it exists today (Suhrawardy, 1941, p. 120).

The *Sunnah* (Traditions) is a record of everyday actions and comments of the Prophet compiled by his followers over the 23 years of his ministry. Each item in the Sunnah is called a *hadith* (although the title *Hadith* is also used as a synonym for *Sunnah*). Unlike the Qur'an, the Sunnah is not found in a single official version. Instead, multiple variations have appeared over the years, with no version containing the exact same assemblage of sayings as any other.

> It is therefore not to be wondered that there are no less than 1,465 collections of the Prophet's sayings extant, of which the more generally used amongst the Sunnis are the "Six Correct" collections, and those amongst the Shiahs, "the Four Books." (Suhrawardy, 1941, p. 18)

Items have been included in the Sunnah only if they could be traced back through "an unbroken chain of absolutely reliable narrators . . . to one of the chief companions of the Prophet. The task of collecting these traditions was undertaken within 11 years of the death of the Prophet" and continued for many years thereafter (Suhrawardy, 1941; Juynboll, 1969).

Personality Structure and the Life Span

As in Judaism and Christianity, a human being consists of a physical form (the perishable body) and of an ethereal essence (the soul that lives on after the body has expired). According to one of the *hadiths*:

The grave is the first stage of the journey into eternity. The faithful do not die; perhaps they become translated from this perishable world to the world of eternal existences. Death is a bridge that uniteth friend with friend. (Suhrawardy, 1941, pp. 67-68)

However, in contrast to typical Christian doctrine, the soul is not initially encased in the body at the moment of conception but, rather, it is placed there 120 days after conception. Until that time, the fetus is without a soul and thus is not truly human. When the soul enters the body, four crucial features of the individual's life are predestined, as suggested in this passage from the Sunnah:

Everyone of you is made [into a fertilized ovum] which stays in the womb of his mother for 40 days. Then he is made into a clot of congealed blood for another 40 days, then into a lump for 40 days. Then God sends an Angel to put a soul into him, and the Angel issues four words [foretelling] his earnings, his death, his deeds, and whether man is going to be happy or miserable. (Munzudi in Obeid, 1988, p. 157).

According to Husain and Ashraf (1979), children are not born carrying the burden of original sin, as fundamentalist Jews and Christians often maintain. Rather, the neonate, by its original nature, is morally unmarred.

Islam emphasizes that every child, like his primordial grandfather, is born in a state of innocence and if it succumbs to evil later, it is because of its failure to rise above temptation. But for every one man who yields to temptation, there are scores who do not, a fact which points to man's capacity for good. (Husain & Ashraf, 1979, p. 36).

Moral Values

Like Judaism and Christianity, the moral goal in Islam is to abide by the Lord's commandments. Two *hadiths* in the Sunnah proclaim:

God saith, "O, Man, only follow thou My laws and thou shalt become like unto Me. . . ." The key to heaven is to testify to the truth of God and to do good work. (Suhrawardy, 1941, pp. 82, 85)

The commandments to which Muslims subscribe are found in the Qur'an and the Sunnah. All commandments published in the Qur'an are considered immutable and obligatory. The ones appearing in a version of the Sunnah are likewise binding if they have been properly verified. "A Muslim may question the genuineness of an individual saying; but once its authenticity is proved, it is as binding upon him as the injunctions and prohibitions of the Qur'an" (Suhrawardy, 1941, p. 17).

Because the commandments extend into the hundreds, it is not practical to list all of them here. However, it is possible to suggest the diversity of moral values by sampling areas of life they address. The following items, extracted from the Qur'an (Dawod, 1974; Shakir, 1988) and Sunnah (Suhrawardy, 1941), illustrate the three general types of moral and social-interaction principles featured in Islamic tradition: positive behavior (thou shalts), negative behavior (thou shalt nots), and guidelines to courteous and prudential behavior.

Positive Values from the Qur'an*

The most essential obligations Muslims bear are known as the Five Pillars of Islam: (1) affirming belief in the unity of God and recognizing Mohammed as God's messenger, (2) praying five times daily, (3) fasting during the designated month of the lunar year, (4) paying the *zakat*—a tax for relief of the poor and needy, and (5) visiting the holy city of Mecca at some point within one's lifetime (if financial means and family obligations permit).

Other positive moral acts include:

(*Righteousness*) Righteousness is this: that one should believe in Allah and the last day and the angels and the Book and the prophets, and give away wealth out of love for Him to the near of kin and the orphans and the needy and the wayfarer and the beggars and for (the emancipation of) captives, and keep up prayer and pay the poor-rate; and believe the performers of their promise when they make a promise; and aid the patient in distress and affliction and in time of conflicts—these are they who are true (to themselves) and these are they who guard (against evil). (2:177)

(*Various virtues*) True believers are those who set aside a due portion of their goods for the needy and the dispossessed; who truly believe in the Day of Reckoning and dread the punishment of their Lord (for none is secure from the punishment of their Lord); who restrain their carnal desire (save with their wives and slave-girls, for these are lawful to them: he that lusts after other than these is a transgressor); who keep their trusts and promises and bear true witness; and who attend to their prayers with promptitude. (70:20)

(*Memorizing the Qur'an*) Recite from the Koran as many verses as you are able. Allah knows that [this is sometimes difficult, because] among you there are sick men and others traveling the road in quest of Allah's bounty; and yet others fighting for His cause. So just recite from it as many verses as you are able. (73:20)

(*Orphans, fair business dealings, justice*) Do not tamper with the property of orphans, but strive to improve their lot until they reach maturity. Give just weight and full measure. Speak for justice, even if it affects your own kinsmen. (6:152)

(*Alms, forgiveness, repentance*) Paradise as vast as heaven and earth is prepared for the righteous: those who give alms alike in prosperity and in adversity; who curb their anger and forgive their fellowmen (Allah loves the

---

*The chapter and verse of each item from the Qur'an are given in parentheses, with the chapter number preceding the verse number, such as (66:9). Quotations are from translations of the holy book by Dawod (1974) or Shakir (1988).

charitable); who, if they commit evil or wrong their souls, remember Allah and seek forgiveness of Him and do not knowingly persist in their misdeeds. (3:134).

(*Humility, generosity*) Give good news to the humble, whose hearts are filled with awe at the mention of their Lord; who endure their misfortunes with fortitude, attend to their prayers, and bestow in charity of that which we have given them. (22:35)

(*Marriage*) Lawful to you are the believing women and the free women from among those who were given the Scriptures before you, provided that you give them their dowries and live in honour with them, neither committing fornication nor taking them as mistresses. (5:4)

(*Defending the faith*) The believers who stay home [from holy wars]—apart from those that suffer from a grave impediment—are not equal to those who fight for the cause of Allah with their goods and their persons. Allah has given those that fight a higher rank than those who stay home. He has promised all a good reward; but far richer is the recompense of those who fight for Him. (4:95)

(*Debtors*) If your debtor be in difficult straits, grant him a delay until he can discharge his debt; but it will be better if you waive the sum as alms. (2:276)

Positive Values from the Sunnah

(*General virtues*) When you speak, speak the truth; perform when you promise; discharge your trust; commit no fornication; be chaste; have no impure desires; withhold your hand from striking others and from taking that which is unlawful and evil.

(*Nine obligations*) My Lord commanded me to (1) reverence him, (2) speak the truth in prosperity and adversity, (3) be moderate in affluence and poverty, (4) benefit my relations and kindred who do not benefit me, (5) give alms to him who abuseth me, (6) forgive him who injureth me, (7) silently attain a knowledge of God, (8) mention Him when I speak, (9) be a proper example to others.

(*Patience, forgiveness*) Thus saith the Lord, "Verily, those who are patient in adversity and who forgive wrongs are the doers of excellence."

(*Priorities in charitable acts*) A man's first charity should be to his own extended family, if they are poor.

(*Treatment of animals*) Verily there are heavenly rewards for any act of kindness to a live animal.

(*Just responses*) Do not say that if people do good to us, we will do good to them; and if people oppress us, we will oppress them; but determine that if people do you good, you will do good to them; and if they oppress you, you will not oppress them.

(*Courage, gentleness*) Two qualities which God and His messenger love are fortitude and gentleness.

(*Repentance*) Do a good deed after every bad deed that it may blot out the latter. A sincere repenter of faults is like him who hath committed none.

As a general policy, the Sunnah also offers the same virtue as the Christians' Golden Rule: "Do unto all men as you would wish to have done unto you, and reject for others what you would reject for yourself. . . . No man is a true believer unless he desireth for his brother that which he desireth for himself" (Suhrawardy, 1941, pp. 49, 72).

Negative Values from the Qur'an

(Fighting, blocking the Mosque, persecuting) Fighting is a grave matter, and hindering (men) from Allah's way and denying Him; and (hindering men from) the Sacred Mosque and turning its people out of it, are still graver with Allah, and persecution is graver than slaughter. (2:217)

(Drink, gambling) They ask you about intoxicants and games of chance. Say: In both of them there is a great sin and means of profit for men, and their sin is greater than their profit. (2:219)

(Killing) You shall not kill except for a just cause. You shall not kill your children because you cannot support them. (6:149)

(Forbidden foods) You are forbidden carrion, blood, and the flesh of swine; of strangled animals and of those beaten or gored to death; of those killed by a fall or mangled by beasts of prey; also of animals sacrificed to idols. (5:3)

(Charging interest) Do not live on usury, doubling your wealth many times over. (3:126)

(Slander, wealth) Woe to all back-biting slanderers who amass riches and sedulously hoard them, thinking their treasures will render them immortal. By no means. They shall be flung into the Destroying flame. (104:1-4)

Negative Values from the Sunnah

(Adultery) The adultery of the eye is to look with an eye of desire on the wife of another; and the adultery of the tongue is to utter what is forbidden.

(Adultery, drunkenness, stealing) He is not a good Muslim who commits adultery or gets drunk, who steals, plunders, or embezzles.

(Begging) Do not beg unless absolutely compelled, then beg only from the virtuous. For every man who shall beg in order to increase his property, God will diminish his property. . . . God is gracious to him that earneth his living by his own labour, and not by begging.

(Mischief-making) The worst of God's servants are those who carry tales about, do mischief and separate friends, and seek for defects in good people.

(Envy) Keep yourselves far from envy; because it eateth up and taketh away good actions, like as fire eateth up and burneth wood.

(Unkindness, vanity) It is unworthy of a Muslim to injure people's reputations, to curse anyone, to abuse anyone, or to talk vainly.

Courtesy and Prudence from the Qur'an

Verses in the Qur'an sometimes serve as prudential advice rather than as commandments.

(*Kindness*) A kind word with forgiveness is better than charity followed by insult. (2:263)

(*Humility*) To be charitable in public is good, but to give alms to the poor in private is better and will atone for some of your sins. (2:268)

(*Courtesy*) Tell my servants [the faithful] to be courteous in their speech. (17:50)

(*Moderation*) Be neither miserly nor prodigal, for then you should neither be reproached nor be reduced to penury. (17:21)

Courtesy and Prudence from the Sunnah

In a similar way, many of the Prophet's remarks qualify more as guides to courtesy and prudence than as moral rules. They concern general character traits that promote amicable social relations rather than acts that are morally right or wrong.

(*Modesty in doing good works*) Meekness and modesty are two branches of faith; and vain talking and embellishing are two branches of hypocrisy. . . . Humility and courtesy are acts of piety.

(*Insulting others*) Abuse nobody; and if a man abuse thee and lay open a vice which he knoweth in thee, then do not disclose one which thou knowest in him.

(*Offending others*) When three persons are together, two of them must not whisper to each other without letting the third hear . . . because it would hurt him.

(*Respect for the dead*) Do not speak evil of the dead. . . . When the bier of anyone passeth by thee, whether Jew, Christian, or Muslim, rise to thy feet.

(*Muslim fellowship*) When you meet a Muslim, greet him; and when he inviteth you to dinner, accept; and when he asketh you for advice, give it him; and when he sneezeth and saith, "Praise be to God", do you say, "May God have mercy on thee"; and when he is sick, visit him; and when he dieth, follow his bier. . . . Muslims are brothers in religion and they must not oppress one another, nor abandon assisting each other, nor hold one another in contempt.

Stages of Moral Development

According to Ragaa Obeid:

Development in Islam is not viewed as a series of stages with the characteristics of one stage significantly different in moral principles form those of another. Rather, development is regarded as a continuous process extending throughout the entire life span. Therefore, seldom are distinctions made between one age level and another. (Obeid, 1988, p. 172)

Nevertheless, Suzanne Haneef has identified types of knowledge and kinds of responsibilities that Muslims are to acquire at different times of life. By the age of five or six, children are expected to have learned about

> God's absolute power and sovereignty, man's total dependence on Him and his place in the scheme of things, the existence of angels and also of Satan and his forces . . . the purpose of his life, the certainty of death and of returning to God when he or others die, and the future Life in the Garden or the Fire. (Haneef, 1993, p. 150)

By early adolescence, the young are regarded as accountable to God for their own actions, "fearing God in all they do and trying their best to stay away from what they know to be harmful and prohibited" (Haneef, 1993, p. 151)

In their mid-teens, youths should gradually prepare themselves for their roles as husband and wife and as parents. When they become adults, they are expected to marry and to bear children and rear them as dedicated Muslims. Ultimately, late in the life span, as parents

> get older and their vitality diminishes, this is not seen as the signal to put them away somewhere where they will not be a nuisance or make demands. In Muslim countries there is virtually no such institution as an old-age home; the aged are cared for as a matter of course or by other relatives if there are no children. (Haneef, 1993, p. 152)

Conclusion

With the advent of the 21st century, the worldwide Islamic community faces a pair of interrelated crises that bear implications for moral-development theory. One crisis concerns a conflict between Islamic doctrine and modern science as science is practiced particularly in Europe, the Americas, and parts of East Asia. Muslim scholars, endeavoring to resolve the conflict, have been proposing interpretations of the Qur'an and Sunnah that might accommodate Islamic tradition as well as the logic and findings of empirical science (Farah, 1968, pp. 229-252) or interpretations showing modern science to be in error (Nasr, 1982).

This dogma/science debate is linked to a controversy over the impact of Western European civilization on traditional Islamic life. In seeking to distance themselves from Western ways, conservative Muslims have rejected psychological models created by European and American theorists, including models of moral development, rather than attempting to adapt Western methods of investigation and interpretation to Islamic tradition.

JUDAIC-CHRISTIAN-ISLAMIC THEORY ASSESSED

By using the standards from Chapter 2 for judging the Judaic-Christian-Islamic patterns of theory, I arrived at the following assessment.

On clarity of description (item 1), I marked the religious doctrines in the moderate range. I readily understood the aim of moral development, the way the moral domain is delineated, most of the commandments, the general consequences of obeying and of disobeying God, stages of development, and length of development. However, I found numbers of other matters confusing and self-contradictory. One is the problem of God's predetermining people's destinies, yet people are said to have free will—the capacity to make their own moral decisions. How can these two proposals be reconciled? Another puzzlement is the effect that obeying God's commandments will have on one's afterlife when the decision about a person's assignment to Heaven or Hell ultimately rests on God's "grace" rather than strictly on a person's record of moral and immoral behavior. And how can an omnipotent God permit an evil force, Satan, to cause so much harm in the world? I believe that these issues and others of like nature—all of which have been the focus of debate for centuries—reduce the clarity of the theories to only a moderate level.

The Judaic-Christian-Islamic Line

How well do I think each theory meets the standards?

The Standards	Very Well	Moderately Well	Very Poorly
1. Is clearly understandable		X	
2. Explains past and predicts future moral behavior		X	
3. Offers practical guidance in coping with moral matters	X		
4. Is readily verifiable and falsifiable			X
5. Accommodates new evidence		X	
6. Stimulates new discoveries			X
7. Is durable	X		
8. Is self-satisfying		X	

I find the theories' explanation of a person's past behavior and their prediction of future moral behavior only moderately satisfactory. If children innately carry original sin, then their tendency to misbehave is readily understood. Or even if the child is not burdened with original sin, misdeeds can be accounted for by Satan's efforts to tempt the young into unrighteous acts. At the same time, God and His emissaries, the guardian angels, invigorate people's souls with the Holy Spirit that arms them against evil thoughts and actions and motivates them to obey His commandments. By assuming this contest between supernatural good and evil forces, as played out in people's lives, the Judaic-Christian-Islamic line can theoretically explain past and, in a general sense, predict future moral behavior. However, exactly how the good and evil forces operate is not at all clear, as evidenced by the inability of even the most pious and learned clerics to predict accurately how people will behave in the future. Hence the dependence on such phrases as "The Lord acts in mysterious ways."

On item 3 (offers practical guidance in coping with moral matters), Judaic-Christian-Islamic theory deserves high marks. The moral values espoused by these traditions are cast in the form of commandments to guide moral decisions. Particularly when the precepts are stated as specific rules, either in holy writ or through interpretations drawn by clergy, people know how to distinguish good from bad daily behavior. Furthermore, they know how to absolve themselves of sins by acts of penance and by resolutions to reform.

If a theory's validity or falsifiability must depend on empirical evidence and tests, then the Judaic-Christian-Islamic persuasions warrant a rating of *very poor*. Belief in the substance of the theories depends on faith in the word of authoritative documents, individuals, or groups. However, whether a document (Jewish Bible, Christian Bible, Islamic Qur'an) is to be considered authoritative depends on confidence in the those who have declared the document canonical. People who assume the position of ecclesiastical authorities do so on the claim that they speak from divine inspiration, a claim that cannot be empirically tested. Debates among the clergy about the validity of religious assertions are typically settled—or at least argued—according to logic grounded in the declarations of earlier authorities (Moses, the pope, Martin Luther, the third Islamic caliph) who are credited with direct guidance from God (Ott, 1974). Thus, the validity of Judaic-Christian-Islamic theory is established by faith in authorities and because "it makes sense" and "is intuitively convincing" rather than empirically confirmed.

Perhaps the greatest strength of religious traditions is that they represent eternal truth that is not altered by the vagaries of changing times. New events must be interpretable by the existing tenets of the theory rather than casting doubt that requires revisions of the theory itself. This matter of accommodating new evidence is often at the core of disagreements between fundamentalists and modernists in religious communities. Fundamentalists are apt to hold staunchly to the literal interpretation of holy writ and custom, whereas modernists or liberals are likely to readjust traditional theory to fit new conditions. A case in point is the debate over the creation of living species. While fundamentalists cleave to the best-known of the descriptions of creation in Genesis (1:1-31, 2:1-5), modernists are prone to accept Charles Darwin's theory of evolution (Darwin, 1859) or at least to declare the issue unresolved (*A New Catechism*, 1969, pp. 9-10). As a second example, what is described as a world wide Islamic crisis has been caused by the problem of accommodating traditional doctrine to modern social conditions (Husain & Ashraf, 1979; Nasr, 1982). Although religious authorities—the Catholic pope, ecclesiastical councils, and individual rabbis or pastors or imams—periodically issue directives intended to keep doctrine up with the times, rarely do such proclamations alter any basic tenets of the faith. Hence, in view of the cavalier fashion in which religious authorities—and fundamentalists in particular—often dismiss new evidence about human development, I have rated the Judaic-Christian-Islamic line below the midline on item 5.

Consider next the standard bearing on innovation. Our three religious theories are essentially conservative. Their purpose is to maintain intact centuries-old explanations of moral development rather than stimulating the discovery of new explanations or encouraging variations of established dogma. Thus, they earn a low mark on item 6.

In contrast, the Judaic-Christian-Islamic line deserves a top mark for durability. Not only have the three faiths survived over the centuries, but they continue to enlist a growing quantity of followers. Billions of people today explain moral development in terms of these religions' doctrines.

Finally, standard 8, which concerns the self-satisfying quality of theories. My own upbringing throughout childhood and adolescence was in a deeply dedicated Christian family that required daily prayer, reading the Bible, and attendance at several church services each week. As a young adult I began to study other religions and to adopt canons of scientific inquiry as a way to acquire knowledge and test its validity. This habit has persisted over five decades, causing me (a) to wonder which of the many conflicting religious theories that claim divine inspiration is correct and (b) to seek empirical evidence in support of authorities' claims. The habit has left me without acceptable answers about a variety of matters at the core of religious theories, such as the existence and characteristics of one or more supernatural beings (God, Satan, angels), the presence and nature of *soul*, life after death, and the inevitability of reward and punishment for one's moral behavior. Without adequate empirical means (at least at the present time) for verifying these matters, I simply admit my ignorance and hold such issues in abeyance. In doing so, I do not contend that people who do accept authorities' descriptions of those matters are wrong. Possibly they are right. But for myself, I find the present evidence for such claims unconvincing. For that reason, on item 8 I marked Judaic-Christian-Islamic models low as persuasive explanations of moral development. This does not mean that I reject the moral values that these religions espouse. Indeed, I strongly subscribe to many of those values. It means, instead, that I question the underlying conception of development as proposed in the Judaic-Christian-Islamic line.

11

Hinduism and Derivatives— Buddhism, Jainism, and Sikhism

Judaism, Christianity, and Islam comprise a sequence of connected religious beliefs. The four traditions inspected in the present chapter represent a similar pattern of development. Hinduism not only evolved over the centuries into its modern-day form, but it also served as the source of divergent sects that departed from the Hindu fold at various junctures in history. The three derivative belief systems described in the following pages are those of Buddhism, Jainism, and Sikhism. They have since achieved the status of doctrinal and organizational structures separate from Hinduism, yet faithful to several fundamental Hindu convictions.

Hinduism, as the foundational set of religious tenets, traces its beginnings back perhaps 4,000 years. At present, there are an estimated 764 million adherents of the Hindu faith throughout the world, most of them in India. Buddhism appeared 2,500 years ago as a protest to aspects of traditional Hinduism that were judged by the creator of the Buddhist movement to be both false and harmful. By the latter 1990s, followers of Buddhism numbered 339 million, located primarily in China, Burma, and Thailand. Jainism also originated more than 2,500 years ago as a further variant of Hinduism designed to alter what Jainists considered to be faulty features of traditional Hindu doctrine. Jains currently number nearly 4 million. Sikhism, which arose 500 years ago, was another attempt to remedy what its founders viewed as mistaken aspects of the Hindu belief system. Today there are more than 20 million members of the Sikh community, most of them in the Punjab region of India (Barrett, 1995, p. 275).

Because the worldviews espoused by these four traditions share a variety of elements in common, we can profitably begin by identifying beliefs on which they all agree, then continue to inspect each of the four in turn, describing elements unique to their particular conceptions of moral development.

COMMON FEATURES OF THE FOUR TRADITIONS

The four religions agree on the following components, although they may differ regarding the components' details.

1. *Sources of evidence.* The evidence supporting the four sects' theories of moral development is found in the traditions' written dogma. In three of the sects (Hinduism, Buddhism, Jainism) multiple documents comprise their canonical literature. In Sikhism, the dogma is found in a single volume. Sages who pose as authorities within the first three sects do not always agree on which of the numerous sources are true accounts of reality, of the good life, and of how it should be lived. However, in all four, questions about moral development are answered by reference to the canonical sources rather than through the empirical collection of data and its analysis by the application of scientific logic.

2. *Personality structure.* Humans are constructed with a body and a soul. Each person's body has been newly created nine months before birth by the mating of a man and woman. The ultimate demise of the body comes with corporeal death that normally occurs after six to eight decades unless ended sooner by accident or illness. Following death, the body decomposes into the four elements from which all physical matter is constructed—earth, air, fire, and water. The soul, in contrast, was not conceived anew at the time the body was created. Rather, each person's soul was created at some indefinite time in the far distant past. Across the centuries the soul has inhabited numerous other bodies, periodically passing out of one deceased frame to enter another newly conceived one. This process of a soul's vivifying one body after another over eons of time is known as *metempsychosis* or *the transmigration of the soul.* Beliefs about the exact composition of the soul vary somewhat from one sect to another, but all of them subscribe to the concept of metempsychosis.

3. *The goal of moral development.* The aim of moral development can be divided into two parts—the immediate and the ultimate. Hinduism and its derivatives teach that life on earth is fraught with pain and tribulation. Therefore, the ultimate goal of life is to win release from this burden of pain so as to enter a state of everlasting peace. That goal is reached through accomplishing the intermediate aim of abiding by the precepts of moral thought and conduct laid down by one or more of the supernatural forces that control the world.

4. *The moral domain.* The realm of morality is defined by the rules dictated by the supernatural forces. In effect, the moral domain can be delineated by listing all of the particular sect's moral precepts.

5. *Reality.* All matter in the universe—animate and inanimate—is organized according to a hierarchy of blessedness or nearness to moral perfection. Such inanimate objects as stones and trees are very low in the system—far distant from moral purity. Above the inanimate objects are the earth's animals, with some species higher than others on the scale. Cats are above insects, monkeys above mice. Humans, being morally closer to perfection than animals, reside on the uppermost levels of this edifice of moral goodness.

Reality includes not only the visible objects and events of the everyday world but also such invisible forces as spirits and gods. However, the exact nature of these supernatural entities varies from one creed to another.

6. *The influence of consequences.* A core concept shared by the four faiths is that of *karma* or *karman*, a term that literally means *deeds*. Karma can be viewed as both a process and a product. The process is founded on the following convictions:

(a) People's actions can be either morally good (faithful to the revered rules), or morally bad (in violation of the rules), or neutral (unrelated to the rules).

(b) Good behavior produces a positive effect or residue in the soul, bad behavior produces a negative effect, and neutral behavior produces no effect.

(c) Karma, as a product, consists of the algebraic sum of the positive and negative effects in a person's soul up to the present time. Karma is thus a kind of moral bank balance, with the bad deeds subtracted from the good deeds to yield a total that can be either dominantly negative or dominantly positive.

(d) At the time of a person's earthly death, the ratio of good to bad deeds—the karmic algebraic sum—determines two outcomes.

The first outcome concerns the kind of body the soul will next occupy. Karma that has been produced chiefly by sinful acts relegates the soul to a new body that lies low in the moral stratification system—perhaps in the form of an insect or worm. Karma burdened with somewhat fewer sinful acts may assign the soul to a species higher on the scale—an elephant or horse. Karma with a higher ratio of good than bad deeds can result in the soul's entering a human body for its next sojourn on earth.

The second outcome concerns the advantages and disadvantages (pain and pleasure) that the next inhabited body will experience during its lifetime. Differences among humans in the quality of their lives depends to a great extent on the karma they have inherited. More pain and travail are endured by people whose souls are burdened with a higher ratio of negative effects than by people whose souls carry less negative residue.

7. *Just deserts.* As the description of karma illustrates, the keystone of Hindu moral theory and its derivatives is the concept of justice. In people's development, they get what they earned—exactly what they deserve. Whatever they sow, that they will reap, even though the harvest is postponed until the soul's subsequent life on earth.

8. *Moksha.* A person who manages to live a perfect life by adhering to all of the moral rules attains the ultimate goal of release (*moksha*) from the cycles of birth and death. Never again will the soul be obliged to return to earth. Having attained *moksha*, the soul is finally at peace. Its development is now complete.

9. *Original moral nature.* The original moral status of the neonate is governed by the karma the soul brings to the new body from the soul's former existences. Thus, all infants are not born with the same tendencies toward either good or bad behavior. Some will be more prone to morality than will others who are laden with more negative karma.

10. *Causality.* In Hindu theory and its offshoots, a person's moral development results from three sources of cause—karma, free will, and the forces that control the operation of the universe. By dint of the karma process, people

produce the material and moral condition to be experienced by the soul's next life on earth. However, even in people's present state which they predestined by their behavior in a previous life, they still have the freedom of will to decide how faithfully they will abide by the moral rules and thereby generate karma that will improve their lot during a subsequent life on earth. Religious instruction is intended to guide people in making wise decisions about how to behave. The third source of cause is the set of forces—spirits, gods—that establish the manner in which the universe functions. These forces determine the rewards and punishments to be expected for different types of behavior. Much of moral development consists of people learning the rules by which the universe is governed and then seeking to guide their lives in accordance with such knowledge.

HINDUISM

Aryan tribes, which apparently originated in the steppes of southern Russia, invaded northern India, perhaps around 1500 BCE, bringing with them an evolving philosophical tradition that became the Vedic religion. It derived its name from the Sanskrit word *veda*, meaning "sacred knowledge." Today the term *Vedas* refers to the collection of about 120 texts that have been passed down over the centuries (Bloomfield, 1908, pp. 17-18). The Vedic tradition ultimately developed into the Hinduism of more recent times.

A large body of Hindu literature has accrued over the centuries, the product of many authors and editors. The following description is drawn from only a portion of that collection. The most valuable resource has been the *Manu Smriti*, a title meaning the laws or memorized traditions of Manu. This work provides a condensation of the religious rules, maxims, and ethical precepts that a person of the upper Hindu castes must follow in order to lead a successful life. According to Hindu lore, the contents of the *Manu Smriti* were received by Manu, the primordial man and representative on earth of the Supreme Being, as revelations direct from that Being, who is often referred to as Brahman, the Cosmic Soul. A similar work in two volumes, the *Grihya-Sutras*, is a compilation of rules governing the conduct of daily domestic life and thus serves as a further guide to Hindu notions of moral development. To supplement these volumes, I have drawn lightly on segments of the *Rig-Veda,* the *Atharva-Veda,* the *Upanishads*, the *Ramayana*, and the *Mahabharata*. Because the version of moral development offered here is one I inferred from such a selection of material, that version cannot be considered *the* Hindu theory but, rather, as only one rendition of Hindu belief.

Hindu concepts of moral development extracted from these texts are addressed in the following order: (1) the nature of reality, (2) the hierarchy of social castes, (3) moral values, (4) personality structure, (5) stages of development, and (6) questions of cause.

The Nature of Reality

According to Hindu tradition, reality has two aspects: (a) the visible but ephemeral and illusory impression of what is real and (b) the invisible but unchanging spiritual essence of existence. The first of these aspects consists of people's everyday experiences—the kaleidoscope of events that pass minute by minute. In Hindu theory, those events are like dreams. People delude themselves into thinking such experiences are what life is all about. However, the true reality of life is spiritual, not material. Its basic nature is found in what some might call God but in Hindu parlance is more often referred to by such names as Brahman, the Divine Self-Existent, the Cosmic Soul, the Everlasting, the Absolute, or the Supreme Reality. The obligation of a Hindu is to renounce the visible world with its deceptive succession of lives and deaths in order to achieve relief from both the pains and the joys of mortality. The key objective is not to attain pleasure or success in a worldly sense but, rather, to win release from life. This goal of liberation is attained by mastering knowledge of the sacred writings, by practicing austerities, and by performing a multiplicity of rites.

Hindu doctrine employs the terms *kama* and *moksha* to distinguish between worldly happiness and ultimate release from successive lives on earth. Whereas *kama* denotes the happiness sought by ordinary mortals during their illusory lifetimes, *moksha* is the supreme, unalloyed, eternal happiness experienced when the soul is ultimately merged into the Cosmic Soul after the accumulation of sufficient positive karma relieves the soul of further mundane embodiments (Iyer, 1969, pp. 9-15).

The Hierarchy of Social Castes

The caste system that has so dominated social life in India over the centuries is founded on the conviction that one's social status in the world is properly determined by a divinely ordered hierarchy of social classes or castes. The caste structure in its most basic form consists of four well-defined upper strata, plus one almost ignored lower stratum occupied today by an estimated 20 percent of the Indian population. This lowest group of outcasts has been referred to as *untouchables* or, in more recent and less degrading terms, as the *scheduled castes*.

When I speak of a Hindu theory of moral development, I mean a theory that gives sole attention to how the upper four classes develop. Thus, the theory essentially denies the existence of the lowest one-fifth of India's Hindu population. As the *Manu Smriti* points out, "there is no fifth caste" (Buhler, 1886, p. 402). Theoretically the caste system is comprised of only the four strata or *Varna* (colors), kept pure by restrictions against marriage across caste boundaries. But in reality, ever since the Aryan tribes first invaded India 3,500 years ago, there has always been a substantial amount of intermarriage, recognized by names assigned to the resulting mixed castes. Consequently, today there are 3,000 recognized subcastes produced by complex permutations of marriage combinations across class lines, with most of the subcastes associated with particular occupations (Renou, 1961, p. 53).

The four main castes, ranging from the most privileged and honored at the top to the least privileged and least respected at the bottom, follow this order: (a) the Brahmins (sometimes called Brahmanas) or priests, who exercise spiritual power; (b) the Kshatriyas (Ksatriyas) or warriors and administrators, who wield secular power; (c) the Vaisyas or artisans and cultivators, who perform business and production functions; and (d) the Sudras who are expected to serve the three higher castes. The three top castes are said to be Aryan, descended from the original invading tribes, while the Sudras are viewed as non-Aryan. According to present-day estimates, the upper three classes make up about 20 percent of India's Hindu population, while 60 percent of the population are Sudras and 20 percent are in scheduled classes or tribes (Shinn, et al., 1970, p. 154).

Although the government of India has officially outlawed caste distinctions, any cultural pattern that has dominated social relations for so many centuries can hardly be erased by government edict. At the level of daily customs and attitudes, caste still influences social intercourse.

In relation to moral development, the caste system is significant in two ways. First, each person is considered to be bound to his or her caste by birth. People cannot move out of their inherited caste by virtue of good deeds, education, political connections, economic success, or religious conversion. Second, the rules of living which influence the karma that the soul carries into the next lifetime vary somewhat from one caste to another. The greatest difference in moral precepts is found between Sudras and the upper, Aryan castes. And even though the rules for the three highest groups have much in common, they do differ from each other in several respects, especially in modes of social interactions, in marriage practices, in rites to perform, and in responsibilities to bear. As the *Manu Smriti* declares:

> The Brahmin must know the means of subsistence prescribed by law for all [the rest of the people], instruct the others, and himself live according to the law. On account of his preeminence, on account of the superiority of his origin, on account of his observance of particular restrictive rules, and on account of his particular sanctification, the Brahmin is the Lord of all castes. (Buhler, 1886, p. 402)

Caste also affects the way a person is to be greeted. Upon encountering a Brahmin and asking about his health, the greeter is to use the word *kusala* in his inquiry. For a Kshatriya the word is *anamaya*; for a Vaisya, *kshem*; and for a Sudra, *anagrogya*. If people of different castes are in the same house at mealtime, Brahmins are to eat before the others do. These distinctions are not simply matters of etiquette but, rather, are serious moral concerns, since how faithfully a person abides by them influences the karma that he or she will carry into the soul's next period on earth.

Moral Values

The moral domain is defined by the values espoused in Hindu doctrine, values that appear in two forms—as personality traits and as specific behaviors that hasten one's progress toward final redemption.

The traits lauded in Hindu writings are not unique to Hinduism but are found in other ethical systems as well. However, through emphasizing certain virtues over other possible ones, Hinduism lends its value system a recognizable spirit or flavor. The principal traits can be clustered into five groupings. The exemplary Hindu is (a) studious and knowledgeable, particularly well versed in the religion's sacred literature; (b) disciplined, dutiful, devoted, loving, and obedient; (c) humble, self-effacing, unselfish, and self-sacrificing; (d) even-tempered, chaste, free from both desire and aversion, exempt from hate and inordinate affection, and pure of speech and thought; (e) trusting in the correctness of Hindu doctrine and, as Iyer (1969, p. 14) has put it, "confident in eternity" (Bloomfield, 1908, pp. 269-287; Buhler, 1886, pp. 29, 59; Iyer, 1969, pp. 13-15).

Some distinction among castes is expected in the traits that are valued. Obedience is considered more appropriate for a Sudra servant and studiousness of little or no importance, because only the three upper classes are qualified to peruse the Vedas. Likewise, greater self-assertiveness and less humility, at least in worldly matters, can be expected for the warrior/administrator class of Kshatriyas than for the priestly class of Brahmins.

In the following manner, Shastri (1994, p. 18), has summarized virtues and vices described in the Hindu epic *Mahabharata:*

> Twelve virtues are: knowledge, truth, self control, scholarship, tolerance, shame for vices, patience, absence of jealousy, sacrifice, charity, courage, and calmness.
> Twelve vices to be avoided are: wrath, lust, greed, delusion, too much desire for worldly pleasure, non-compassion, jealousy, shamelessness, sorrow, desire, envy, and disgust.
> Seven pitfalls of human mind are: seeking only sensual pleasure, being immersed in trivialities, regretting after giving, miserliness, feeling of weakness, vanity about one's lineage, and hate for or distrust of women.

In addition to identifying desirable personality characteristics, Hindu lore lists a great host of specific behaviors that contribute to the karma a person acquires. The following examples from the *Manu Smriti* illustrate typical facets of living that involve moral acts (Buhler, 1886, pp. 47, 51, 63, 67, 121).

Sublimation of appetites. Those organs which are strongly attached to sensual pleasures cannot so effectively be restrained by abstinence from enjoyment as by constant pursuit of true knowledge [of the Veda literature].

Displays of respect. A student shall first reverentially salute that teacher from whom he receives knowledge referring to worldly affairs, to the Veda, or to the Brahman [Divine Self-Existent].

Improper oral behavior. Let him not, even though in pain, speak words cutting others to the quick; let him not injure others in thought or deed; let him not utter speeches which make others afraid of him, since that will prevent him from gaining heaven [*nirvana*].

Improper social behavior. A student should abstain from gambling, backbiting, and lying; from looking at and touching women; and from . . . doing injury to living creatures.

Improper disposal of remains of sacrificial feasts. The foolish man who, after having eaten a Saddha dinner, gives the leavings to a Sudra, falls headlong into the Kalasutra hell.

In conclusion, the desired direction of moral development is depicted in Hinduism in three forms—as the general goal of liberation from the cycle of rebirths and deaths, as valued personality traits, and as behaviors that convey the individual toward ultimate liberation.

Personality Structure

For present purposes, personality structure is defined as "the organization of the major elements that compose a functioning human being." Such a definition does not limit the concept of personality to the psychic or spiritual person but includes also the soma or physical self. Thus, we are concerned with both body and soul and with the relationships among their main components.

Traditional Hindu literature offers not a single version of personality structure but, rather, several versions that have evolved over the centuries and have varied somewhat from one theorist or sect to another. However, most versions hold certain characteristics and assumptions in common, so it is possible to construct one rendition that I feel represents a general Hindu viewpoint, though it differs in some details from other renditions. Throughout the following discussion, the aspects of personality are described in terms of body-soul components and their interrelationships.

In assembling material from different sources, I have taken the liberty of casting the elements of personality in a graphic form (Figure 11-1), a form more familiar to information-processing theorists than to Hindu scholars.

As explained earlier, in Hindu theory the body is perishable but the soul is eternal. The individual soul or self is connected with, or is a part of, the Cosmic Soul, which is the Supreme Reality. However, the ancient texts do not agree on the exact nature of the individual soul and Cosmic Soul relationship. Nor is there consensus on why Brahman produced individual selves to live in the world in the first place. One version from the *Upanishads* holds that "the Supreme soul becomes individual in order to experience life in the world as well as eternal verity" (Keith, 1925, p. 553).

Authorities also agree that key features of the body-soul configuration include the senses, which vary in different accounts from eight to ten in number. Each sense is a seeker or grasper (*ghraha*) or a particular sort of experience (*atigraha*). In contrast to Western conceptions, the senses in Hindu theory include both receptors, such as the eyes, and executors of deeds, such as the hands. The senses and their external experiences form pairings like the following from the *Kausitaki Upanishads*: Ear is paired with sound, tongue with taste, eye with visible form, smell with odor, speech with name, hands with action, feet with movement, the body in general with pleasure and pain, the sex organs with delight and procreation (Keith, 1925, p. 556).

A typical way Hindu theory interrelates these pairings is to envision mind as the integrating center for the senses and to assign mind the tasks of governing "desire, judgment, belief, doubt, unbelief, firmness, weakness, modesty, knowledge, fear . . . . Mind, therefore, is responsible for forming into ideas the impressions of the senses (sight, hearing, taste, smell, touch), which mind then—in the form of *will* motivated by *desire*—transforms into resolves that are carried out by the organs of action" (Keith, 1925, pp. 554-555).

What, then, is the relation of mind to soul? While answers to this question are not consistent throughout Hindu texts, one common view is that the senses and mind are in the service of the soul. Eliot's interpretation suggests that:

> The soul (*atman*, or *perusha*) uses the mind and senses: they are its instruments rather than parts of it. . . . If we talk of a soul passing from death to another birth, this according to most Hindus is a soul accompanied by its baggage of mind and senses, a subtle body indeed, but still gaseous, not spiritual. (Eliot, 1921, p. lxiii)

It is also necessary to assume a storage function for a person's karma—the accumulation of good and bad deeds that decides one's fate in a next embodiment.

One way that the components of personality change with the passing of time is in the maturation of the mind—the accumulation of knowledge cultivated by the study of the Vedas, by daily experiences, and by introspective meditation. In addition, a person's karma is expected to change as thoughts and deeds add to, or subtract from, the existing sum of karma.

Stages of Development

In Chapter 1, I noted that the phrase *stages of development* is typically used in secular theories to identify a series of periods into which the life span is divided, with each period identifiably different from all the others. Furthermore,

Figure 11-1

One Version of Hindu Personality Structure

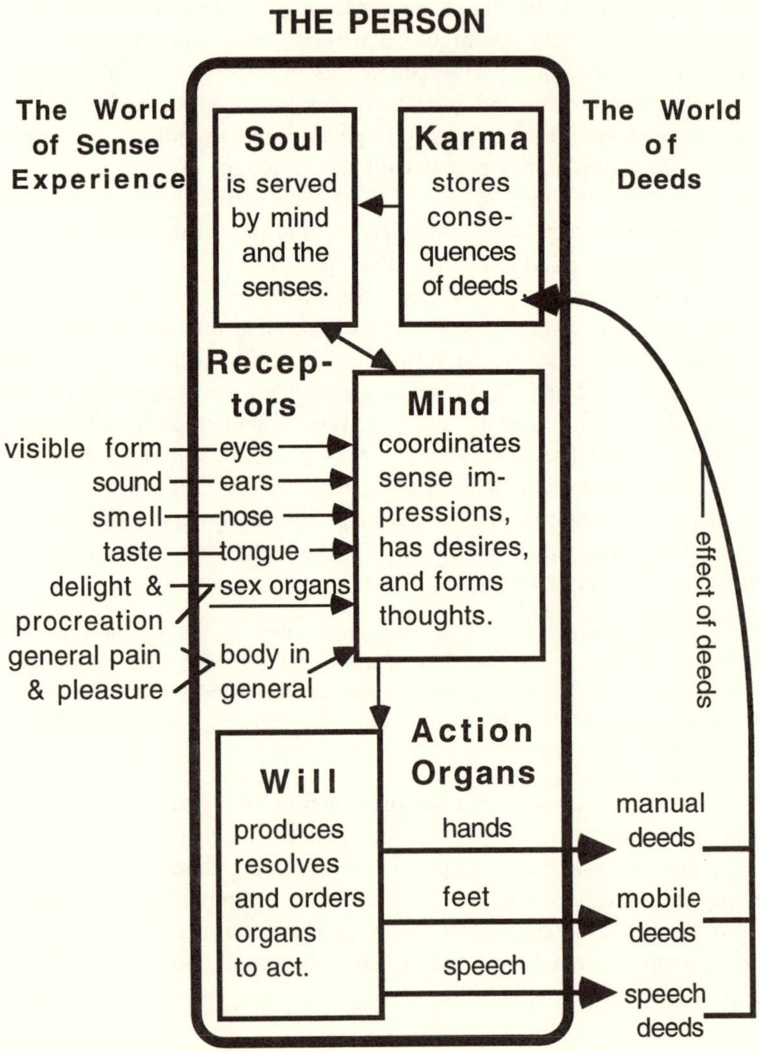

THE PERSON

The World of Sense Experience	**Soul** is served by mind and the senses.	**Karma** stores consequences of deeds	**The World of Deeds**

Receptors

	Mind coordinates sense impressions, has desires, and forms thoughts.
visible form — eyes →	
sound — ears →	
smell — nose →	
taste — tongue →	
delight & procreation — sex organs →	
general pain & pleasure — body in general →	

Will produces resolves and orders organs to act.

Action Organs

hands	→ manual deeds
feet	→ mobile deeds
speech	→ speech deeds

effect of deeds

such stages are regarded as being universal, sequential, and irreversible. But when this definition is applied to Hindu theory, we recognize that the soul's succession of lifetimes on earth in different bodies cannot be viewed as stages, since these visitations to the world are not universal (the same for everyone) or irreversible (since people can slip back to an earlier form of life by accumulating enough negative karma). However, there are clearly defined stages during a person's single life span—or, more accurately, during the span for people in the three Aryan castes.

Although the traditional stages are four in number (beginning at the time a youth becomes a student), I have cast the following description as five, preceding the later four with a preparatory stage that covers the first decade of life.

The Preparatory Stage

A key distinction between the preparatory stage and the four that follow concerns the agent who is chiefly responsible for the individual's moral development. In each of the periods beyond childhood, the person herself or himself is responsible for moral acts, so that the prescriptions for virtuous thoughts and deeds are directed at the individual who is developing. In contrast, the prescriptions for promoting desirable growth during the prenatal and early-childhood period are directed at the child's caretakers, mainly at the parents. This distinction is perhaps based on the same concept that underlies the idea of "age of reason" in Western societies. Prior to the onset of puberty—an event commonly marked in nearly all cultures by initiation rites of some sort—children are considered not responsible for their own acts, and thus they must be cared for and their behavior must be monitored. But by the time of adolescence, they should have achieved sufficient ability to learn, to make decisions, and to realize the consequences of their actions to be regarded as reasonable and responsible individuals.

Therefore, during the preparatory phase prior to studentship, the milestones of development take the form of periodic tasks parents perform to influence such characteristics of the child as its sex, length of life, quickness, intelligence, morality, religious brilliance, and general welfare. Both the timing and form of the tasks bear important implications for the child's destiny.

A rite to ensure the safety of the embryo in the months after conception consists of offering up "a cooked mess [of food] and rubbing butter on the limbs of the wife" (Keith, 1925, p. 367). The expectant mother's hair-parting cere-mony, which takes place in the fourth month or later, is intended to promote the overall well-being of the unborn child. Among the complexities of this rite are the husband's adorning his wife's neck with an umbara branch having an even number of unripe fruits and parting her hair from front to back with darbha grass, virantara wood, and a porcupine's quill, while looking at a serving of rice, sesame, and ghee (liquid butter) in which she seeks to see offspring (Keith, 1925, p. 367).

In like manner, ceremonies are prescribed for the event of birth. To secure a long life and increase the child's intelligence, the father in one rite breathes three times on the newborn and feeds it a mixture of butter, honey, and sour milk that may include rice, barley, and the whitish-black and red hairs of a black bull.

Between birth and adolescence, further rituals are specified to promote the child's growth and readiness for studentship.

The Student

The purpose of studentship is to equip the youth with an in-depth understanding of the voluminous holy scriptures so that he will know how to live a moral life. Caste affects the time an Aryan becomes a student. A Brahmin can be initiated as early as age 5 but no later than age 16, a Kshatriya as early as 6 but no later than 22, and a Vaisya as early as 8 but no later than 24 (Buhler, 1886, p. 36). Becoming a student who is assigned to a particular teacher (*guru*) signifies the child's spiritual birth. The phrase "twice born man" refers to this event. An individual's first birth was entirely physical—the infant issuing from the mother's womb. However, the second is the more important, for in it the youth begins the study of the Vedas that explain the complex moral requirements for compiling the positive karma that eventually releases the soul from the cycles of birth and death.

This studentship stage is divided into a series of study terms, each lasting from four to six or more months. Every term is devoted to mastering a particular body of the sacred writings. Depending on the learner's aptitude and the depth of detail of the particular scriptures, this stage can last a few years or as many as 48, wherein 12 years are devoted to each of the four major bodies of knowledge (Keith, 1925, pp. 370-373).

The Householder

Upon completing the studentship period, the individual is ready to wed and assume the burden of supporting the members of the other three stages—the student, the ascetic who has advanced beyond marriage, and the aged mendicant who has passed beyond asceticism. Householders are the class of people who keep the workaday world operating by assuming the roles of parents, administrators of government, producers of goods, traders, warriors, and educators.

To compile positive karma, householders must carry out a great number of special rites. The most basic are the five daily sacrifices: (a) teach and study the holy books, (b) scatter food and water on the ground in honor of the seers, (c) offer a burnt oblation to one's forefathers, (d) offer grain to animals, and (e) hospitably receive guests and give alms to students and ascetics (Buhler, 1886, p. 87). Typical of a broad range of behaviors that a householder is required to avoid are those of looking at his wife while she eats or sneezes, stepping over a rope to which a calf is tied, viewing his own reflection in water, blowing a fire with his mouth, looking at a naked woman, and urinating on ashes or in holes inhabited by living creatures (Buhler, 1886, pp. 124-137).

After several decades of faithfully performing his duties as a householder, the twice-born man "sees his skin wrinkled, and his hair white, and the sons of his sons; then he may resort to the forest" (Buhler, 1886, p. 198).

The Hermit in the Forest

To enter the stage of asceticism, the householder abandons all his belongings, takes with him the sacred fire and implements for domestic sacrifices, and lives alone in the forest, either assigning his wife to the care of the sons or taking her with him into seclusion. He dresses in a tattered garment and lets his hair, nails, and beard go uncut.

The ascetic's time is spent reciting the scriptures, performing rites, and observing strict austerities, making no effort to obtain things that give pleasure. His goal is to attain complete union with the Supreme Soul—a sense of oneness with Brahman. This state is attained by obeying the tenfold law of contentment with one's lot, forgiveness, self-control, refraining from unrighteously taking anything, obeying purification rules, controlling the organs, wisdom, knowledge of the Supreme Soul, truthfulness, and refraining from anger (Buhler, 1886, p. 215).

Although separated from normal social contacts, the ascetic remains available to offer guidance and advice to those who seek it.

The Sannyasin—A Roving Almsman

The ideal devout Hindu does not remain a hermit for long, but abandons the ascetic state to enter the final stage of a holy life, that of a wandering mendicant known as a *sannyasin*. No longer must he observe the complex array of rituals of the earlier stages, since the function of the rituals has been to convey the believer closer to union with the Cosmic Soul; the *sannyasin* has now passed that brink. He need no longer observe caste distinctions and can live anywhere he chooses. His physical needs are cared for by others. Because the crowning glory of Hinduism is the renunciation of the material world that is personified in the mendicant, "all Hindus bow before a sannyasin and think it a privilege to serve him" (Sarma, 1953, p. 20). This stage ends with death, but the soul continues on, with its fate in the future determined by the karma accumulated during the lifespan just completed.

As a final observation about the Hindu stage theory, Sarma (1953, p. 20) has explained that:

> this scheme of four stages of life is only an ideal. In practice, not even one in a thousand traverses the entire path and goes regularly through all the stages. Though technically the scheme is supposed to hold good for the first three

castes, it is an ideal accepted by all Hindus. There are now sannyasins from all castes, and they are revered by all without distinction.

Questions of Cause

From a Hindu perspective, people's moral development is determined by the interaction of four variables—heredity, environment, intention, and divine intervention.

Heredity

Nearly every aspect of a person's current life span is inherited—physical appearance, condition of health, personal abilities, caste, and socioeconomic status. Thus, with few exceptions, all facets of an individual's life have been preordained. Caste and physical attributes are unalterable. Only in the realm of physical skills and moral behavior can environmental conditions or the person's current efforts slightly alter the predetermined course of the present lifetime.

People inherit their characteristics from two sources—themselves and their parents. Of these two agents, the person herself or himself is by far the more significant. Whereas to some degree the sins and virtues of parents are visited on their children, it is chiefly people themselves whose deeds in previous life spans have generated the karma that results in their present life condition. In this sense, people become both their own progenitor and their own heir.

The smaller portion of one's inheritance—that derived from one's parents—is of three kinds. The first results from parents' deeds in their own earlier life spans. "If the punishment falls not on the offender himself, it falls on his sons; if not on the sons, at least on his grandsons" (Buhler, 1886, p. 156). The second type consists either of wrong deeds parents committed or of right deeds they failed to commit in preparation for the birth of the child.

> If a man wishes that a son should be born to him who will be a famous scholar, frequenting assemblies and speaking delightful words, a student of all the Vedas, and an enjoyer of the full term of life, he should have rice cooked with the meat of a young bull or of one more advanced in years, and he and his wife should eat it with clarified butter. (Nikhilananda, 1956, p. 375)

The third kind of parental legacy is in the form of direct bequests of character traits or talents passed on in the same manner that a dying person intentionally endows the next generation with worldly goods. For instance, the parent says something like "I endow you with my intelligence and my strong will," and the son or daughter replies, "I accept your intelligence and your will" (Renou, 1961, pp. 100-101).

Whereas parents' legacies to their children are in the form of deeds and bequests, children's legacies to themselves result from both deeds and thoughts during previous lifetimes, that is, from the transport of karma from one life span to the next.

Environment and Intention

For the Hindu, the question is not whether events in the environment will affect an individual's moral development, because the events will surely do so if the person lets them. In other words, people are free to choose how to think and act in each moral encounter. Their choice is determined by two factors—their knowledge and their intentions. Insufficient knowledge can be cured by study of the Vedas and by meditation that equips one to comprehend the nature of one's soul (*atma*), the soul that originally was part of Brahman, the Cosmic Soul. Intentions are motivated by two underlying causal factors, fear and desire—fear of dreadful punishments for failing to abide by the precepts of the Vedas and the desire to end life's suffering by reuniting with the Cosmic Soul.

Thus, people can affect their current destiny during this lifetime to a limited extent by adhering faithfully to Hindu teachings. As a modern-day interpreter of Hinduism has explained, if a person has "predestined himself [by dint of his karma] to be the possessor of a bad temper, he cannot suddenly change it into a good one; but he can gradually alter it by right desire and right thought" (Besant, 1908, p. 152).

Divine Intervention

Although people are ultimately responsible for their own moral development by reason of the karma they accrue to shape their destiny in lives to come, they do not directly exert this influence on their own lives. Instead, the effects are mediated through Brahman or other spirits. None of the rites and penances that people perform are direct causes of outcomes. Intoning prayers or eating a concoction of milky rice and bovine hairs has no direct logical connection with ensuring one's good health or obtaining higher-caste status in an upcoming life on earth. Rather, the rituals are intended to placate supernatural beings that, in turn, are empowered to produce the desired changes in the person's life.

In summary, moral development results from the interaction of four principal factors—heredity (carried through the karma to which the person has contributed in earlier lives), knowledge of the holy scriptures, personal intention that is driven by fear and desire, and the action of supernatural forces.

Conclusion

In Hindu theory, morality consists of (a) engaging in a multiplicity of rites and austerities so as to appease the supernatural forces that control one's destiny and (b) complying with rules of social relations. Throughout the centuries and down to the present day, this theory has been accepted, either totally or in large part, by millions of adherents. However, over the decades of the 20th century, elements of Western secular theories appear to have made inroads on traditional Hindu beliefs, particularly among India's city dwellers who have attended schools modeled on British institutions. Furthermore, the Indian government's denunciation of the caste system and the emphasis on egalitarian, democratic ideals in the nation's constitution and legal system have served to weaken the discriminatory moral aspects of the caste structure. For example, interviews with a sample of 99 Hindus living in the vicinity of the city of Delhi led researchers to conclude that:

> Accurate and detailed knowledge of traditional Hindu doctrine relating to human development has markedly deteriorated among members of the population from which our respondents were drawn.   Likewise, the goals of desirable development for sons and daughters were chiefly secular, worldly ambitions [rather than the goals of mastering the Vedas and achieving release from cycles of birth and death].   Nevertheless, belief in traditional personal and social values for males and females still persists, although far less among modernists (educated urbanites) than among traditionalists (less educated villagers). . . . In keeping with the observation that the villages follow the lead of the towns in social change, we would   expect that people in even distant regions will increasingly give up Hindu beliefs in favor of theories of development popular in Western industrialized societies. (Marek & Thomas, 1988, pp. 210-211).

BUDDHISM

In northeastern India during the middle of the sixth century BCE, a young prince—Gautama Siddhartha—of the Kshatriya warrior/administrator caste stepped out of his much-sheltered social environment to see how ordinary people lived. He was so appalled by the misery he witnessed that he renounced his life of luxury in order to discover a way that humans could transcend the suffering that dominated their lives. This search, begun at age 29, led him through six years of study with religious seers and through enduring severe austerities, meditating, and living among people of every caste and circumstance. At age 35 he achieved his goal of discovering the truth about human existence, suffering, and death. In doing so, he attained the status of a buddha—an enlightened one. He then dedicated the remaining 45 years of his life to instructing members of the rapidly growing community of Buddhists. Those who faithfully applied his teachings could reach a state of perfect insight and thereby also earn the title *buddha*. However, the term *Buddha*, when spelled with a capital B, still refers solely to Gautama Siddhartha, the founder of the creed.

The following description of a Buddhist theory of moral development focuses on (1) sources of evidence, (2) basic tenets, and (3) moral values and stages of development.

Sources of Evidence

Like the teachings of Jesus and Mohammed, the doctrine espoused by the Buddha was memorized and disseminated orally by disciples well before it was cast in written form a century or more after the master's death. Ever since that time a large volume of literature has been produced by proponents of the two major schools of interpretation—the Theravada and the Mahayana—and by members of many minor variants of Buddhist tradition. The account of moral development offered in the following pages is drawn chiefly from Marek's (1988) analysis of the Thai version of the Theravada canon, supplemented by several additional sources (Gard, 1961; Guenther & Reynolds, 1994; Johansson, 1969; Rahula & Reynolds, 1994).

Basic Tenets

In the Buddha's revision of Hindu theory, he accepted certain features of traditional Hinduism and rejected others. Among elements he retained were the beliefs in karma, in the transmigration of the human essence from one body to another, and in the goal of ultimately achieving release from the cycles of birth and death. Personality structure as portrayed in Buddhist writings is very similar to that found in Hindu sources.

Aspects of Hinduism that the Buddha rejected were the caste system, the concept of a permanent *self*, and most of the rites and austerities deemed necessary for redemption. He also offered a variety of important innovations, including the *Three Jewels*, the *Four Noble Truths*, the *Middle Way*, the *Noble Eightfold Path*, and a novel conception of the soul. Among significant basic tenets of the theory are the Buddha's conception of reality, the goal of moral development, and the impermanence of the soul.

Reality and the Goal of Moral Development

Two core convictions of Buddhism concern suffering and permanence.

Suffering—The Curse of Existence. At the center of the Buddha's teachings is the conviction that everyone's life is plagued by continual suffering and sorrow.

Birth is painful, in old age we suffer from various illnesses and from realizing that death is near, and throughout [the life span] we experience continual physical and mental distress—loss of limb, the death of a friend, a broken marriage, and more. We suffer from wanting things and not obtaining them. To those who say they have experienced joy in their lives, the Buddha explains that even moments of joy are cause for sorrow because we know the moments are fleeting and will soon be over. . . . [Thus] the ultimate goal of development in Buddhism is to eliminate rebirth and suffering. (Marek, 1988, p. 98)

Achieving this goal is experienced as enlightenment or *nirvana*—a state of nothingness, of freedom from all thought and emotion. The basic key to moral enlightenment is found in the Four Noble Truths: (1) that existence consists of suffering; (2) that suffering originates in such traits and emotions as desire, bodily appetites, acquisitiveness, sloth, envy, hate, and the like; and (3) that suffering can be eliminated by achieving enlightenment and omniscience; (4) which is attained by advancing through the stages of the Noble Eightfold Path to nirvana.

The Impermanence of Soul. The Buddhist principle of impermanence derives from the observation that everything in the universe—material and immaterial, somatic and psychic—is continually in transition. From one instant to the next, nothing remains precisely the same. Life in all its forms is thus simply a fleeting spectacle, constantly in motion. Rahula (in Gard, 1961, p. 114) contends that from a Buddhist perspective, every "being is nothing but a combination of physical and mental forces or energies" driven by "will, desire, thirst to exist, to continue, to become more and more. . . . [In addition,] this force does not stop with the non-functioning of the body, which is death; but it continues manifesting itself in another form, producing re-existence which is called rebirth." In recognition of such impermanence, the Buddha rejected the proposal that the soul is a substantive, permanent "thing"—a spiritual container that conveys karma from one lifetime to another. He asserted, instead, that there is no such soul (*atman*) or self, and that karma passes only as a flow of energy linking one body's death with the next body's birth.

Nevertheless, whether karma is carried by a substantive soul, as in Hinduism, or by energy impulses, as in Buddhism, the practical results are quite the same. In both theories, an individual's behavior during one lifetime affects the fate of that individual in subsequent periods on earth.

Moral Values and Stages of Development

Moral virtues that adherents of Buddhism are expected to pursue are in the form of character traits, stages of awareness, and actions to avoid.

The most basic value is that of renouncing the material world. Conze has observed that in Buddhism:

> It is true that this world . . . is emphatically regarded as wholly ill, as wholly pervaded with suffering, as something to be rejected totally, abandoned totally, for the goal of Nirvana. . . . [Thus, Buddhists] believe that man is a spirit ill at ease, a soul fallen from heaven, a stranger on this earth. His task is to regain the state of perfection which was his before he fell into this world. Self-denial is the highest law and duty of man. (Conze, 1951, pp. 21-22)

Examples of desired qualities of character that convey the faithful toward nirvana are the 10 great virtues (*paramitas*), in the form of personal traits, that the Buddha perfected en route to enlightenment—charity (generosity), morality, renunciation, wisdom, effort, patience, truth, determination (vigor), universal love, and equanimity (Rahula & Reynolds, 1994, p. 265).

Moral virtues are also reflected in actions to avoid, such as destroying living things, stealing, lying, committing adultery, imbibing intoxicating liquors, eating between meals, attending secular entertainments, using unguents and jewelry, sleeping on high or especially luxurious beds, and dealing in money (Coomaraswamy, 1964, p. 130).

In Buddhism, the closest thing to stages of development is the Noble Eightfold Path that must be traversed if a person is to win redemption. The stations along the path represent the sequence of virtues whose attainment releases a person from cycles of birth and death. Marek's (1988, p. 100) summary of the stations as found in the *Digha Nikaya* scripture portrays the virtues as:

1. *Right views* consist of knowledge of the Four Noble Truths, that is, knowing the existence of suffering, its origin, its end, and the path to end it.

2. *Right aims* are ones free from lust, craving, hatred, or cruelty.

3. *Right speech* involves not lying, gossiping, or using harsh or filthy language.

4. *Right action* means not killing or stealing, and refraining from sexual misconduct.

5. *Right livelihood* involves earning a living in a way that does no harm to living things (so being a butcher is an unacceptable livelihood).

6. *Right effort* means mobilizing one's strength to foster right views and to reach a worthy goal.

7. *Right mindfulness* consists of consciously observing all of one's own bodily and mental processes, that is, focusing fully on whatever one is engaged in at the moment.

8. *Right concentration* involves nine progressive levels of mental activity.

The nine levels, as described by Johansson (1969, pp. 99-100), can be summarized in terms of each higher level's unique characteristics and of each prior level's features that now have been eliminated from the thought process (Table 11-1). Advancing through the levels carries the individual eventually to nirvana. In brief, the person's mental focus progresses from reasoning about worldly matters, past joy and pain, past a neutral awareness of self and worldly space, past infinite consciousness, and ultimately to cessation of all thought and feeling.

Causality

Four causal factors that contribute to the growth of people's moral thought and action are karma, knowledge of the scriptures, meditation, and willpower.

Table 11-1

Nine Levels of Mental Focus

Characteristics Present	*Previous Features Now Eliminated*
1. Joy and ease born of seclusion Reasoning and investigating	Sensuality, lust, unskilled mental processes
2. Inner tranquillity, singleness of mind, joy and happiness born of concentration	Reasoning; investigating; joy and happiness born of seclusion
3. Happiness of neutrality, equanimity, even-mindfulness, self-possession	Joy born of concentration
4. Pure neutrality of thought and feeling, equanimity	Happiness and pain, elation and dejection, happiness of neutrality
5. Sphere of infinite space	Consciousness of form, of sense reactions, of diversity
6. Sphere of infinite consciousness	Sphere of infinite space
7. Sphere of nothingness, of unreality	Sphere of infinite consciousness
8. Sphere of neither ideation nor nonideation	Sphere of nothingness
9. Cessation of ideation and feeling	Ideation and feeling

The ratio of good to bad karma inherited from one's previous lives establishes the sort of body that the soul inhabits during the present life span and determines the rewards and punishments a person can expect during the current lifetime. Knowledge of the holy scriptures—especially the details of the Noble Eightfold Path—reveals the behaviors that lead to nirvana. Studying the scriptures under the guidance of a teacher not only informs people of acceptable and proscribed actions but also trains them in the techniques of meditation that can produce a spiritual state approximating the nonthought and nonfeeling of nirvana. In addition, such tutelage heightens the self-discipline necessary for treading the Eightfold Path.

Conclusion

The ethical ideal in Buddhism is that of renouncing the world in order to save oneself from recurrent births and deaths. According to Coomaraswamy, the religion was never intended to be a social-reform movement.

Nothing could have been further from [the Buddha's] thoughts than the redress of social injustice, nor could any more inappropriate title be devised for Him than that of democrat or social reformer. . . . [Nevertheless, it is] a positive social and moral advantage to the community that a certain number of its finest minds, leading a life that may be called sheltered, should remain unattached to social activities and unbound by social ties. (Coomaraswamay, 1964, pp. 128-129)

Therefore, the Buddhist ascetic, in seeking to achieve nirvana, inadvertently offers a constructive example of virtues to be pursued by the majority of people who do not reject the workaday world in order to complete the journey to nirvana. Hence, the ascetic sage, while pursuing his or her own salvation, concomitantly serves as a type of social conscience, as a reminder to society of moral values that everyone could profitably adopt.

JAINISM

The Jaina variant of Hinduism was introduced early in the sixth century BCE by a sage who would become known as Mahavira. This reformation movement represented a revolt of the Hindu Kshatriya warrior/administrator caste against the Brahman priesthood's tight grip on religious affairs. Just as the words *Christ* (Messiah or Savior) and *Buddha* (Enlightened One) are titles rather than names, so also the term *Mahavira* (Great Hero) is an epithet applied to the man credited with shaping the Jaina order in the form in which it has functioned over the past 2,500 years. And, like the titles *Christ* and *Buddha*, the term *Mahavira* has become so closely attached to the man that it now serves as his name.

According to Jaina dogma, Mahavira did not invent Jainism. Rather, he was the final *jina* (possessor of infinite knowledge) of the 24 seers appearing in the most recent of the Jaina time cycles that extend back into the beginningless past. A *jina* is therefore not the founder of a sect but is:

the propagator of a truth and a path which have been taught in the same manner by all teachers of this ever-present, imperishable tradition. . . . The teachings are neither received through divine revelation nor manifested through some inherent magical power (as, for instance, the Vedas are alleged to be). It is the individual human soul itself which, aided by the earlier teachings, comes to know the truth. (Jaini, 1979, pp. 2-3)

The following rendition of Jaina theory treats (1) sources of evidence, (2) reality, (3) the goal of moral development, (4) moral values, (5) stages of development, and (6) causality.

Sources of Evidence

A Jaina theory of moral development can be extracted from the 60 texts that comprise the faith's canon. Originally the texts were in the form of an oral literature that disciples recited. Eventually the recitations were compiled in written form. Although the oldest of the texts were lost centuries ago, brief summaries of their contents can be found in volumes of more recent vintage. Some of the existing material is attributed to Mahavira himself, whereas other portions are the work of disciples (*ganadharas*) who lived in later times.

Unlike religions which claim that their holy books are of divine origin, Jainas say their texts were created by humans who had gained such purity of insight that they attained omniscience during their current lifetimes (Jaini, 1979, p. 42).

The Nature of Reality

Jaina theory recognizes both material and animate aspects of reality. Material objects are composed of atoms, each possessing four qualities: color, taste, smell, and palpability (can be touched). Animate objects are immaterial—not composed of atoms. The most significant animate entity is the human soul (*jiva*), which is characterized by such qualities as cognition, knowledge, bliss, and energy that can increase and decrease but never entirely disappear.

> The first and most important characteristic of the soul (*jiva*) is its capability of cognition. If the soul is completely free from the disturbing influence of matter, it is capable of recognizing everything in the present, past, and future. . . . If it is however infected with *karma*-matter, this absolute cognition disappears. [Negative karma-matter] veils the omniscience of the soul as a dense veil of clouds hides the light of the sun. But . . . in spite of the influence of matter, a fraction of the faculty of cognition is preserved to the *jiva;* for if the *jiva* would also lose this, it would no longer be a *jiva*. This fraction of cognition is of different dimensions in different beings. In some it is very large: they are capable of perceiving absent material things and even the thoughts of others by means of transcendental perception; in most of them, however, it is only small, as they can only perceive by means of their senses. (Glasenapp, 1942, p. 43)

The existence of the soul requires no empirical proof, since a person's self-awareness is proof enough. Because the qualities of the soul are so vast in number and so complex in their aspects, they cannot all be known by an ordinary person. The ordinary individual is able to comprehend no more than a few aspects of reality at any given time. Only the rare individual who ultimately completes the journey to enlightenment acquires the omniscience needed to recognize all facets of reality.

A significant characteristic of reality is the contradictory nature of many pairs of concepts concerning life, such as *eternal and momentary, perfect and imperfect, bound and free, pure and impure.* But these seemingly conflicting pairs can be rationalized in Jaina theory by recognizing that each term in any such pairing will be true "in some respect" or "from a particular vantage point," so that they are not really in opposition For instance, the soul as a substance—a conveyor of karma—is eternal, but its karma changes with people's experiences, so the karma aspect of soul is ephemeral, not everlasting. Viewed from these two perspectives—the conveyor and the conveyed—the soul is simultaneously both eternal and temporary.

> The Jaina maintains that every assertion, whether positive or negative, is made within the framework of a certain situation defined by four factors: the specific being [person, object], the specific location, the specific time, and the specific state [activity, behavior] of the referent. (Jaini, 1979, p. 95)

Thus, judgments about moral incidents are not absolute and unchanging from one episode to another but, instead, are relative to the conditions of each particular incident. Every episode must be judged on the basis of the conditions obtaining at the time, a judgment affected by the vantage point that the observer adopts on that occasion.

The Goal of Moral Development

The ultimate goal of moral development—indeed, the goal of life itself—is to win freedom from the bondage of the soul's recurrent earthly lives of suffering. To reach this goal, it is necessary for people to overcome the causes of bondage, which can be summarized as:

Perverted views, meaning false notions about reality—beliefs about the soul, (anger, pride, self-pity), deities, one's ability to change other people's lives, and more.

Nonrestraint of urges to perform acts harmful to others or to oneself.

Carelessness, in the sense of apathy and a lack of dedication to observing one's vows (see "vows" under Stages of Development).

Passions, such as desire, lust, hatred, jealousy, and anger.

These causes result from destructive karmas, which Jaina dogma identifies under four broad classes. The first class involves delusions of insight (perverted views) and delusions of conduct that produce the major passions of anger, pride, deceit, and greed as well as subsidiary passions (laughter, pleasure, sorrow, fear, disgust, sexual cravings). The second set of karmas obscures knowledge by obstructing the function of the senses and the mind (distorted reasoning ability, impeded clairvoyance, curtailed ability to interpret other people's modes of thought). Karmas in the third cluster disturb people's perceptions, causing them to misjudge moral situations. The fourth set restricts the energy needed to direct the body, mind, and speech (Jaini, 1979, pp. 131-132).

Study of Jaina doctrine, meditation, and the observance of austerities are prescribed for eliminating the causes as one progresses through the stages of moral enlightenment.

Moral Values and Stages of Development

Negative, harmful karma is added to a person's soul each time that individual fails to heed the moral values advocated in Jaina dogma. The way to rid the soul of harmful karma is to work one's way through the stages of moral purification that lead to *moksha*.

Jaina Moral Virtues

Moral values prescribed in the Jaina scriptures appear as both virtues to adopt and sins to avoid. The principal virtues are five ethical principles that Mahavira taught his followers—nonviolence, seeking and telling the truth, nonstealing, celibacy, and freedom from possessing things (Gopalan, 1973, p. 159).

From a negative perspective, moral values espoused in Jainism are reflected in sins committed in violation of values. Stevenson (1915/1970, pp. 116-139) has cited 18 varieties of sin proscribed in Jaina dogma. In Table 11-2, I have included Stevenson's set of sins in the left column and paired it in the right column with my estimate of the virtues that have been breached by the commitment of those sins.

However, simply listing general types of sin fails to convey the complexity of the Jaina value system. For instance, Jaina doctrine includes 25 subtypes of false faith, such as believing in the Hindu gods Genesha and Hanuman (whom the Jaina believe are not gods at all) and insincerely offering vows to Jaina saints or gurus in order to gain one's wishes. The Jaina canon also describes 82 kinds of dire results that sins can produce for one's next life on earth, such as physical deformities, mental aberrations, bad dreams, lethargy, poor housing, general unluckiness, rebirth as a vegetable or detested animal rather than as a human, and far more (Stevenson, 1915/1970, pp. 130-139).

Jaina Stages of Moral Purification

As in Buddhism, stages of development in Jainism consist of a series of levels through which the dedicated Jaina advances to win release from the bondage of rebirths. Two sets of stages are defined, one set for ordinary people—the laity—and the other for the most devout members of the order—the ascetic mendicants.

The 11 stages prescribed for the laity advance in the following sequence: (1) adopting the right views, (2) taking the 21 vows (see below), (3) practicing the *samayika* chant, (4) fasting on holy days, (5) adopting pure kinds of nourishment, (6) being continent (self-restraint) by day, (7) displaying absolute continence, (8) abandoning all household activity, (9) abandoning acquisitiveness (disposing of one's possessions), (10) withdrawing approval of all activities related to household life, and (11) renouncing all connections with one's family.

These steps of abandoning the work-a-day world are guided by the 21 vows prescribed at stage 2, which include: renouncing certain edibles (meat, alcohol, honey, figs); refraining from false speech, theft, illicit sexual engagements, hunting, and gambling; limiting one's possessions; restricting such items of enjoyment as favorite foods and clothing; and adopting positive acts—fasting and giving food and medicine to mendicants (Jaini, 1979, pp. 186-187).

The stages that mendicants are expected to master are similar in kind but more austere than the stages for laypersons.

Progressing through the entire series of stages may be far too demanding a task to finish during a single life span. Hence, the soul may need to return to the world many times to complete the journey.

Table 11-2

Sins and Virtues in Jainism

Sins to Avoid	*Virtues to Pursue*
1. Killing—destroying any living thing	Permitting living things to exist
2. Untruthfulness—telling lies	Speaking the truth
3. Dishonesty—theft, smuggling, law-breaking, treason, sharp business practices	Honesty, veracity
4. Unchastity—illicit sexual affairs	Chastity—fidelity to one's spouse
5. Covetousness—undue attachment to one's possessions	Freedom from attachment to material goods and honors
6. Anger—the frequent source of sins	Calmness, forgiveness
7. Conceit—pride of caste, family, wealth, reputation, learning, or being a landed proprietor	Humility
8. Intrigue, cheating	Candidness, honesty
9. Greed, avarice	Generosity, unselfishness
10. Overfondness of a person or thing	Moderation in fondness for individuals or objects
11. Hatred, envy that often springs from desiring possessions	Kindheartedness, altruism
12. Quarrelsomeness	Agreeableness
13. Slander—false accusations that destroy the peace of family life	Truthfulness
14. Gossiping—telling tales that discredit others	Speaking well of others or refraining from talking about them
15. Criticism—finding fault in others	Correcting one's own failings
16. Loss of self-control in the presence of either joy or sorrow	Even-tempered, undemonstrative in either joyful or sad circumstances
17. Hypocrisy	Forthright truthfulness
18. False faith, false beliefs	True dedication to Jaina doctrine

Causality

Jainism, more than any of the other religions inspected in Part III, locates the cause of moral development in the individual person. Whereas the Judaic-Christian-Islamic tradition recognizes that characteristics inherited from one's forebears can affect one's present moral condition, Jainism proposes that what a person has appeared to inherit is actually the karma earned during previous lifetimes. Ancestors cannot be either credited or blamed for any part of one's present moral fate. And whereas both Hinduism and the Judaic-Christian-Islamic line recognize the influence of spirits and gods on one's moral destiny, Jainism rejects the notion of supernatural intervention.

> The Jaina believe strongly in the duty of forgiving others, and yet have no hope of forgiveness from a Higher Power for themselves. They shrink from sin and take vows to guard against it, but know of no dynamic force outside themselves that could enable them to keep those vows. They see before them an austere upper path of righteousness, but know of no Guide to encourage and help them along that difficult way. (Stevenson, 1915/1970, p. 289)

Environment can be a significant influence on moral development by (a) the kinds of temptations it offers for leading people into sin and (b) the opportunities it provides for gaining spiritual guidance from Jaina teachers and Jaina literature. Thus, one person's task of progressing toward deliverance from the cycle of rebirths will be more difficult than another's because of their different environments. However, the core cause of moral development is still the individual person's knowledge of Jaina doctrine and his or her strength of determination to abide by the vows and bear the austerities required for attaining nirvana.

Conclusion

One curious feature of Jainism is the social class from which the sect has drawn a majority of its followers. The community of Jains is composed chiefly of members from the prosperous Hindu Kshatriya caste, people who are apt to possess a substantial quantity of the worldly goods that Jaina dogma holds in contempt. Although hesitant to divest themselves of their property, such adherents are well equipped to provide the mundane support needed by members of the faith who have chosen to tread the path of the ascetic mendicant.

SIKHISM

Among movements designed to reform Hinduism, Sikhism was a late comer, founded in the 15th century CE by a man of upper-caste lineage known as Guru Nanak Dev (1469-1539). Revered in the present-day Sikh community as an embodiment of the sect's monotheistic God, Guru Nanak is described as being "born with divine status, thus, his teachings were heavenly" (*Sikh Religion,* 1990, p. 15).

Sikhs cite the sociopolitical and religious climate of 15th-century India as the motive force behind Guru Nanak's reform efforts.

> When Buddhism was driven out of India, the Hindu society set up their own gods and goddesses and began to worship their stone images. The Hindu priests, who had been for centuries the self-made custodians of religion and its teachings, had reduced religion to a mockery, performing rites and rituals and superstitious ceremonies devoid of any sense and meaning. . . . Hindu society was over-ridden with the caste system. . . . Religious reading, writing, and teaching were strictly the monopoly of the Brahmans [priesthood caste]. (*Sikh Religion,* 1990, p. 10)

On the occasion of Guru Nanak's death in 1539, the leadership of the sect was inherited by his chief disciple, Guru Angad, who in turn would later pass the authority to his own disciple, Guru Amar Das. Thereafter, responsibility for the Sikh community would be delegated to a succession of seven more gurus until the death in 1708 of the tenth leader, Guru Gobind Singh, the "last Guru forever" (*Sikh Religion,* 1990, p. 245).

Sikhs are critical of the popular use of the term *guru* to mean a teacher or expert. The term, they explain, is a combination of the two words *gu* (darkness) and *ru* (light), so together they mean the "divine light that dispels all darkness." Hence, Guru (with a capital G) identifies a religious sage who directs people toward salvation.

The Source of Evidence

The teachings of the Sikh Gurus were compiled in 1604 by the fifth of the 10 seers, Guru Arjun, and have remained in that original form until the present day. This 1,430-page collection of holy scriptures is entitled *Guru Granth Sahib* (The Divine Word). It contains advice directly transmitted to the Gurus by God. The aim of the book is to help people "live by certain directives or moral codes which are necessary for salvation"—that is, for release from all their prior sins, sorrows, sufferings, and cycles of birth and death. The *Guru Granth Sahib* "initiates a disciple on the path of spiritual progress and guides him at various stages of his journey to God" (*Sikh Religion,* 1990, pp. 250-251).

In several ways, Sikh dogma agrees with Hindu belief—the transmigration of souls, the role of karma in determining the sorts of bodies the soul will inhabit in its successive lives on earth, the moral goal of achieving release from cycles of birth and death, and the superiority of spiritual life over material life and worldly possessions. However, in other respects Sikhism differs from Hinduism. Sikhs denounce the caste system; they regard people from all walks of life as equally worthy of kind treatment and salvation. Sikhs also recognize people from all religious faiths as deserving respect, because "understand thou that mankind is all one" (*Akal Ustat* in Singh, 1974, p. 85). Furthermore, Sikhs reject the policy of nonviolence advocated by Buddhists and Jains. According to Sikh doctrine, the faithful should fight to rectify injustice.

Reality and Components of Personality

Sikh cosmology holds that the universe consists of two sorts of components, the material (tangible, physical) and the immaterial (invisible, spiritual). The material world is constructed from the four elements of Hindu lore—fire, water, earth, and air. The bodies of sentient beings—all animal life—are material and decompose into the constituent elements following their mundane death.

As in Hinduism, souls in Sikh theory are the most significant immaterial aspects of the universe. Souls migrate from one body to another as the result of karma compiled during a particular body's lifetime.

At the center of Sikh theology is a single God. As the opening lines of the *Guru Granth Sahib* declare: "There is but One God, Who is All Truth, the Creator, devoid of fear and enmity, Immortal, Unborn, Self-existent, Great, and Bountiful" (Singh, 1974, p. 77). There are neither angels nor such a specific pernicious being as the devil in Sikh theory. However, human personality contains a functionary called *Haumain* that represents *free will*, which can operate either for good or for evil, depending on which of these tendencies the person lets dominate moral decisions. When driven by selfish, egocentric motives that ignore God's will, Haumain causes people to be "false, evil, sad, defiled, unwise." But when focused on God's will, Haumain makes people "truthful, good, happy, pure, wise, etc." (Singh, 1969, p. 138).

> When man performs an evil act, an inner voice tells him that he is doing evil. This inner voice is of pure conscience, of God Himself. Man hears this voice and sometimes acts accordingly. But often he performs evil acts in spite of that voice which he ignores. (Singh, 1969, p. 150)

> > "Mind of man knows full well
> > And yet performs evil acts;
> > How odd it is that, while holding
> > A lamp, he falls into the well"
> >   (*Guru Granth Sahib* in Singh, 1969, pp. 150-151).

The Goal of Moral Development

The ultimate aim of moral development is for the soul to merge with the Supreme Soul or God and thereby enjoy eternal bliss. However, unlike Hindus, Buddhists, and Jains, the Sikhs do not expect to achieve this state by retreating from the workaday world into asceticism and painful austerities. Instead, while rejecting the pursuit of luxurious materialism, Sikhs still value active engagement in the conduct of society, doing good works and thereby garnering spiritual bounty.

> Sikhism holds out no alluring promises of eternal happiness on the mere adoption of certain rites or belief in any particular person or dogma, but enjoins upon its followers to live a life of purity, not as ascetics living upon public charity but as worldly men living upon the fruit of their honest labour. . . . The salvation of the Sikh is not obtained by renouncing the world, residing in forests and there torturing and annihilating the body by austerities and penances. (Singh, 1974, p. 79)

> [The complete enlightenment of *moksha*] is a stage reached while living in the everyday world . . . shining out brilliantly in the midst of the darkness of the world, thereby enlightening the paths of others around. . . . This moksha is not breaking connections with the world but is something which increases connections with the family of man. The outlook of complete aloofness is replaced by a sense of social and corporate life. (Singh, 1969, p. 163)

The *Guru Granth Sahib* condemns begging and extols self-reliance and hard work.

> Touch not at all the feet of those who call themselves *gurus* and *piers* and go about begging. They alone who eat the fruit of their own labour and share it with others, says Nanak, recognize the right path. (*Sarang K. Var* in Singh, 1974, p. 79)

Moral Values

Morality in Sikh theory is portrayed chiefly as personality traits rather than as specific behaviors to adopt and sinful acts to avoid. Among the qualities to be acquired are such virtues as truthfulness, kindness, altruism, self-reliant hard work, and humility (though not servility).

The five principal evils to avoid are those of lust, covetousness, attachment, anger, and pride (self-aggrandizement, conceit). The first three of these are human characteristics acceptable in moderation but evil when in excess.

> The question arises: From where do the evil forces originate if God is not their source. The answer is that . . . they are natural instincts produced in man through the organs given to him by God. [Lust] as a natural instinct is not evil so long as it is confined within the limits of any accepted law of morality. Without this instinct, the human race would have come to an end. . . . But natural instincts become evil when they are acted upon by the Haumain [egocentrism]of man. Haumain in its bad sense stimulates natural instincts to desire more of everything and by means which may not be consistent with the law of morality. (Singh, 1969, p. 149).

Causality

In Sikh theory, the causal factors behind moral thought and action include (a) heredity (carried through the karma to which the person has contributed in earlier lives); (b) knowledge of the holy book, *Guru Granth Sahib*; (c) the environmental setting determining one's social, material, and financial opportunities; (d) personal intention, driven by the desire for release from the cycles of birth and death; (e) conscience; and (f) supernatural forces.

By their heavy dependence on prayer, Sikhs show their high regard for the power of supernatural intervention. Singh (1974, p. 91) asserts that Sikhs "do nothing important without invoking the Lord for His protection and guidance." However, unlike Hindus, Sikhs abjure the practice of rites and austerities that are intended to mollify the gods. Instead, Sikhs focus on performing good works in their day-to-day social life as a means of accumulating positive karma.

Conclusion

Commenting on the influence of Sikhism on present-day life in India, Hasan has written:

> One of the significant features of Indian culture is its capacity to absorb different trends. . . . When different traditions have combined together, what has grown is not merely the aggregate of these traditions—the interaction has led to the emergence of something which is much more and is characterised by freshness and vigour. Among the finest fruits of this process of cultural synthesis has been the rise of Sikhism. Guru Nanak not only imbibed various teachings of Hinduism and Islam, but his own teachings have a quality whose mark on the personality of India remains very deep. (Hasan, 1979, p. ix)

AN ASSESSMENT OF THE FOUR PERSPECTIVES

As in previous chapters, the appraisal of the theories in the present chapter focuses on the standards introduced in Chapter 2.

On the first criterion—how readily the theories can be understood—I rated the four Asian models in the lower "moderately well" range. Although I believe the gist of the theories can be grasped by typical readers, I question whether some of the most essential concepts can accurately be understood in the ways the authors of the doctrines intended. There are at least three reasons for this problem of understandability. First, with the exception of Sikhism, the holy scriptures were written in ancient times and in languages not readily understood today. Therefore, modern-day audiences must read the scriptures in translations that may not accurately convey the original authors' meanings, particularly since the cultural conditions of ancient times differed significantly from present-day conditions. Second, the Hindu, Buddhist, and Jain canonical literature is volumi-

Hinduism, Buddhism, Jainism, Sikhism

How well do I think the theories meet the standards?

The Standards	*Very Well*	*Moderately Well*	*Very Poorly*
1. Is clearly understandable		X	
2. Explains past and predicts future moral behavior	X		
3. Offers practical guidance in coping with moral matters	X		
4. Is readily verifiable and falsifiable			X
5. Accommodates new evidence			X
6. Stimulates new discoveries		X	
7. Is durable	X		
8. Is self-satisfying			X

nous and appears in different versions that often contain conflicting accounts. Thus, there is the question of which accounts are the authentic ones. Third, descriptions of such key concepts as *soul, moksha,* and *punishments* are often vague and differ from one version to another, or sometimes even within the same version. Furthermore, each of these sects faces unresolved issues, such as that of rationalizing the idea of an omnipotent god with the notion of human free will. The question is: Are people's destinies entirely preordained by an all-powerful god or do people have some control over their fate? It would appear that this matter has not been settled satisfactorily in any of the dogma.

Linked to the issue of understandability is the problem of verifying many of the models' key proposals. I marked the theories low on falsifiability (item 4) because there seems to be no empirical method for either verifying or disconfirming numbers of their most essential assertions. Such is the case with the concepts *soul, karma, transmigration, nirvana,* and *Brahma* or *God.* In addition, other core notions, such as the efficacy of prayer or of rites and austerities, are likewise not amenable to empirical verification. Belief in such tenets rests entirely on faith in the infallibility of the holy scriptures.

I rated the four theories high for their ability to explain the past and predict the future (item 2) and for their usefulness in guiding people's daily behavior (item 3). The concept of karma explains how and why people's present fate was predetermined by their behavior in earlier lifetimes, and the notion of karma makes clear what future destiny people can expect on the basis of their behavior during their current life span. In Hinduism, how people should conduct their daily lives in order to achieve salvation is detailed in the religion's extensive catalog of rites and austerities to perform and forbidden acts to avoid. In Buddhism, Jainism, and Sikhism, the personality traits that people should display and the ones they should eschew in their pursuit of *moksha* are amply depicted throughout the scriptures.

The four theories' ability to accommodate new evidence (item 5)—such as the findings of empirical science (physical and social)—seems limited either to ignoring or rejecting such evidence outright or to interpreting it in ways that maintain the theories' structures without completely answering the questions that the data evoke.

The fact that Buddhism, Jainism, and Sikhism originated as reactions against putative shortcomings of Hinduism implies that Hinduism did stimulate new discoveries (item 6). And Sikhism also represented a reformation of ostensible inadequacies of Buddhism and Jainism. Thus, at least to a minor extent, such theories stimulate thinkers to propose alternative models featuring elements that might be regarded as "new discoveries."

In durability (item 7), all four of these belief systems deserve high marks. After many centuries, they continue to serve as the conceptions of moral development to which millions of people subscribe.

My assessment of the self-satisfying quality of these four models of moral development is the same as in the case of the Judaic-Christian-Islamic line. The Hindu, Buddhist, Jain, and Sikh models depend too heavily on the speculations of ancient authorities rather than on empirical investigation to suit my tastes. I do not contend that people who do accept authorities' descriptions of moral development are wrong. Possibly they are right. But for myself, I find the present evidence for such claims unconvincing. Therefore, on item 8, I marked the Hindu, Buddhist, Jain, and Sikh models low as persuasive explanations of moral development. This does not mean that I reject the moral values that the religions espouse, for I subscribe to many of those values. It means, instead, that I question the underlying conception of development as proposed in the four creeds.

12

Confucianism and Shinto

Although Confucianism and Shinto originated as separate philosophical systems (Confucianism in China, Shinto in Japan), they have shared important elements ever since Confucian beliefs (along with Buddhist teachings) were introduced into Japan during the fifth and sixth centuries CE. The following description of Confucianism and Shinto as theories of moral development opens with a summary of beliefs held in common, then continues with a sketch of characteristics unique to each system, beginning with Confucianism and closing with Shinto.

COMMON FEATURES OF THE TWO TRADITIONS

Six sets of belief that characterize both Confucian and Shinto doctrine concern (1) the goal of moral development and its temporal focus, (2) people's innate moral nature, (3) the importance of an individual's willpower in development, (4) the influence of the spirits of dead ancestors, (5) methods of investigating the process of development, and (6) a nation's worldview.

1. *The goal and its temporal focus.* Unlike the theories reviewed in chapters 10 and 11, neither Confucianism nor Shinto portrays life on earth as merely preparation for a life after death. Both persuasions are chiefly concerned with the here and now, particularly with how the moral behavior of the individual affects society as a whole. The quality of a person's morality is judged by how the individual's behavior influences the peace and prosperity of the group.

2. *People's innate moral nature.* In Confucian and Shinto belief, humans are born pure and cheerful. However, this positive, optimistic view of life is at risk in an immoral world. The challenge children face in growing up is to arm themselves against evil influences in order to protect their inherent righteousness.

3. *The importance of willpower.* In moral development—and, indeed, in all mental and physical endeavors—the principal cause of success is how hard people have tried. Although inherited abilities and environmental opportunities or constraints are accorded some recognition as causes, the most important is hard work. Wrongdoers are not excused on the grounds of unfavorable environments, their family's social status, or their biological inheritance. They themselves bear the blame for their misdeeds.

4. *The spirits of dead ancestors.* In their modern-day form, both Confucianism and Shinto hold that an invisible essence of departed ancestors can hover about and in certain ways may affect the outcome of moral events.

5. *Methods of investigation.* In both traditions, the truth about moral development is to be found in the canonical literature and in the interpretations given by the creeds' authoritative figures—sages and the priesthood—rather than in empirical investigations.

6. *A nation's worldview.* Stripped of their specifically religious accoutrements—such as a theology and rituals—each tradition in its moral precepts and notions of causality represents a general attitude toward life shared by an entire nation's citizenry. Core beliefs of secular Confucianism are shared by virtually all citizens of the Republic of China in Taiwan and by a great many inhabitants of the People's Republic in mainland China. The central tenets of secular Shinto are embraced by the population of Japan, even those who subscribe to some form of Buddhism. In effect, Confucianism and Shinto—unlike Christianity, Islam, and Buddhism—are to a great extent national rather than international belief systems. During the Tokugawa regime in Japan (1603-1867) the influence of Confucian belief was particularly strong as its "emphases on such simple virtues as honesty, frugality, filial piety, and the veneration of [sacred spirits] and the throne prepared the ground for the resurgence of ethnocentric Shinto in the 19th century" (Kitagawa, 1987, p. 164). In the subsequent Meiji regime (1868-1945) an imperial rescript required all elementary schools to include a course on moral teaching (*shushin*) designed to "inculcate 'Japanesed' Confucian ethics in order to strengthen faith in the national [political] policy" (Kitagawa, 1987, p. 168).

With such common elements as a background, we now consider key features of each of these faiths, beginning with Confucianism.

CONFUCIANISM

At first glance, Confucian philosophy may appear to have originated with the man whose name the tradition bears—Confucius or Kung Fu-tzu (551-479 BCE). However, the belief system that he synthesized, improved, and taught actually derived from earlier beginnings. Although Confucianism today is often described as a religion, it was initially in the form of a social philosophy. Confucius' concerns were not theological and other-worldly, but instead centered on the mundane matter of human nature as it influences social interactions in a political state. Later, his philosophical notions were transformed into a variety of religious doctrine. People who assert that Confucianism is indeed a religion support their argument with reference to rituals and the worship of ancestors that have been practiced by many who regard themselves as Confucianists. On the other hand, those who believe original Confucianism is solely a social philosophy say that the rites which have become associated with Confucianism are borrowings from Taoism or Buddhism, embellishments that have no necessary connection with the essence of Confucian belief. They point out that Confucius himself has never been officially deified, but has been known simply as the Sagest of Sages.

The following version of a Confucian theory of moral development addresses (1) the sources of evidence about development, (2) the goal of development, (3) personality structure, (4) moral values, and (5) matters of cause.

Sources of Evidence

Like so many other ancient philosophers and religious leaders, Confucius did not present his ideas about social organization and human nature in the form of a logically argued written treatise. Instead, he expounded his ideas orally to his students, and it was they who compiled the teachings as a collection of disconnected aphorisms and brief anecdotes that then were published as the *Lun yu*—Confucian *sayings* or *analects* (Lin, 1988).

The *Analects of Confucius* is the earliest of four books that, over the centuries, have been the most fundamental sources of this philosophical tradition (Waley, 1938; Ware, 1955). The second of the four is *The Book of Mencius*, written by the sage Mencius or Meng-tzu (Master Meng) (372?-289? BCE), who was taught by a disciple of Confucius' grandson. The third book, *The Great Learning*, appeared in different versions over the centuries, eventually assuming its present form, arranged by the scholar Chu Hsi into a basic text and a series of commentaries. Chu Hsi declared that the text was Confucius' own words as handed down by his pupil Tseng Tsan (505-436 BCE) and that the commentaries were the views of Tseng-tzu as recorded by his pupils. The last of the four books is *The Doctrine of the Mean*, attributed to Confucius' grandson, Kung Tzu-ssu (492-431 BCE), though some scholars doubt that Tzu-ssu was really the author (Chai & Chai, 1965; Lin, 1988).

Today these classics continue to be viewed by adherents of Confucian philosophy as offering the most authentic prescription for the conduct of a political state and of the state's individual members. Hence, the four can serve as our basic source of information about a Confucian theory of moral development.

The Goal of Moral Development

According to Mencius, people are innately inclined to virtuous thought and action. However, from infancy onward, this righteous nature is subject to the influence of the environment, an influence that can either support or corrupt an individual's inborn goodness. The aim of moral development is to cultivate the original heaven-endowed nature and thus make the person *truly human*, a condition known as *jen*, which means *human goodness* and *a desire to help people*—"extending one's heart to include others." When people's natural goodness is thus developed and extended, they feel no distinction between themselves and others. They identify themselves with the entire universe (Chai & Chai, 1965, p. 146).

Jen is not a simple virtue that can be directly observed. Instead, it is a complex unity that can be understood only through analyzing its constituent moral "hearts."

Personality Structure

From a Confucian perspective, human nature is divided into two general aspects, the physiological and the virtuous. The physiological represents lower-quality characteristics disposed toward types of overt behavior—the mouth disposed to tastes, the eye to colors, the ear to sounds, the nose to odors, and the four limbs to ease or rest. The qualitatively higher level of personality is that of virtue, which makes the difference between humans and brutes. Unlike animals, humans innately possess a heart that is sensitive to the suffering of others. This sensitive heart is a composite of four hearts related to virtues—hearts of compassion, of shame, of courtesy and modesty, and of a sense of right and wrong.

The heart of compassion is the seedbed of *jen*. The heart of shame is the basis for righteousness (*i*). The heart of courtesy and modesty is the source of the observance of the Confucian rites (*li*). And the heart of right and wrong is the origin of wisdom (*chih*). These four are the source of all other virtues that people acquire (Lin, 1990, p. 149).

Moral Values

The precepts championed in Confucian writings are a mixture of moral and prudential advice. As moral guides, the precepts describe what is just and humane in social intercourse. As prudential maxims, they suggest the sorts of behavior that maintain amicable social relations and lead to success with one's ventures.

As already noted, the aim of moral development is to achieve *jen*. The most basic foundation of *jen* is love, meaning love for one's parents, for one's neighbors, and ultimately for all of humanity.

> As a process, *jen* represents the way to build social relationships, that is, the way to establish reasonable, harmonious interactions with others. Of the two parts that make up the process, the first focuses on oneself and the second on others. In regard to oneself, an individual should always be honest and engage in no self-deception. As for others, a person should base all social relations on *li*, that is, on courtesy and modesty. *Li* is the set of rules or traditions that guides proper relations among people. In social interactions, a person displays *jen* through sincerity and honesty in speech and action. What people say and do are true expressions of what they think. (Lin, 1988, pp. 122-123)

As more precise guides to moral development, specific maxims that define *li* are distributed throughout the Confucian canon. For example, among his sayings Confucius identified traits to be acquired by people who wish to maintain and enhance their innate virtuous nature and thereby become *superior humans* or *humans-at-their-best*.

> He who is unflinching, bold, simple, natural, and unhurried approximates manhood-at-its-best.
> Great Man is sparing in words, but prodigal in deeds.
> He who in this world can practice fine things may indeed be considered man-at-his-best . . . humility, magnanimity, sincerity, diligence, and graciousness. If you are humble, you will not be laughed at. If you are magnanimous, you will attract many to your side. If you are sincere, people will trust you. If you are diligent, you will be successful. If you are gracious, you will get along well with your subordinates. (Ware, 1955, pp. 88, 94, 111)

The practical, mundane nature of Confucian moral values is reflected in the foregoing advice. Rather than advocating traits or rituals that might please the gods and earn credit toward a better life after death, Confucius espoused moral traits that would help achieve desired consequences in this life. Ezra Pound (1969, p. 191) quoted Voltaire as saying, "I admire Confucius. He was the first man who did *not* receive divine inspiration." Pound then observed that Confucius "was not born of a dragon, not in any way supernatural, but remarkably possessed of good sense."

And the rewards of goodness do not await an after life but can be expected in the present world. As promised in *The Great Learning,* "Virtue is the root; wealth is the result" (Legge, 1893, p. 375). Furthermore, the results of virtue include psychological as well as material dividends. In the *Analects* Confucius declared, "The wise are free from perplexities; the virtuous from anxiety; and the bold from fear" (Legge, 1893, p. 225). *The Doctrine of the Mean* proposed that when people—especially those in positions of authority—are "sincere and reverential, the whole world is conducted to a state of happy tranquillity" (Legge, 1893, p. 433).

Nearly all the values that people are to acquire are expressed in the *Analects* as character traits, either stated outright or reflected in positive and negative examples (Legge, 1893).

Fortitude. To see what is right and not do it is want of courage.

Sincerity. In the ceremonies of mourning, it is better that there be deep sorrow than a minute attention to observances.

Honesty, integrity. Riches and honours are what men desire. If they cannot be obtained in the proper way, they should not be held.

Goodness. The superior man thinks of virtue; the small man thinks of comfort.

Lack of egocentrism. He who acts with a constant view to his own advantage will be much murmured against.

Humility. I am not concerned that I am not known ; [rather,] I seek to be worthy to be known.

Carefulness. The cautious seldom err.

Logical stalwartness. Chang is under the influence of his passions; how can he be pronounced firm and unbending.

Equanimity. Admirable indeed was the virtue of Hui. With a single bamboo dish of rice, a single gourd of drink, and living in his mean narrow lane, while others could not have endured the distress, he did not allow his joy to be affected by it.

Dutifulness. Let the will be set on the path of duty.

Propriety, moral obligation. Without the rules of propriety, respectfulness becomes laborious bustle; carefulness becomes timidity; boldness becomes insubordination; straightforwardness becomes rudeness.

Dignity, humility. The superior man has a dignified ease without pride. The inferior man has pride without a dignified ease.

Reciprocity. What you do not want done to yourself, do not do to others.

One of the most honored Confucian values is obedience to parents.

During a father's life time, do what he wants; after his death, do as he did. If a man can go along like his father for three years, he can be said to be carrying-on filially.

Young men should be filial in the home, and brotherly outside it; careful of what they say, but once said, stick to it; be agreeable to everyone, but develop friendship further with the real men. (Pound, 1969, pp. 195-196)

Mencius said: "Of the services of men, which is the greatest? The service to parents is the greatest."

The Doctrine of the Mean, addressing the question of relations between a sovereign and the populace, describes desired traits for anyone in authority.

It is only he who shows himself quick in apprehension, clear in discernment, of far-reaching intelligence, and all-embracing knowledge, fitted to exercise rule; magnanimous, generous, benign, and mild, fitted to exercise forbearance;

impulsive, energetic, firm, and enduring, fitted to maintain a firm hold; self-adjusted, grave, never swerving from the Mean, and correct, fitted to command reverence; accomplished, distinctive, concentrative, and searching, fitted to exercise discrimination.

It is the way of the superior man to prefer the concealment of his virtue, while it daily becomes more illustrious; and it is the way of the mean [inferior] man to seek notoriety, while he daily goes more and more to ruin. (Legge, 1893, pp. 428, 431)

In Confucian literature, moral values are also reflected in characteristics that disciples noticed in their master. Followers of Confucius wrote that he was entirely free from egoism, obstinacy, foregone conclusions, and arbitrary predeterminations.

To summarize, *jen* is the core virtue to which more specific desirable traits contribute. As such, *jen* comprises the perfect personality that is the goal of moral development and the source of success in day-to-day social interactions.

Causality

In accounting for the moral characteristics that people acquire, Confucian writings allude to (a) inherited tendencies, (b) environmental forces, and (c) a person's intellect and willpower.

Inherited Tendencies

Mencius is credited with developing the doctrine that humans, by their very nature, are disposed to behaving morally. He taught that people are innately endowed with propitious "instinctive feelings—such as those of love and compassion, shame and dislike, modesty and yielding, and right and wrong—that lead to positive efforts for the good of others" (Chai & Chai, 1965, p. 148).

Environmental Forces

The most significant environmental influences are (a) the models of morality and styles of life that a person witnesses and (b) the sources and amounts of knowledge the individual utilizes.

A story about Mencius' mother tells of her changing residences in order to offer her son suitable examples of occupations. Mother Meng and her young son first lived near a cemetery until she discovered the boy playing at burying and mourning the dead. She then moved near a marketplace, where Mencius was soon mimicking the merchants' sharp business dealings. This displeased his mother, so they moved to the vicinity of a school, which produced the desired result of Mencius patterning his behavior after that of the pupils and their teachers (Chai & Chai, 1965, p. 93).

Models of proper and improper conduct also play a central role in moral development. For instance, Confucian literature alludes to the importance of people in authority setting examples of traits that others can profitably adopt. *The Doctrine of the Mean* declares that "the superior man does not use rewards [to influence others, but by his example] the people are stimulated to virtue. He does not show anger, and the people are awed more than by hatchets and battle-axes" (Legge, 1893, p. 432). In the *Analects*, Confucius advises that:

> When we see men of worth, we should think of equaling them; when we see men of a contrary character, we should turn inwards and examine ourselves.
>
> When I walk along with two others, they may serve me as my teachers. I will select their good qualities and follow them, their bad qualities and avoid them.
>
> There are three friendships which are advantageous, and three which are injurious. Friendship with the upright; friendship with the sincere; and friendship with the man of much observation—these are advantageous. Friendship with the man of specious airs; friendship with the insinuatingly soft; and friendship with the glib-tongued—these are injurious. (Legge, 1893, pp. 170, 202, 311)

The *Analects* also suggest that "A gentleman . . . associates with decent people so as to adjust his own decencies" (Pound, 1969, p. 197).

Confucius was a great advocate of learning—of observing life, of studying writings from the past, of listening to people of experience, and of thinking deeply about all such matters. In Confucian theory, well-informed thought is essential for moral development.

> The superior man, extensively studying all learning, and keeping himself under the restraint of the rules of propriety, may thus likewise not overstep what is right.
>
> There may be those who act without knowing why. I do not do so. Hearing much and selecting what is good and following it: seeing much and keeping it in memory—this is the . . . style of knowledge.
>
> [Moral behavior requires] extensive study of what is good, accurate inquiry about it, careful reflection on it, the clear discrimination of it, and the earnest practice of it.
>
> There is the love of being benevolent without the love of learning—the beclouding here leads to foolish simplicity. . . . There is the love of being sincere without the love of learning—the beclouding here leads to an injurious disregard of consequences. There is the love of straightforwardness without the love of learning—the beclouding here leads to rudeness. (Legge, 1893, pp. 193, 203, 323, 413)

Intelligence and Willpower

Not only did Confucius place great store in the usefulness of knowledge, but he located the responsibility for failure and immorality on the person himself rather than on the individual's heredity, on the physical environment, on other people, or on supernatural forces.

> When the archer misses the centre of the target, he turns round and seeks for the cause of his failure in himself. . . . He rectifies himself, and seeks nothing from others. . . . He does not murmur against Heaven, nor grumble against men. (Legge, 1893, p. 396)

The Progression of Moral Development

The Confucian model is not a stage theory that pictures people developing through a defined set of levels. However, Confucius in his old age did see himself as having advanced through phases of maturity.

> At 15 I thought only of study. At 30 I was playing my role. At 40 I was sure of myself. At 50 I was conscious of my position in the universe. At 60 I was no longer argumentative. And now at 70 I can follow my heart's desire without violating custom. (Lin, 1988, p. 117)

As explained in *The Great Learning,* Confucius envisioned a process through which a society becomes well ordered and moral through a succession of expanding circles that extend from the individual person outward to embrace ever-larger groups of people.

The process begins with individual people perfecting their own minds and hearts. This feat is accomplished by means of several steps. The first consists of investigating daily objects and events and thinking deeply about them in order to understand the principles by which the world operates. It is by thus apprehending the quality of each object and event for a long time that a person extends his or her knowledge to the limits. Throughout this process, individuals are to make their wills sincere by engaging in no self-deception—being true to themselves and extending true understanding and sincerity to other people. Next, it is necessary to control the emotions of wrath, fear, fondness, and anxiety that reside in the heart. Such emotions, when uncontrolled, lead to irrational, harmful behavior. This ability to regulate the emotions is called "cultivating one's personal life" (Lin, 1990, p. 126).

When people have thus perfected their knowledge and cultivated their lives, they are prepared to carry out their responsibilities within the family in a wise and amicable fashion. This phase of social development is termed "regulating the family." During this process, members of the family learn to operate efficiently as a small social system.

Confucian belief holds that since the state is composed of families, if every family is well regulated, then the state will be properly regulated as well. Individual family members' knowledge, sincerity, self-cultivation, and skills of living within the social system of the home form the elements which ensure that the state will function effectively. And when each state operates efficiently, peace and enlightenment result for all of humanity.

In summary, the moral fate of the society depends on the moral development of each member of the society.

Conclusion

Confucian theory, after originating in China, thrived in its homeland and subsequently exerted influence over neighboring peoples, particularly the Koreans and Japanese. Although in the middle decades of the 20th century Confucian doctrine was officially outlawed by the Marxist government of the People's Republic of China, Confucianism beliefs have continued to be held by many of the billion Chinese living on mainland East Asia. Furthermore, Confucian doctrine has served as the official philosophical foundation of the Republic of China on Taiwan, where the population had reached 21 million by the mid-1990s. Consequently, by the end of the 20th century, a very large portion of East Asians subscribed—either in whole or in part—to a Confucian version of moral development.

SHINTO

Shinto or Shintoism is a national rather than international theory of moral development. The Shinto depiction of life, in effect, is confined to Japan. As an ethos of ancient origin, it continues to exert a powerful influence over the moral development of individual Japanese and over the political-social character of Japanese society.

Whereas the influence of Shinto is widely recognized, the nature of the philosophy itself is difficult to describe in concise terms because Shinto appears in a variety of forms and has no recognized founder, no established dogma, no list of ethical behaviors or commandments, and no sacred scriptures, although certain historical accounts function somewhat as scriptures. Furthermore, the mystical aspects of Shinto cannot readily be conveyed in words.

The word *Shinto* has been translated variously to mean the Divine Way, the Way of the Gods, and the Way of the Kami. Holtom (1938, p. 6) sought to capture the essence of Shinto by defining it as "the characteristic ritualistic arrangements and their underlying beliefs by which the Japanese people have celebrated, dramatized, interpreted, and supported the chief values of their national life." Ueda (1972, p. 29) called Shinto "the basic value orientation of the Japanese people." Ono (1962, pp. 2-3) declared that "Shinto is more than a religious faith. It is an amalgam of attitudes, ideas, and ways of doing things that through two millenniums and more have become an integral part of the way of the Japanese people." Kitagawa (1987, p. 139) called Shinto "the *ensemble* of contradictory yet peculiarly Japanese types of religious beliefs, sentiments, and approaches, which have been shaped and conditioned by the historical experience of the Japanese people from the prehistoric period to the present." For the purposes of this book on moral development, Shinto can be considered a theory of the proper conduct of life.

Historically, Shinto has been affected by religions imported from China, principally by Confucianism and Buddhism. Confucianism appeared in Japan at least by the fifth century CE and perhaps even earlier. Buddhism came first in the sixth century CE, and in its more influential Zen version in the 12th century. Thus, present-day Shinto consists of an integration of these belief systems and others into what can be considered a Shintoist view of life in modern Japan.

> It is with ample justification that a Japanese Confucian scholar has recently said that the national educational system, the social order, and the political institutions of Japan are all based upon the doctrines of Confucius. (Holtom, 1938, p. 205).

It is important to recognize that there are several varieties of Shinto. First, *koshitsu shinto* is a set of traditional rituals practiced only in the emperor's Imperial House and not open to public view. Second, shrine Shinto (*jinja shinto*) is a general system of beliefs, rituals, and festivals held at shrines around the nation in honor of the gods or spirits. Third, sect Shinto (*kyoha shinto*) is a collection of 13 religious groups that arose in the 19th century as offshoots of the Shinto tradition. Fourth, folk Shinto (*minkan shinto*) is "a portfolio term for the amalgam of superstitious, magico-religious rites, and practices of the common people" (Agency for Cultural Affairs, 1972, p. 32). However, none of these varieties has been my primary focus in extracting a Shinto theory of moral development. Rather, my attention has centered chiefly—though not exclusively—on *basic Shinto*, defined as the pervading value orientation of the Japanese people. In this sense, Shinto is a foundation stratum of beliefs undergirding not only the four religious types described above but all of Japanese society. Even those people who officially subscribe to Buddhism or Confucianism or Christianity will typically be adherents of basic Shinto. In essence, Shinto is a racial religion, with its theory of moral development centered exclusively on the people of Japan.

The following description of the theory addresses (1) sources of evidence, (2) the *kami*, (3) human nature and the goal of moral development, (4) moral values, (5) personality structure, (6) causality, and (7) stages of moral development.

Sources of Evidence

Even though there are no orthodox Shinto scriptures, a substantial body of literature analyzing and interpreting Shinto belief has accumulated over the centuries. This literature serves as the source from which a theory of moral development can be distilled. The two oldest references that I used were the

Kojiki or *Furu-koto-bumi* (Records of Ancient Matters) (1958) that was completed in 712 CE and the *Nihongi* or *Nihon-shoki* (Chronicles of Japan) (1958) which was finished in 729 CE (Chamberlain, 1932, pp. i, xxii). Additional sources have included such works as Jean Herbert's *Shinto: At the Fountain-head of Japan* (1967), Joseph J. Spae's *Shinto Man* (1972), D. C. Holtom's *The National Faith of Japan* (1938), Genichi Kato's *A Historical Study of the Religious Development of Shinto* (1973), and J. M. Kitagawa's *On Understanding Japanese Religion* (1987).

Much of Shinto belief is expressed in the form of myths representing a condensation of wisdom acquired by ancient sages who astutely observed life and extracted from their observations a series of convictions about the kind of individual behavior that best maintains an efficient, satisfying social system. Such convictions, when cast as a mixture of actual history and myths, are considered easier to understand and to apply in daily life than abstract philosophical generalizations would be (Herbert, 1967, pp. 227-228).

The principal methods of study and investigation in Shinto today are not those of scientific experimentation and observation but, rather, consist of learning the traditional myths, studying interpretations offered by recognized Shinto authorities, and privately meditating in order to perceive more clearly the truths found within one's inner self.

The *Kami*

To begin, it is useful to recognize the role assumed by *kami* in Japanese thought. At the core of Shintoism is the belief that spirits or deities, known as *kami*, influence people's destinies. The *kami* also serve as models of proper moral development, thus explaining why Shinto has been called the Way of the Kami.

The precise meaning of *kami* is rather elusive. The distinguished 18th century Shinto authority Motoori Norinaga (1730-1801) admitted that:

> I do not yet understand the meaning of the term *kami*. Speaking in general, however, it may be said that *kami* signifies, in the first place, the deities of heaven and earth that appear in the ancient records [*Kojiki* and *Nihongi*] and also the spirits of the shrines where they are worshipped. . . . In ancient usages, anything whatsoever which was outside the ordinary, which possessed superior power or which was awe-inspiring was called *kami*. Eminence here does not refer merely to the superiority of nobility, goodness, or meritorious deeds. Evil and mysterious things, if they are extraordinary and dreadful, are called *kami*. (Spae, 1972, p. 43)

In Shinto legend, there are well over a thousand deities in addition to many thousands of ancestors who have been accorded a kind of *kami* status. Some accounts place the total number of heavenly and earthly *kami* as high as 8 million (Kato, 1973, p. 15). Many *kami* are guardians, protecting people from evil influences, with certain ones in charge of particular affairs, such as people's health, fortune, and longevity, as well as earthquakes, pestilence, fertility, and other social and natural events (Kitagawa, 1987, p. 141). There is a separate guardian assigned to every day of the ten months between a woman's conception and the birth of her baby, with each of these *kami* bearing a specific name (Kato, 1973, pp. 21-23). From ancient times, *kami* have been associated with geographical regions, such as villages and provinces. Some are believed to reside in mountains, trees, forests, rivers, or celestial bodies (Kitagawa, 1987, p. 141).

Whereas most *kami* are benevolent and foster people's development, a minority are malevolent, blamed for misfortune in individual's lives and for such disasters as drought, earthquake, famine, and flood. Therefore, the characteristic that all *kami* share in common is not kindness or compassion but, rather, power and cleverness, which humans are wise to respect, even in the mischievous and evil spirits. The majority of *kami*—the benevolent ones—all display such virtues as generosity, faithfulness, patience, kindness, and compassion.

The significance of the *kami* for moral development is twofold. First, the character traits of the admirable *kami* define the goal toward which proper human development should be directed. Hence, the benevolent *kami* (and even the evil ones, in the case of power and cleverness) serve as models for people to emulate. Second, the *kami* are able to affect people's destinies, so it is well for humans to solicit the goodwill of the *kami*, encouraging these guardians to arrange life's conditions in ways that further a person's development and happiness.

Human Nature and the Goal of Moral Development

The Japanese word *seimei* or *akaki*, meaning purity and cheerfulness of heart, describes the Shinto notion of basic human nature. Each infant's original bent is toward acting in a moral, socially constructive fashion. However, this innate goodness is always threatened by the imperfections of society and by evil spirits called *magatsuhi*.

> Evil . . . is an intruder. Evil comes from without. The source of temptation and evil is the world of darkness. . . . Moral evil is thus an affliction, a temporary affliction. While man's soul is good, the flesh and senses readily succumb to temptation. Man commits evil because he has lost, has been deprived of, the capacity for normal action. (Ono, 1962, p. 106)

In most of the religions inspected in Part III, the ultimate aim of moral development is to enjoy a satisfying afterlife—to reach heaven, experience nirvana, or achieve oneness with the Cosmic Mind following one's earthly demise. In this sense, then, death is not a tragedy, but instead can signify a transformation to an infinite state of bliss. But in Shinto the goal of life is quite the opposite. Life on earth is viewed as good. Death is an evil, dreaded curse (Ono, 1962, p. 108). As Kitagawa (1987, p. xii) explains, "Japanese religion has been singularly preoccupied with *this* world, with its emphasis on finding ways to cohabit with the *kami* (sacred) and with other human beings."

Therefore, what is sought in Shinto is success and happiness in one's present life. This happiness is achieved through preserving one's original purity of soul and clarity of mind, which have been inherited through the ancestral line. To nurture such purity and clarity:

> man must strive, in both public and private life, to serve the kami and ancestral spirits, and to make contributions and import blessings to the world through his own work in life. The greatness of the character of a man is based on the greatness of this service and these contributions. . . . A man's virtue is formed by his training himself to play such a role. (Shinto Committee, 1958, p. 32)

Moral Values

Because of the conviction that the soul is inherently pure, Shinto theorists have considered it unnecessary to prepare a list of rules for good behavior, such as commandments of *dos* and *don'ts*. To decide the proper way to act, people need only search their souls, since, as Motoori proposed, humans "are naturally endowed with the knowledge of what they ought to do and what they ought to refrain from" (Motoori in Herbert, 1967, p. 69).

Shinto literature offers no set of commandments, no code of ethics, and no list of virtues that people are to display. Indeed, a specific list of dos and don'ts would be quite out of character, for Shinto is founded on a conditional view of human behavior. What constitutes proper action depends on the conditions existing at the time. Such acts as killing, taking another's property without permission, and not telling the truth are not proscribed in a list of dicta, because on certain occasions these may be the right ways to act. What is important is that a person's behavior always be expressed in the spirit of *kannagara-no-michi* or the way that the *kami* would act in such situations. "A man of *michi* is a man of character, of justice, of principle, of conviction, obedient to the nature of his humanity" (Hirata in Herbert, 1967, p. 70). The word *zen* connotes a similar attitude by meaning not only *good* in a moral sense, but also the "happiness and superiority of the nature or value of a thing" (Herbert, 1967, p. 70).

Shinto thus espouses a situational ethic that necessarily refrains from prescribing a single way of doing right. It teaches an ethic of purpose, emphasizing that one's actions should stem from noble intent (Ross, 1965, p. 109).

So, theoretically, people in close touch with their original pure nature will know instinctively how to act without being directed either by a list of rules or by orders from others. However, Japanese culture is actually replete with specific expectations about behavior. Such agents of society as parents, teachers, club leaders, and religious workers continually monitor how well the growing child and youth fulfill these expectations. Therefore, Japanese children develop morally under constant reminders of how people should behave in service to the *kami* and to their racial heritage. This means that in everyday living people's actions are judged against a multitude of specific values that they are expected to exhibit. Historically such virtues have been depicted in the behavior of kings and *kami*. The *Kojiki* and *Nihongi* both illustrate in the behavior of *kami* and of competing princes the trait of cleverness in exerting power, with the cleverness including the use of deception. Hence, deceit, when in the service of a noble end, is pictured as laudable and thus an example of the conditional nature of Shinto morality—whether or not an action is virtuous depends on the circumstances at the time. Other desirable character traits reflected in the ancient histories include trustworthiness, patience, bravery in the face of great odds, and the relentless pursuit of a lofty cause, such as avenging the oppression of one's family or one's emperor by enemy forces.

> Further specific traits are taught in present-day moral-education materials and in the contents of such mass communication media as books, magazines, radio, and television. These additional virtues include *makato* (sincerity of purpose), which itself is composed of such elements as *shojiki* (honesty or strict avoidance of error in word or deed), *koto-dama* (the right use of words, extending to affection and tenderness), and *kotomuke* (directing words toward bringing peace). Another desired characteristic is *kansha* (thankfulness directed toward the *kami*, the family, and the nation). Still others are *kenshin* (willing offering of oneself for the common interest), *kwan-yo-sei* (tolerant generosity), *tsui-shin* (industriousness), and *koko* (devotion to the emperor and faithfulness to friends). *Koko* also implies the filial piety that traditionally has played a strong role in Japanese society. (Thomas & Niikura, 1988, p. 142)

Personality Structure

In Shinto belief, a human being consists of a multifaceted soul encased in a physical body. The generic term for soul is *tama* (or *mitama*, with the honorific prefix *mi*). Although there is no agreement among Shinto scholars on the precise composition of the soul, one frequent distinction is made between the soul or personality itself (*tama*) and its active power (*tamashii*), with the power representing a nobler part of the personality that lives on beyond the death of the body to be continually "creative and growing into the higher dimensions" in contrast to a lower part of the soul (*mono*) that is a sort of mundane spirit that animals also possess (Herbert, 1967, p. 60). Possibly the *tamashii*, as the more exalted aspect of the soul, can eventually achieve *kami* status.

An alternative interpretation of *mitama* holds that the soul consists of four parts arranged as two pairs. The first pair—*ara-mitama* and *nigi-mitama*—are counterpart forces that create and direct the human body and other objects in the visible world. The second pair—*saki-mitama* and *kushi-mitama*—are forces affecting the unseen mental world. Herbert (1967, pp. 61-62) explains that within the first pair, the *ara-mitama* is wild, raging, and raw, serving as the power that destroys evil and sustains what is divine in humans, empowered to rule with authority. In contrast to the *ara-mitama,* the *nigi-mitama* is mild, quiet, refined, and peaceful, a spirit engaged in maintaining harmony and unity in life. In the second pair, the *saki-mitama* is described as emotional—the happy and flourishing source of pure love, creation, and blessings. The other aspect of this pair, the *kushi-mitama*, is the force behind both the intellectual and the mysterious in life, "variously described as wonderful, hidden and also hideous, the inside spirit, wisdom, invention, discovery, and [the cause of] mysterious transformations" (Herbert, 1967, p. 62).

The moral differences among people result from the particular pattern of interaction among these four forces within each personality.

A key conviction in Shinto is that the individual's soul is intimately connected with the souls of all other Japanese, past and present. As Spae (1972, p. 30) explains:

> Shinto primarily sees man as a being-in-community and not as an individual. . . .
> He is not personified to the extent that he becomes easily distinguishable from
> his milieu; he is not individualized to the point where he might decide upon a
> course of life irrespective of others in his past, present, and future. Man's dignity
> is derived from the totality of the macrocosmos in which he lives, not from the
> microcosmos which is the self.

Perhaps this conviction that the individual personality is a component of a racial personality can explain the strong commitment to filial duty and social obligation that figures so prominently in Japanese culture. Abiding by societal standards and acting responsibly in support of the group is not, therefore, simply an unselfish altruistic act but, rather, it is enlightened self-interest—fulfilling one's social obligations meets the demands of one's own extended soul.

Causality

As noted earlier, Shinto theory proposes that people are innately pure, born morally good. Thus, Shinto is a theory of *moral maintenance* rather than *moral growth* or *moral progression*. The aim of life is to sustain one's primal purity in the face of environmental influences bent on soiling the soul. Thus, *moral development* from a Shinto perspective means both (a) the unfolding of one's original righteousness and (b) the acquisition of the skills and strength of character needed to maintain this righteousness against forces in the environment that seek to divert people from the way of the *kami*. As Isaku Kanzaki (in Herbert, 1967, p. 78) suggests:

We are recipients from the *kami*, by direct descent though the ancestors, of a specific endowment of tendencies and capacities, and if we permit this innate disposition to find normal expression, we achieve spontaneously filial piety, loyalty, and love of fellow-men. . . . As a race, we are one with our ancestors, a part of divine nature. It is thus involved in the natural unfolding of the Way of the Gods within us that we should be prudent regarding self, that we should contribute to national progress and anticipate the future peace of the whole world.

Therefore, one's heredity is conducive to moral goodness.

The environments that a person inhabits can act as either positive or negative moral influences. Environments, in Shinto theory, are of two general sorts—the visible people and events of daily life and the invisible *kami*. Shinto authorities agree that some *kami* promote moral goodness and others foster evil. Thus, a person's good behavior and bad behavior may both result—at least partially— from the actions of spirits.

Visible environments consist of episodes within the family, in school, among companions, in the community, and in the mass media (books, television, films) that a person witnesses and either imitates or rejects as guides to moral thought and action.

A question now can be asked about how environments interact with one's original morally pure inclinations to produce either moral and immoral behavior. In other words, to what extent does evil arise within individuals' personalities? Shinto theorists have not agreed on the answer. The most frequent reply is that the person is blameless, since immoral behavior is generated from without, thrust on people by their inauspicious surroundings. "Moral evil must be expressed passively as the result of [the person's] having been deprived of normal moral consciousness and having been caused to do evil" (Ono in Ross, 1965, p. 109). However, other writers have proposed that evil lurks within the soul, yearning for expression. It is each person's responsibility to reject these vile cravings. "Though a man wash off his bodily filth, he will yet fail to please the Deity if he restrain not his evil desires" (Tomobe in Herbert, 1967, p. 80). From this second perspective, people are not entirely victims of externally imposed wickedness. Hence, they are obliged to bear some blame for allowing their deviant tendencies to take command of their actions.

No matter which of these explanations is offered to account for wrongdoing, both hold the same implications about the methods people must adopt to be true to the *kami* way—or, if once strayed off course, to return to the path. The methods include physical purification techniques, meditation, and the conscientious performance of societal obligations. Whereas the underlying cause of proper moral development is a person's natural purity of soul inherited from the *kami*, the more immediate causes are purification, meditation, and the diligent performance of social duties. By means of such acts, people avoid becoming mere pawns manipulated by their environments.

The likely causes of individual differences among people in their moral development are accorded little or no attention in Shinto theory. Thus we are left to speculate why such differences might occur. Because everyone is assumed to be born in a condition of moral purity, the variations in people's moral characters and destinies apparently arise from (a) the quality of nurturing and guidance provided by the child's caretakers; (b) the models of behavior offered by caretakers, companions, and the mass-communication media; (c) environmental events produced by the *kami*, such as disasters or strokes of good fortune that affect moral thought and action; and (d) the individual's own evolving moral character—the intent, motivation, and strength of will that determine how faithfully the person carries out filial and social obligations, self-betterment efforts, and acts of purification and meditation (Thomas & Niikura, 1988, p. 150).

Stages of Moral Development

Shinto insistently claims to be a religion of the 'middle-now', the 'eternal present', *naka-ima*, and that is certainly true. Its main stress is on what should be done at the present instant, without much concern for what happened before or for what will happen later, whether in this life or in afterlife. (Herbert, 1967, p. 32)

While focusing on the middle-now, Shinto theory also recognizes points of transition in human development that denote a shift from one stage of life to a subsequent stage of greater maturity. Nevertheless, moral development is not pictured simply as progress through stages that represent fixed levels of maturity. Instead, there is a strong commitment to *shojin*, a belief in incessant progress, a continual state of "becoming," so that people are obligated to continue striving toward greater moral perfection throughout their lives. "Man is a finite being but he is capable of growth, creativity, and development" (Ross, 1965, p. 49).

In popular Shinto belief, biological conception does not mark the beginning of human life. The unborn baby is recognized as human only after it receives its soul (*tamashii*) four months before birth. "Little, if any, remorse is felt about abortion induced before the third month of pregnancy. It is popularly believed that the fetus is not a living being until its stirrings are felt" (Spae, 1972, pp. 36-37).

Periodic celebrations mark transition points in both physical and moral development. One week after birth the child is given a name. When 120 days old, infants are given their first solid food at a party attended by family and friends.

At age 3, the passage from infancy to early childhood is celebrated by a visit to the child's assigned shrine, where prayers are offered for his or her protection. A subsequent visit to the shrine at age 5 marks the advance from early to middle childhood. On the ninth birthday, a child's hair is cut in the fashion of an adult, symbolizing the end of middle childhood and the assumption of greater responsibility for their own moral behavior. At age 13, a child may participate in a mid-April ceremony at Shinto temples to pray for wisdom.

In early adulthood or later, marriage symbolizes entrance into the most important stage of moral responsibility—the obligation to care faithfully for a spouse and for offspring.

The final stage of development appears with the individual's death, when the soul may assume any of a number of forms, even appearing as a ghost, a monster, or a shining ball gliding thorough the night air. Souls of those who have died violently "are particularly restless; they could be dangerous to the living unless placated by food and purification" (Spae, 1972, p. 37). Such appeasement of souls is a sacred duty that the remaining family members bear, particularly during the 49 days following death, when the deceased member's soul is thought to linger within the house before leaving for a place of comfort. At some point in time after death—which may vary from one to 33 years—the soul may become a *kami*, a spirit entering its ultimate stage of rapture when it serves to protect and bless those in the family who are still alive.

In summary, Shinto tradition does not offer an elaborately described set of stages of moral development, as does Hinduism. Rather, Shinto theory posits periodic occasions over the life span that signify a transition from one level of development to another. By implication, the phase of life following a given occasion is a more advanced level of moral growth than the one preceding it.

Conclusion

As mentioned earlier, basic Shinto is a worldview or attitude toward life shared by virtually all Japanese. This means that by the latter 1990s, there were over 125 million people who subscribed—at least in some degree—to a Shinto theory of moral thought and action. It seems likely that in the future, Shinto will continue to have widespread appeal in Japan, since the theory's tenets and its ethical values derived from Confucianism appear compatible with the nation's remarkable economic success of recent decades. Belief in hard work, frugality, and sacrificing for the good of the group (family, company, nation) promotes economic success. Filial piety, which ensures that citizens and workers abide by their leaders' decisions, is an additional moral conviction contributing to the controlled operation of the social system.

AN ASSESSMENT OF THE THEORIES

In keeping with the procedure adopted in previous chapters, the criteria from Chapter 2 for judging the adequacy of theories are used as guides to the appraisal of the Confucian and Shinto conceptions of moral development. On each scale line of the assessment chart, the letter C shows where I located Confucianism and the letter S indicates where I placed Shinto.

In judging how readily the two theories can be understood (item 1), I rated both in the "moderately well" region. The moral values espoused in Confucian doctrine are specifically stated in the tradition's four great books. Furthermore, the process by which people can maintain their original moral goodness is made clear, a process consisting of (a) continuous study of the Confucian canon, (b) steady guidance by elders and people in positions of leadership (parents, statesmen, employers), and (c) the firm application of one's own willpower. However, it is also the case that certain of Confucius' pithy sayings lend themselves to a variety of interpretations about how the epigrams should be applied in moral situations. Over the centuries, this ambiguity has led to scholars sometimes reaching different conclusions about precisely what the master's aphorisms imply for human behavior.

Confucianism and Shinto

How well do I think the theories meet the standards?

The Standards	Very well	Moderately well	Very poorly
1. Is clearly understandable		C S	
2. Explains past and predicts future moral behavior	C S		
3. Offers practical guidance in coping with moral matters	C S		
4. Is readily verifiable and falsifiable	C	S	
5. Accommodates new evidence		S C	
6. Stimulates new discoveries			S C
7. Is durable	C S		
8. Is self-satisfying		C S	

I placed Shinto somewhat lower than Confucianism on the understandability scale, because Shinto teaches a situational morality, requiring each person to decide how to act in each moral situation. Thus, in their moral judgments, people can reflect different understandings of what Shinto belief means for human conduct under different sorts of environmental conditions.

The two theories enable people to explain past moral development (item 2) by citing environmental influences that have formed the character traits reflected in people's moral behavior. In the case of Shinto, accounting for the past includes speculating about how the *kami* have apparently affected a person's moral decisions and destiny. Of the two theories, Confucianism would appear to be the better forecaster of future behavior, because the basis for its predictions seem grounded strongly on judgments of a person's present moral traits. Furthermore, the older the individual who is being judged, the more deep-seated those traits are expected to be and, thus, the more accurately future behavior can be estimated. However, using Shinto theory for guessing about upcoming moral events leads to less confident estimates, since the ways that helpful or mischievous *kami* might affect moral incidents cannot adequately be judged ahead of time.

Both Confucian and Shinto theories serve as effective guides to moral action (item 3), with much of Shinto's advice about desirable moral traits derived from the Confucianism imported from China in centuries past.

On item 4 (verifiable, falsifiable), I ranked Confucianism higher than Shinto because the predictions offered by Confucian doctrine lend themselves more readily to empirical testing than do predictions derived from Shinto theory. Consider, for example, the Confucian proposals about (a) the responsibilities of the leader of a social unit to ensure that members of the unit abide by moral precepts and (b) the series of expanding social units that influence the morality of an entire society. Confucian theory not only empowers the head of a social unit (family, clan, neighborhood, city, province, nation) with the authority to control the people within that unit but also obligates the leader to exemplify the characteristics of "humans at their best." Thus, by dint of this combination of authority and example, the leader fosters proper moral conduct among members of the social unit. The most basic unit is the family. If it is in proper order, then each of the wider circles of social units will display proper moral behavior as well. These propositions are empirically testable. Observations of the moral decisions of leaders and of members of their social units can reveal the extent to which the propositions are true and the theory itself is valid. In like manner, it is possible to test Confucius' belief that most people are very much alike in innate physical and intellectual abilities, so the observed differences among individuals result from differences in their environments (how they are treated by others, what examples are available to them) and in their willpower. However, in addition to these verifiable/falsifiable aspects of Confucian theory, some elements do not lend themselves to empirical testing. Such is true of the rituals and the belief in unseen spirits that have become attached to Confucius' theory of social organization. In consideration of each of the above factors, I rated Confucianism between "very well" and "moderately well" on item 4.

I located Shinto lower on scale 4, primarily because the existence and functions of *kami*, which play such an important role in the religion, are not amenable to direct, empirical verification. Furthermore, in the Shinto system of situational morality, the application of moral guidelines depends heavily on each person's interpretation of the moral episode being faced at the moment. Under such a system, testing the validity of the theory can be most difficult, since it involves such a large measure of subjective judgment on the part of both the assessor and the person being assessed.

The two theories seem much alike in their ability to accommodate new evidence (item 5). That is, if the term *new evidence* can mean a philosopher's innovative observations about human nature and about societies—including novel explanations of unseen forces in the world—then both Confucianism and Shinto have displayed a degree of accommodation. For instance, following the compilation of Confucius' analects, the present-day version of Confucianism evolved through the addition of refinements in *The Book of Mencius, The Great Learning,* and *The Doctrine of the Mean.* In like fashion, original Shinto has been altered by incorporating elements of both Buddhism and Confucianism.

From the viewpoint of speculative philosophy, both Confucianism and Shinto have stimulated the creation of somewhat varied interpretations of human nature, the purpose of life, and of the conduct of societies. In effect, both have been the source of a substantial body of literature. However, from the perspective of empirical science, neither Confucianism nor Shinto has been the source of a notable number of new discoveries. Each tends to be conservative rather than progressive in regard to new knowledge. For this reason, I have ranked them rather low on item 6.

Like other long-lasting religious and philosophical systems, both Confucianism and Shinto score high on durability (item 7). The Confucian ethos, with its history extending at least 2,500 years into the past, continues today as a potent influence over the moral convictions of many millions of Chinese, Koreans, and—with Shinto and Buddhist modifications—Japanese. Even though the recorded version of Shinto can be traced back no further than the sixth century CE, the theory in that written form can still boast of a life span nearly equal to that of Islam. Today, Shinto continues to represent the perspective from which most Japanese appear to view moral matters.

Finally, in judging how satisfying I find the two theories overall (item 8), I have rated them both relatively low. I quite agree with most moral values that each of these systems promotes, I agree with their emphasizing the importance of environmental influences on moral development, and I find the Shinto situational-morality position reasonable. However, I am not convinced by two of the theories' key proposals. The first is that people are born promoral, innately bent on good behavior. On the basis of observing quantities of young children, I am more inclined to believe that humans are born amoral, with no penchant for either good or bad actions. Rather, I see them as innately motivated to fulfill their needs, with some of their attempts at need fulfillment deemed proper by their societies and others considered improper. The second belief that I find unsatisfactory is the proposal that unseen spirits—*kami* in Shinto, shades of ancestors in certain versions of Confucianism—affect people's moral development. I suspect that blaming or crediting supernatural forces for humans' moral thought and action is more an expression of frustration at the complexity of moral development than it is a constructive explanation of moral matters.

13

Representative Minor Religions

The four theories inspected in Chapter 13 are all local religions, each specific to a particular people in a particular place. The Navajo belief system is held by an American Indian population living in the southwestern United States. The Zulu variety consists of the convictions of tribal groups of South Africa. Vodou is an interpretation of life employed by most inhabitants of the Republic of Haiti in the Caribbean. The Okinawan theory is a conception of moral development embraced by people living on the largest of the Ryukyu Islands in the East China Sea.

Although the four traditions are widely separated in their locales and historical antecedents, they are much alike in several important respects. All four:

1. Envision the universe as consisting both of tangible, visible entities (such as people, animals, places, objects) and of unseen spirits that affect events in the visible world.

2. Propose that when the elements of the universe are in proper balance, nature is at peace and people are free of pain and stress. When the elements are out of balance, natural disasters occur (earthquakes, floods, drought, and the like) and people suffer social disorder, illness, injury, and emotional stress.

3. Contend that the disrupted harmony of the universe can be remedied by people's (a) performing rites and austerities that mollify the offended spirits and (b) displaying the moral values considered proper for adherents of the faith. Whereas some of these values are embraced in all four traditions, others are specific to a particular faith.

4. Hold that the goal of moral development is that of promoting the harmony of the universe. The specific nature of this harmony and how disorder can be restored may differ somewhat from one of the belief systems to another.

The principal differences among the four theories appear in the number and attributes of their invisible spirits, certain of the behaviors deemed suitable and unsuitable for an ideal moral person to display, the specific rituals performed to pacify the spirits, and the sorts of consequences people can suffer for violating moral principles.

THE NAVAJO VIEW

For centuries, the Navajo Indians have inhabited a region of North America that lies in the present-day states of New Mexico, Arizona, southeastern Utah, and southwestern Colorado. By the late 20th century, Navajos were the most populous Indian group in the United States, numbering well over 100,000.

The Navajo moral code derives from the conviction that the universe is a complex system of elements operating according to rules of the universe's unseen holy authorities, rules designed to maintain balance and harmony in personal development and social relations. When the equilibrium among the elements is disrupted, illness, personal distress, and social friction result. The purpose of Navajo moral principles and rules is to avoid or rectify disorder and thereby promote personal serenity and social harmony.

> It is a basic Navajo belief that the welfare of each individual is dependent on the welfare of every other individual. . . . This belief results in the view that no one is in competition with his fellows. Quite the reverse in fact—the success of others is thought to contribute to one's own welfare; and doing good for oneself is inseparably related to doing good for others. Indeed, the welfare of others is a *necessary condition* of one's own welfare. This concept of welfare implies that the Western philosophical distinction between egoism and altruism is not, and cannot be, recognized as either valid or intelligible by the Navajo. (Little & Twiss, 1978, p. 127)

In keeping with such a worldview, the Navajos' moral behavior is guided by three interlinked principles: (1) care for yourself, (2) avoid and correct trouble with others, and (3) assist others as if they were close kin (Little & Twiss, 1978, p. 131). From these principles Navajos derive a set of specific moral rules intended both to benefit oneself and to foster the welfare of others. The rules include prohibitions against such behavior as gambling, drunkenness, laziness, killing, fighting, stealing, adultery, ridiculing others, and all forms of deception. However, these acts are not disapproved because they are considered inherently bad. Instead, it is because behaving in such ways so often leads to undesirable consequences. Gambling wastes the money needed to support the family, and drunkenness causes a person to neglect kinship responsibilities and to say and do things that damage personal relations. Stealing or lying is not condemned if one can get away with it.

> Young men, when questioned, said, "We are told not to steal, not because it is sinful but because if someone saw it, the thief would get a bad reputation in the community. . . . " [Being] caught with stolen goods or in attempts at cheating are humorous situations—they have no ethical connotation; they merely

indicate the discomfiture of the culprit at getting caught. (Reichard, 1963, pp. 131-132)

In effect, morality among the Navajos is pragmatic and situational. The moral status of an act is not judged by the actor's intent but, rather, by the consequences of the act. Behavior that brings bad consequences, such as causing illness or destroying the harmony of human relations, is immoral.

In addition to proscribing socially damaging behavior, the Navajo code extols the value of altruism and self-sacrifice, of never abandoning anyone in serious need (Ladd, 1957, p. 295).

Specific rules are not adequate guides to behavior in all situations. Thus, Navajo morality is generally cast in the form of character traits that govern people's decisions, enabling people to adjust their actions to the conditions of the present moral encounter. Three character traits in concert with the code's moral principles are personal prudence, self-control in social situations, and benevolence (Little and Twiss, 1978, p. 134). Child-rearing practices in Navajo communities are aimed at developing these virtues in the young.

The causal factors behind moral development include both natural and supernatural forces. The natural ones are those carried out by humans themselves. Such forces consist chiefly of instructing the young in the Navajo belief system and of conducting ceremonies intended to placate beneficent supernatural spirits and thwart the efforts of malevolent ones. The supernatural forces comprise a large array of invisible spirits and visible beings (certain animals and people accused of practicing witchcraft) that command unusual powers. According to Reichard (1963, pp. 50-79), the Navajos' pantheon of supernaturals includes (a) benevolent deities, such as the Sun, whose aid can be solicited by means of rituals; (b) messenger deities and mythical protagonists that mediate between the supernatural Holy People and humans and that instruct people in rituals; (c) undependable, mischievous spirits whose help is difficult to obtain by rituals; (d) evil deities (monsters) that must be dealt with through exorcistic rites; (e) deities that are intermediate between good and evil (Old Age, Poverty); and (f) certain natural phenomena (lightning, wind, rain) that are sometimes dangerous and other times beneficial.

Sickness and accident are intimately involved with morality, since illness and mishaps are believed to result from the operation of evil spirits or from humans' disturbing the harmony of social relations. Methods of putting matters right can involve offering prayers, applying herbs, observing taboos, and performing dances and chants that recount ancient myths.

A Navajo chantway myth describes the origin of the associated curing ceremony, how it was obtained from supernaturals and made available for the use of earth people. The myths are revealed as teachings to the Navajos about how they should relate to each other, families, and strangers. They learn the possible consequences for failing to live up to these standards. In sum, the stories provide a thorough education for those who will heed them. (Iverson, 1981, p. xxxi)

Moral development in Navajo society consists of the young gradually learning the myths and taboos, their abiding by these action guides, and their soliciting the aid of medicine men who are expert in the more complex rituals, chants, dances, and sandpainting. The young acquire their moral knowledge from the time of infancy by means of parents teaching them rituals, by the elders narrating myths, and by themselves attending public ceremonies conducted by medicine men—ceremonies that may last from a few hours to a week or more.

> During the period from babyhood to adolescence there is little difference in the ritualistic treatment of male and female children.   At adolescence, however, there is a definite change. The girl, because there is physical evidence of her maturity, becomes a tribal symbol of fecundity at her adolescence ceremony . . . [but] no particular moment marks the transition from boyhood to manhood.
>
> Knowledge must be ripened by experience, which takes time to acquire. Youth is tried [in terms of moral behavior] and repeatedly teased, ridicule being a major form of discipline. Gradually, by a subtle process difficult to define, the young man grows into a position of responsibility in the various social groups—first his own family, clan, clan group, and after marriage, his wife's groups [within the Navajo matrilineal social structure]. (Reichard, 1963, p. 39)

To summarize, moral behavior in traditional Navajo society is guided by belief in fulfilling one's own needs while, at the same time, maintaining amicable interpersonal relations through aiding others who are in want. Rather than abiding by a set of rules governing how to act in specific moral encounters, Navajos are expected to determine for themselves the proper way to behave in the circumstances of the moral situation at hand. Of great importance in the Navajo moral ethos is the throng of invisible supernatural spirits that can either foster or impede the conduct of people's lives, spirits whose support is solicited by means of rituals and ceremonies.

ZULU BELIEFS

The Zulu are a Nguni-speaking people located principally in the Natal region of South Africa, who form a branch of the southern Bantu culture. They were traditionally grain farmers who also kept large herds of cattle on lightly wooded grasslands. However, during the 19th century, European settlers took most of the Zulu land through extended warfare. In modern times the Zulu mainly work in cities or depend on wage labor on farms owned by whites.

Zulu lore teaches that the world was created by a supreme being known as Nkulunkulu (the Great One) who subsequently stood apart from the conduct of the world, seldom intervening in its operation and rarely meddling directly in human affairs (M'Timkulu, 1977, p. 14).

In Zulu theory, reality consists of tangible people and objects as well as spiritual beings. These two aspects of the universe are not really separate but, rather, form a unified whole. Hence, the society of mortals is continuous with the society of the spirits of dead ancestors. People's personality characteristics and social status as mortals continue in the spirit realm after death. A woman who is cantankerous during her lifetime will be fractious in her spirit state. A man of high social position in life will enjoy the same position after death.

Each individual's spirit is symbolized by breath, so that people are not declared dead until it is assumed that their breath has left them to dwell somewhere "just around" in shadow form. When people are still alive, their spirit may temporarily wander from the body and engage in activities at some distance, with this departure from the body often providing valuable learning experiences. Dreams during sleep are cited as evidence of this wandering.

There are two dominant foci of Zulu moral values. First is the concept of *ubuntu*, the expected proper relationship between one person and another. If any individual or group deviates too far from this relationship, then it becomes the occasion for the Creator, Nkulunkulu, to immediately intervene, punishing the offenders so as to bring them into line. The punishment can assume any of a variety of forms—sickness, mental disorder, loss of property, drought, and more.

The second value focus is on maintaining the integrity and coherence of the group—the family, the clan, and the coalition of clans. Hence, moral behavior is viewed in relation to its effect on group solidarity, as illustrated in the case of homicide.

> When an instance of one man killing another occurs, there is always careful inquiry to break up the God-given coherence of society, he may be removed [by killing] and it is not a murder, for he has ceased to be a man [in that] he had denied himself all the qualities of *ubuntu* and was the type of fellow who disrupts society. (M'Timkulu, 1977, p. 15)

It is also vital in Zulu society to guard the continuity of the group over time. For this reason, it is important for people to have progeny so their family line will endure. And whereas the Creator seldom intercedes in people's affairs, the spirits of ancestors continually affect the lives of their living descendants. It is to these ancestors that the people turn for guidance and support in time of need. However, not all ancestors are honored or solicited for aid. Only those who, while alive, achieved distinction by force of their leadership and longevity will become spirits with power over the fate of the living. The rituals practiced in Zulu culture are designed to curry the favor of these ancestral shades in order to promote the welfare of the group and its members.

The goal of Zulu moral behavior has been to enhance the quality of one's immediate existence rather than to prepare for a life after death. "In their beliefs as to spiritual life there was no trace of [concern for life hereafter]. Their propitiation of ancestral spirits was only to secure [the spirits'] good offices in the ordering of earthly affairs" (Gibson, 1970, p. 61).

The three types of rites performed in Zulu communities have been ones (a) conducted in the routine of daily affairs to show continued respect for the spirits and to recover the spirits' goodwill when they have been offended, since the power of departed ancestors is contingent on their constantly being remembered; (b) performed at the times of the four "great passages of life"—birth, puberty, marriage, and death; and (c) required to cope with large-scale calamities and suffering—epidemics, floods, wars, and the like. Some rites are carried out by the head of the family, some by the head of the clan, and others by the tribal shaman, who has the most profound knowledge of the spirits (M'Timkulu, 1977, p. 21). Dancing, accompanied by drums and chants, and the sacrifice of animals (oxen, goats) play an important role in the sacred rites (Sundkler, 1961, p. 21). By means of frenzied dancing, the shaman summons the spirits to offer advice about how to cure illness, bring rain during a drought, or expose a sorcerer who has put a spell on an individual or group. Curing an illness can involve preparing a small image and dropping blood of the sufferer onto the image. Then the image is cast far off, ostensibly carrying away the transferred disease (Kidd, 1904, p. 146).

As the Zulu conception of reality suggests, the cause of both desirable and undesirable consequences originates in people's moral behavior. The causal process comprises four main steps. First, the Creator has decreed moral virtues in the form of ways people should behave in order to establish amicable relations between individuals and maintain the unity of the group. Second, people's behavior varies in the degree to which it is faithful to the Creator's precepts. Third, the spirits of revered ancestors monitor their living progenies' adherence to the prescribed values, rewarding obedience and punishing deviance. Fourth, people can avoid punishment and can promote personal and group welfare through abiding by the moral dicta and through performing the ceremonies that placate both the ancestral spirits and Nkulunkulu.

Moral values esteemed in Zulu theory are of two general types. One type applies to every member of society; the other applies only to certain kinds of people. The most essential value is that of honoring and obeying the tribal chief. Bravery is a further prime virtue, and loyalty to one's peers is important. For instance, youths within the same age cohort that is circumcised at puberty incur an obligation of mutual loyalty that lasts a lifetime. There are also numerous prohibitions. A particularly heinous crime is that of using sorcery to attain private ends. It is acceptable to employ magic for the benefit of the tribe, but not for personal gain. And some disapproved behaviors appear to be matters of prudence rather than morality. For example, telling a lie is, in itself, not frowned upon, but getting caught telling a lie invites censure (Kidd, 1904, pp. 147-148).

The most prominent moral values that apply only to certain kinds of people are ones involving gender and age.

> To insist that a woman should keep out of the cattle karaal, where men are frequently naked, and to make her keep to certain parts of the hut, and to oblige the mother-in-law to cover her breasts in the presence of her son-in-law—all tended to safeguard a man from temptation. (Kidd, 1904, p. 243)

The process of moral development in traditional Zulu society consists of the young gradually learning the moral and prudential values governing relations among living people and relations with the spirits of deceased ancestors. This process not only involves adults demonstrating proper behavior and punishing infractions during the routine of daily life, but it includes the young observing religious rites and listening to moral precepts that are part of the rich store of tales and proverbs recounted by elders as evening entertainment (Krige, 1950, pp. 345-363). The following are typical Zulu proverbs, accompanied by their translation into similar meanings in Western culture (Kidd, 1904, pp. 294-297).

"The cow licks the one that licks her." —Kindness brings its own reward.
"He milks the cow in calf." —He tells a lie.
"He weeps with one eye." —He is insincere.
"The knife and the meat will never be friends." —a warning against adultery.
"A thief catches himself." —Murder will out.
"Two dogs will not let a fox escape." —Unity is strength.

Finally, to summarize the matter of causation, we can note that nothing in the Zulu world occurs as the result of objective causes. All outcomes are the consequence of how adequately people abide by moral values, even though oftentimes the connection between one's behavior and one's fate is obscure, apparently understood only by the Creator or the ancestral spirits. In Zulu thought, as in other religions, the spirits often work in mysterious ways.

HAITIAN VODOU

Vodou (or Voodoo) has been characterized as the basic view of life among the 6 million inhabitants of the nation of Haiti. The religion's cultural origins are traced back to belief systems conveyed to the Americas in the 16th through 18th centuries by black slaves shipped from Africa to work the colonial plantations of the Caribbean islands. At that time, the western third of the island of Hispaniola was a French colonial possession whose slave population would ultimately win political independence by means of revolution in 1804. However, even after independence, French influence over political, economic, cultural, and religious affairs in the Republic of Haiti continued strong, and it remains strong today. (The eastern two-thirds of the island of Hispaniola—at one time a Spanish colony—is the Dominican Republic.)

Vodou religion claims no individual or group as its founder, has no written doctrine, offers no prescriptive code of ethics or published moral values, and is not organized as a formal ecclesiastical hierarchy. Instead, the religion consists of a central moral goal, a cosmogony, and a complex of rituals that are disseminated throughout the Haitian population orally and by demonstration from one generation to the next. Thus, a description of Vodou belief and practice is not found in official documents of the faith but, rather, in the observations of Haitian daily life and in the interviews with the religion's adepts that have been compiled by such investigators as Michel (1995, 1996), McCarthy Brown (1991), Desmangles (1992), and Laguerre (1980).

Popular literature and movies in Western nations have often depicted Vodou as heathenism, black magic, "mystical incantations, irrational beliefs, and zombies that wander about in a condition of living death," as a religion of "blood and sacrifice . . . sexual orgies and malevolence . . . sorcery and witchcraft" (Michel, 1996, p. 281). Such a portrayal, however, has been severely criticized by such students of religion and culture as Wade Davis (1985, pp. 72-73) who define Vodou as a valuable "complex mystical worldview, a system of beliefs concerning the relationship between man, nature, and the supernatural forces of the universe," providing an attitude that pervades all aspects of daily life.

The apparent stimulus for the creation of Vodou belief in past centuries was the need of the blacks, after being snatched from their African homes by slave traders, to make sense out of their fate as captive workers in a strange and distant land.

> Vodou is the system that [Haitians] have devised to deal with the suffering that is life, a system whose purpose is to minimize pain, avoid disaster, cushion loss, and strengthen survivors and survival instincts. (McCarthy Brown, 1991, p. 10)

The principal forces that arose to unify the diverse tribal groups of the French colony's slave population were the evolving Vodou religion and the recently developed French-Creole language. Vodou early became a syncretic faith, with a foundation of African traditions and a superstructure that included elements of the Catholicism that the French imposed as the society's official religion. Followers of Vodou today usually see no conflict between (a) Vodou's spirit world and elaborate rituals and (b) such Catholic practices as baptism, Holy Communion, marriage in a church, and Catholic funeral rites—"those last rites being particularly important for Vodou adepts who engage in frequent inter-actions with the spirits, ancestors, and the departed" (Michel, 1995, p. 42). However, one significant difference between Catholicism and Vodou theory is in the ultimate outcome that moral virtue is expected to produce. In Catholic doctrine, the prize for righteous living is awarded in one's life after death—in the soul's entering heaven for an everlasting joyful existence. Hence, people's time on earth is viewed as no more than a preparation, as a period of trial that helps determine what their place may be in the hereafter. Vodou theory, in contrast, locates the ultimate aim of virtuous living in the here and now. The reason Vodou's followers comply with the religion's moral guidelines is to help ensure that their current lives will be tolerably free of stress and hardship.

Typical published statistics on the religious affiliation of Haitians place the proportion of Roman Catholics at 81% and Protestants at 16%, with the remaining 3% listed as "other faiths" (Trumbull, 1995, p. 623). Thus, Vodou is generally not recognized as a religion outside of Haiti. However, close observers of the Haitian scene suggest that to some degree everyone accepts certain Vodou beliefs and meld these beliefs with Christian doctrine to form a syncretic faith. Hence, it is said that even devout Catholics will harbor some feeling for Vodou spirits and rites, especially in times of crisis.

In Vodou lore, the universe in which people's current lifetimes are spent features a combination of tangible, visible elements (people, places, objects) and of multiple spirits (*loas*) that function at the behest of a single master God (Bondye). Unlike the Christians' personal God, who periodically may intervene directly in earthlings' daily lives, the master God in Vodou remains aloof, detached from mundane affairs. Therefore, it is through intermediaries—through Vodou's broad array of individual spirits—that the Supreme Being affects people's lives. Certain spirits are assigned responsibility for a particular aspect of worldly affairs. Money is controlled by Azaka, who is envisioned as the peasant, the worker. Power is controlled by Ogu, who will not tolerate injustice. Gédé is the spirit of sexuality and death (Michel, 1995, p. 70).

No elements that comprise the Vodou conception of reality are independent of each other. All entities (people, objects, places, spirits) are bound together to form a harmonious unity. The displacement of a few or even one of the entities can disturb other facets of the configuration. Therefore, the central aim of Vodou, and the principal moral virtue that its adherents are obliged to pursue, is the maintenance of harmony and balance in the universe. A variety of specific moral values that support the principal virtue can be inferred from the sorts of behavior approved and disapproved in Haitian religious life. Prominent among such values are attitudes of benevolence, patience in the face of adversity, forgiveness, cooperation, respect for elders, accepting family responsibilities, encouraging conformity, fostering group cohesion, promoting justice, and displaying general beneficence (goodwill, hospitality, generosity, magnanimity). Behavior reflecting these values is viewed as *serving the spirits*, as placating the unseen powers and thereby cultivating balance among the occupants of the universe (Michel, 1995, pp. 35-39, 75).

Evidence suggesting that events are out of balance can appear in a multitude of forms—friction among family members, conflicts with neighbors, hostilities between nations, illness, injury, starvation, death, financial setback, crop failure, hurricanes, riots, and more. The main cause of this ill fortune is people's failing to abide by the religion's moral imperative, that of maintaining conditions of harmony. Such failure is particularly serious when it involves shirking family responsibilities, jeopardizing communal interests, and neglecting the spirits (Michel, 1995, p. 37).

In order to correct the disharmony that produced the present instance of ill fortune, people are advised to perform a ritual appropriate for the case at hand. If the ritual is conducted properly, the offended spirits will be appeased and further disaster avoided. In addition, it is important for the concerned individuals to heed all moral guidelines in the future so as not to cause other misfortunes.

The process of moral development in Vodou theory involves an individual's learning which kinds of behavior throw life out of balance, which kinds maintain the balance, and which rituals satisfy the spirits and thereby solicit their good-will and protection. Because Vodou pervades all facets of people's lives, learning the belief system occurs in all kinds of settings—the home, the fields, the neighborhood, the market, and the temple. In such environments, a variety of people furnish instruction in a variety of ways. In the home, family members not only caution children about proper and improper ways to behave but they also convey Vodou practices by conducting rites in the children's presence. In the neighborhood the young absorb Vodou convictions from the actions and conversations of adults and older children. Where a high proportion of the populace is illiterate, disseminating religion through oral and visual images is particularly important. Thus, much of Vodou belief is communicated by means of songs, tales, proverbs, prayers, and family recollections. In the temple, children and adults alike learn the complexities of the religion through witnessing rituals and receiving advice and explanations from priests and priestesses.

Vodou temples rarely resemble the sorts of imposing edifices that typically serve as places of worship for Jews, Christians, or Muslims. In fact, Vodou temples are not recognized by outsiders as holy locations at all.

> There is no Vodou *church* per se; instead, all places are sites of worship. The *hounfo*, the Vodou temple, is but one such place where the living gather to communicate with the spirits. It is usually (except when owned by an extremely rich family or by government officials) a very informal place, made of very simple material, not completely enclosed, with sometimes a dirt floor, and having no furniture . . . except for maybe a few chairs and drums, some flags, and pictures. (Michel, 1996, p. 284)

Other important sites of worship include cemeteries—as repositories of spirits— and locations described as *crossroads* where the mortal world intersects with the spirit world.

The level of sophistication in Vodou knowledge and sensitivity that a person displays is formally recognized by a progression of four steps of instruction that confer ascending degrees of control to humans in their relationships with the spirits. The rigorous, extended periods of instruction are intended to equip initiates with mastery over complex rituals and to strengthen their character. By completing the final level, an individual achieves the status of priest or priestess (Michel, 1995, p. 73).

The causes of differences among individuals in their adherence to Vodou theory include:

(a) How thoroughly the person's immediate social environment (family, circle of friends, neighbors) are imbued with Vodou belief
(b) The quantity of ceremonies and rites the person witnesses
(c) The proportion of Christian versus Vodou lore that becomes integrated into the individual's interpretation of life

To conclude, in the Vodou religion the function of moral development is to enhance adherents' abilities to maintain harmonious interactions among all entities of the mortal and spiritual universe—among people, objects, places, and invisible spirits. The process of development entails people (a) mastering the complex ceremonies that are designed to mollify the spirits (*loas*) and (b) consistently adopting the sorts of human behavior that establish amicable and just relationships among the entities of the cosmos. The desired outcome of moral conduct consists of increased strength to endure misfortune and increased freedom from pain, stress, and travail in the daily life of the Vodou community.

THE OKINAWAN VIEW

Okinawa is the largest of the Ryukyu Islands which stretch between Taiwan and Japan. The Ryukyu archipelago was an independent kingdom until the latter half of the 19th century, when it became a prefecture of Japan under the Meiji Empire. The present-day Okinawan population numbers slightly over 1.3 million.

Information about traditional Okinawan religion derives principally from recorded interviews with residents concerning their own and their forebears' beliefs about moral matters (Lebra, 1966; Shimabukuro, 1950; Yanagita, 1951).

The aspects of the Okinawan moral ethos addressed in the following sketch include the nature of reality, causality, moral values, the process of development, and the consequences of violating the culture's moral customs.

In the traditional Okinawan ethos, moral reality consists of two broad categories of phenomena: (a) the objects and people of the natural, visible world and (b) countless supernatural spirits that inhabit every part of the cosmos. The most powerful of the spirits are known as *kami*, similar in several respects to the *kami* of Japanese Shinto. Okinawan *kami* have the power to speak, be seen on occasion, mete out rewards and punishments, and influence events of life. *Kami* are inherently neither benign nor malevolent, but they can affect people's destinies by offering assistance in time of need and, when displeased, by withholding their aid and thus permitting other truly malevolent spirits (ghosts known as *yanamung* or *majimung*) to work their evil ways. Additional ethereal occupants of the Okinawans' shadow world are the spirits of ancestors (*futuki*), spirits that can influence people's welfare, though they are not as powerful as the *kami*. *Futuki* typically act in a supportive, nurturant fashion to foster the welfare of their living descendants. However, when futuki become incensed, they are apt to bring ill fortune on those who have offended them.

The traditional Okinawan view of life does not include the concept of impersonal, objective causality. Therefore, nothing occurs by accident. Everything that happens is believed to result from some personage's intent. That personage is likely to be one of the myriad supernatural powers—*kami, futuki, yamamung, majimung*—which manipulate life's events in ways that determine the fate of living beings.

> Rewards are not capriciously showered upon man; there are few gratuitous windfalls, and man must work for and deserve what he receives. . . . All forms of misfortune are viewed as products of an impaired relationship with the supernatural. . . . In the absence of a concept of impersonal causation, misfortune in the form of human failure, severe economic hardship, suffering, sickness, disease, insanity, disaster, etc., whether visited upon the individual or the group, can be interpreted as resulting from the action of supernatural agencies. . . . Such punishment is always contingent upon failure to act or upon improper action by a group or an individual, living or dead. (Lebra, 1966, pp. 31-32)

Consequently, in traditional Okinawan society, the most basic moral value is that of honoring the supernatural spirits and carrying out their commands. This core value is served by a variety of constituent values and behaviors that, if performed faithfully, bring good fortune and, if neglected, invite punishment and deprivation. Table 13-1 displays a few examples of virtues in their positive and negative forms (Lebra, 1966, pp. 33-43). The values are divided into two principal categories. The first concerns prescribed ritual procedures that directly involve the spirits. The second concerns obedience to, or infractions of, the social norms accorded the greatest significance in Okinawan culture. This second category itself consists of two divisions: (a) behaviors affecting family relationships or the continuity of the family and (b) actions or attitudes important in the Okinawan conception of ideal moral behavior.

A person's ill fortune is not exclusively the result of that individual's own misconduct, since punishment can also be applied for misdeeds committed by ancestors. Thus, immoral behavior bears implications not only for one's present fortunes but for the fate of one's descendants as well.

> Crimes of violence are especially abhorrent to the *kami* (as well as to society) and will inevitably cause endless suffering for descendants. . . . Okinawans consider both murdered person and murderer as suffering punishment for having had ancestors addicted to violence. (Lebra, 1966, p. 39)

Table 13-1

Esteemed Values in Okinawan Moral Theory

Proper Moral Behavior	Improper Moral Behavior
Preserving Respectful Relationships with the Spirits	
Praying sufficiently to ancestors and *kami* on decision-making occasions	Insufficient prayer (*ugwanbusuku*) on decision-making occasions
Priestesses or shamans faithfully performing their duties	Priestesses or shamans being delinquent in their obligations
Correctly performing rituals	Offering incorrect or offensive prayer or worship
Honoring sacred locations	Defiling areas sacred to the *kami*
Maintaining Family Harmony	
Bearing social and economic responsibilities to the family	Neglecting family obligations
In the main, being faithful to one's spouse in sexual behavior	Continually engaging in adultery
Maintaining amicable relations between husband and wife, parents and in-laws, and parents and their first son	Wrangling and displaying ill-will between husband and wife, parents and in-laws, and parents and their first son
Honoring the right of the first son to the family property and leadership of the family	Attempting to alter the order of male succession in the family
Faithfully participating in kin-group rites	Failing to participate in kin-group rites and activities
Displaying Virtuous Character Traits	
Generosity	Greed, inordinate acquisitiveness
Kindheartedness	Jealousy, envy
Altruism	Selfishness

An additional causal factor is the influence of the calendar, which periodically renders a person more or less susceptible to good or bad luck. Finally, a person may commit minor infractions that are not automatically punished by the *kami* but, nevertheless, weaken the person's defenses against misfortune, thereby inviting assault by malicious spirits.

Punishment inflicted by the *kami* can assume any type and degree of inconvenience, loss, or pain. Furthermore, the punishment may be borne by an individual, by a kinship group, or by an entire population. For instance, the *kami* may vent extreme anger by imposing on a community widespread illness, a high death rate, frequent fires or floods, drought, or other calamities. The people who did not participate in the misdeeds may suffer along with the wrongdoers, implying that the innocent can incur guilt by association.

The position of priestess or shaman (*kaminchu*) in Okinawan society is assumed by females assigned to their role by the *kami*. Individuals who reject this destined calling or who neglect to fulfill their ritual duties are apt to be afflicted with a special sort of retribution (*taari*) that typically takes the form of psychosomatic disorders rendering the victim sick and weak, unable to carry out her normal activities, tormented with auditory and visual hallucinations, and troubled by distressing dreams (Lebra, 1966, p. 37). As a consequence of the shaman's misconduct, disaster may also befall members her family. Fear of such punishment gives the priestess a potent reason for being especially diligent in performing her duties.

Moral development in Okinawan theory is not a stagewise phenomenon. Instead, it consists of a person gradually

(a) Learning the religious rituals and the rules of social conduct that promote one's own well-being; that foster amicable relations within the kin group and community; and that avert such disasters as war, pestilence, and drought.

(b) Understanding the penalties to be suffered from failing to honor the *kami* and the ancestral spirits, and from failing to abide by the society's standards of proper social behavior.

(c) Mustering the willpower to fulfill one's moral obligations in the face of the temptation to do otherwise.

Instruction in moral matters is a function of the entire community and takes place chiefly in daily community activities—in the home, the neighborhood, and the shaman's quarters, where people seek aid in coping with difficulties that are assumed to be the consequence of angering the *kami* or ancestral spirits.

Individual differences among people in their moral development and their fate (health, financial welfare, occupational role, social success, kinship amity) result from the combination of factors that determine their destinies. This combination includes the types of *kami* that govern their lives, their ancestors' moral behavior, how effectively they themselves perform religious rites and rituals, and the moral conduct of living kinfolk whose actions may affect their relatives' fate.

Finally, understanding morality in Okinawan culture requires an appreciation that greater concern is felt for the welfare of the group—for kinfolk and the community—than for the welfare of the individual. Consequently, "the primary responsibilities of the individual are to the group. The group, in turn, is accountable for the action of individual members. . . . [And the group] exists in time as well as space, [so] a child may suffer punishment for the action of his parents or ancestors" (Lebra, 1966, p. 42).

CONCLUSION

The principal characteristics common to the four theories sketched in this chapter are shared as well by scores of other minor religions throughout the world. In a host of societies, the belief is widespread that misfortune does not result from impersonal, objective, "natural" causes. Rather, misfortune comes from people's failing to abide by the moral rules decreed by the supernatural powers that control the universe. Evidence that moral matters have gone wrong appears in the form of illness, injury, social discord and disruption, famine, financial loss, war, and the like. To repair the damage and recover personal and societal equanimity, people are obliged to reform—that is, to heed the moral precepts—and to placate the offended spirits by means of prescribed rituals that typically involve accepting blame for one's transgressions and then honoring the spirits in word (speeches, chants) and deed (gifts, sacrifices, dances, displays of asceticism).

Part IV

Afterword

Chapters 3 through 13 have focused on separate theories, with only occasional comparisons drawn between the theories depicted in one chapter and those described in another. Finally, as a closing feature, the single chapter that comprises Part IV adds a more deliberate comparative tone to the book by suggesting how the volume's entire collection of models can be viewed in terms of five cherished human desires.

14

Human Desires and
Theories of Development

This final chapter is a retrospective look at the contents of the earlier chapters from the viewpoints of five desires that people often hold in relation to their conceptions of moral development. The desires are (a) for immanent justice, (b) to understand the causes of the consequences that result from people's behavior in moral situations, (c) to become immortal, (d) to enjoy a happy life, and (e) to understand the moral-development process in order to help others who need moral guidance.

EXPECTING IMMANENT JUSTICE

The desire to have life operate on a principle of immanent justice has been widely held over the centuries. Belief in immanent justice is the expectation—or at least the hope—that the universe, by its very nature, will ensure that wrongdoing is punished and virtue prevails. Such a desire is reflected in the notion of *just deserts*—that people will inevitably experience consequences appropriate to the moral rectitude of their acts. In legal circles that desire appears as the talionic principle (*lex talionis*), which holds that an inflicted punishment should correspond in both degree and kind to the transgressor's offense. The best-known statement of *lex talionis* is the biblical injunction:

> And if any mischief follow, then thou shalt give life for life, eye for eye, tooth for tooth, hand for hand, foot for foot, burning for burning, wound for wound, stripe for stripe. (*Holy Bible*, 1611, Exodus, 21:23-25).

Within certain belief systems, immanent justice is not merely a hope or desire, but is offered as an authentic description of how the world really operates. In the New Testament of the Christian Bible, the apostle Paul warned that people's deeds attract fitting consequences: "Whatsoever a man soweth, that shall he also reap" (*Holy Bible*, 1611, Galatians 6:7). In Chaucer's *Canterbury*

Tales, the conviction that murder will inevitably reveal itself was part of the tale told by the prioress to her fellow pilgrims en route to Canterbury: "Mordre wol out, certein, it wol nat faile" (Morley, 1948, p. 6).

The notion of immanent justice assumes different roles in different theories of moral development. Perhaps all theorists harbor the desire to have life inherently function on the basis of just deserts, but not all theorists incorporate such a desire into their explanations of development and moral events.

Three basic types of belief that link moral development, moral events, and immanent justice are reflected in the theories reviewed in earlier chapters. The three types can be labeled (a) intentionally applied justice, (b) partially comprehended justice, and (c) comprehensible immanent justice.

Intentionally Applied Justice

This type seems implied in, or at least compatible with, most of the secular theories inspected in Part II. It is also in concert with Confucian theory in Confucianism's original form that did not postulate the participation of invisible spirits in human affairs.

From an intentionally applied perspective, the consequences—rewards and punishments—associated with moral events are believed to result either from chance or from people purposely creating the consequences.

The term *chance* or *luck* or *the breaks* is applied when people either (a) cannot identify which, among multiple causal factors, have produced particular outcomes or (b) are not convinced that the world operates on a principle of justice. In other words, they believe the universe is not constructed to ensure that righteousness prevails. Thus, only by chance is a morally admirable motorist killed by a drunk driver. Only by chance does a thief avoid punishment for robbery and murder by escaping unidentified from the scene of the crime. And only by chance is a blackmailer apprehended because he left his fingerprints on a letter mailed to his victim.

However, justice can be intentionally served when people—a jury or parents or peers—provide rewards for virtuous behavior and impose sanctions for wrongdoing. Whereas moral development has nothing to do with consequences resulting from chance, it has much to do with consequences people intentionally apply. The moral values that individuals acquire as they grow up define the kinds of acts they regard as moral and immoral. Those values also define the sorts of consequences individuals deserve for their behavior in moral situations. People subscribing to such values can then reflect those standards when they impose consequences on others for the others' moral behavior.

From this intentionally applied perspective, justice becomes widespread only when people develop constructive moral values and take responsibility for ensuring that appropriate consequences are experienced by the members of their society. In effect, there is no such thing as immanent justice.

Partially Comprehended Justice

Imbedded in most of the religious theories in Part III is a partially comprehended concept of immanent justice. Such a concept involves a belief that the universe functions on a principle of inherent, inevitable justice, but how the system works is not entirely clear.

Among the theories reflecting a partially comprehended position are the Judaic, Christian, Islamic, Shinto, Navajo, Zulu, Vodou, and Okinawan systems. All those theories share the same set of five assumptions. They all assume that:

1. Events in the universe are controlled by supernatural forces in the guise of gods or spirits.
2. Correct moral behavior involves abiding by the spirits' moral dictates.
3. Moral development consists of learning the spirits' moral rules, mastering the rituals for repairing damaged relationships between people and the spirit world, and mustering the willpower to live by the rules.
4. Instances of good fortune that people enjoy are rewards the spirits provide for abiding by the rules. Instances of ill fortune are punishments imposed by the spirits for violating the rules.
5. Justice, as mediated by the spirits, is immanent, in the sense that it is inevitable.

These five convictions represent the portion of the justice system that adherents of the concerned religious groups *do* comprehend. But the part they *do not* understand is precisely how the spirits connect a behavior to a consequence in order to achieve justice. For example, in traditional Christian doctrine, people are warned to live in keeping with the faith's moral principles and, if they breach any principles, to be sincerely penitent and to reform. Ostensibly the faithful will be rewarded for such obedience, if not in the present world, at least in life hereafter. However, Christian doctrine also teaches that a heavenly existence for eternity is not guaranteed by obedience to the Lord's commandments. Instead, the soul's ultimate fate depends on "the grace of God," meaning a decision founded on criteria other than that of conforming to Christian precepts while on earth; and those other criteria are known to God alone.

In the Judaic-Christian-Islamic tradition, this matter of how rewards and sanctions are meted out to produce just deserts has been a source of puzzlement over the centuries. The book of Job in the Jewish Bible (the Old Testament of the Christian Bible) is dedicated to the issue. As a moral man, Job was "perfect and upright," one who "feared God and eschewed evil," yet he suffered extreme misfortune. His cattle and sheep were stolen, his servants slain, his sons killed in a windstorm, and he himself plagued with painful boils from head to foot. In response to his predicament, Job essentially protested, "Why me?" and "What's fair about this?" The story of Job then tells of his friends' attempts to rationalize his ill fortune as actually being justified, but they also found it necessary to conclude that God's reasons were beyond human comprehension. They deemed God's wisdom "unsearchable."

Similar problems of comprehending the link between people's behavior and the consequences they experience are found in the other religious traditions that I would locate in this second category. During severe drought, why may incessant dances and prayers fail to bring rain? When a kind and obedient child's illness led to death, why had the spirits not heeded the supplications and sacrifices offered by the parents and priests? Why were marauding warriors able to rob, rape, and slay members of a peaceful tribe, with the warriors then continuing to enjoy good health and prosperity?

In effect, adherents of such sects generally believe that the gods or spirits will ensure that justice is done. However, puzzling incidents in which virtue is not rewarded and in which wrongdoers are not punished oblige the faithful to conclude that, at least on certain occasions, the spirits act in mysterious ways. So it is that the operation of immanent justice is only partially understood.

Comprehensible Immanent Justice

Hinduism and its derivatives—Buddhism, Jainism, Sikhism—are not only founded on a belief in infallible justice but are prepared to explain precisely how it works. First, it is necessary to accept two elements of religious dogma—metempsychosis and *karma*—as real and true. As noted in Chapter 11, the concept of metempsychosis holds that the human soul does not expire when the body dies. Instead, the soul is transplanted into a new body for a further lifetime on earth. The concept of *karma* asserts that throughout a lifetime, the positive and negative moral deeds a person commits are compiled to produce an algebraic total, a ratio of good to bad deeds that is carried by the soul into the next lifetime on earth. A newborn's fate—social status, intelligence, pain and pleasure to be experienced throughout life—is thus predetermined by the quality of the *karma* accumulated in the soul during its previous sojourns in the world. As Iyer (1969, p. 5) explains:

> The doctrine of Karma emphasizes the principle that as a man sows, so shall he reap and that he is the maker of his own destiny.

Therefore, a Hindu, Buddhist, Jain, or Sikh does not have to wonder whether people will get their due. Clearly, they will—although not now, surely in the soul's next lifetime. It is true that an observer cannot tell which particular sins in an earlier lifetime produced a person's current misfortune or which virtuous acts accounted for someone else's present wealth and happiness. But without doubt, people's current fate is payment for their past deeds.

Hence, the quality of a person's moral development during a given lifetime determines the type of the life that will be lived by the body that the transmigrated soul will next inhabit.

UNDERSTANDING THE CAUSES OF CONSEQUENCES

The great amount of time people spend trying to learn why events occur as they do suggests that humans have a strong desire to understand the nature of causes and of how they operate. It could be argued that this desire arises from the human organism's survival instinct. Knowing the causes of happenings enhances the chance that people can promote their survival and welfare by avoiding harmful causes and by creating and courting propitious ones.

A prominent distinction between typical secular and religious theories is in how they conceive the connection between people's behavior in moral situations and the consequences that result from such behavior. Secular theories usually envision two types of connections—one direct, the other indirect.

In the direct type, a person's actions in a moral encounter yield an immediate (in the sense of *without an intervening medium or agent*) consequence. For example, a wife highly valued her marriage but, nevertheless, engaged in a sexual liaison with a young man. When her husband discovered the affair, he divorced her, thereby directly ending her treasured state of marriage. As a second example, a schoolgirl who returned a lost wallet to its owner was given a cash reward for her honesty. In each of these examples the immediate recipient of the moral act (the aggrieved husband and the wallet's owner) directly provided the consequence experienced by the actor (wife and schoolgirl).

In contrast to the direct variety, the indirect type finds an intermediary or mediator providing the link between the act and the consequence that is ultimately experienced. Such is the case when a jury sentences a murderer to life in prison or a parent assigns a recalcitrant youth to clean out the garage as punishment for staying out too late at night. The jury and the parent are the mediators.

However, the situation is different with religious theories. They typically conceive of all act/consequence connections as mediated by invisible spirits. That is, the aim of moral behavior is to abide by the dictates of the invisible powers—gods or spirits—that control the universe. Violating the dictates angers the spirits, who, in response, impose punishing consequences on the wrong-doers, if not now, then sometime later. On the other hand, when a person obeys the dictates, the spirits are pleased and reward the righteous for their fealty. Thus, both secular and religious theories subscribe to the concept of mediated consequences. However, in secular theories the mediators are observable, mundane agents—judges, juries, parents, teachers, employers, athletic coaches, and the like. In religious theories the ultimate mediators are intangible—gods, spirits, cosmic forces.

Such beliefs about the causes of consequences are important in moral-education efforts. People who believe in a secular theory can be expected to teach about both direct and mediated causes and to focus learners' attention on the kinds of worldly agents who are likely to impose punishments for wrongdoing and to furnish rewards for virtuous acts. On the other hand, people who subscribe to a typical religious theory can be expected to teach a mediated causality, stressing the importance of not alienating the spirits which control the punishments and rewards that mortals experience.

ACHIEVING IMMORTALITY

Rarely do people find their impending death a pleasant prospect. Obviously, there are the exceptions, mainly among individuals who suffer intense physical pain or great mental anguish and yearn to end it. But most people would like their existence to continue well beyond the 70 to 80 years typically allotted, on condition that their health and wit remain reasonably intact. This hope for immortality plays little or no part in some moral development theories but assumes a major role in others.

For convenience of analysis, the theories inspected in earlier chapters can be placed in three categories representing their manner of addressing the issue of immortality.

First are the schemes that avoid mentioning either the possibility of life after death or how moral behavior might relate to such a possibility. This avoidance can derive from various motives. Some authors may reject outright the notion that any aspect of a dead human, such as a soul, lives on after death. And some may shun the issue only because they see no way of empirically testing hypotheses about life hereafter. Still others may assume that immortality is real but believe it has nothing to do with people's moral behavior because the afterlife of the soul is thought to depend on other factors, such as one's ancestry (aristocrat or peasant) or ethnic background (a favored ethnic group or an unfavored one). All of the secular models reviewed in Part II belong in this first category of paying no attention to questions of immortality.

Second are theories that envision a conditioned variety of immortality. That is, only under certain conditions can individuals hope to live forever in a spirit form. Shinto is such a religion since it assumes that only morally superior people will reach the status of *kami*.

Theories that envision all souls achieving eternal existence belong in the third classification. Most prominent among these models are the Judaic-Christian-Islamic and Hindu-Buddhist-Jain-Sikh persuasions. Not only do such theories posit everlasting existence after death for each human soul, but the nature of that afterlife is believed to depend, either wholly or in part, on each individual's moral behavior when on earth.

Questions of *if* and *how* people can become immortal, and of the form immortality might assume, are linked to the question of when the consequences of one's moral behavior will be gleaned. That is the matter we next consider.

ENJOYING A HAPPY LIFE

For present purposes, happiness can be defined as satisfying one's desires. Hence, the measure of people's happiness is the degree to which they fulfill their desires or reach their goals without extended travail. And it is apparent that because people can differ in their desires, what comprises happiness is not the same for everyone. It is also the case that from such a viewpoint, a happy life is not necessarily a carefree one. Clearly, people often take on challenges that require hard work and dedication to overcome obstacles faced in pursuit of their goals, yet they are deemed happy because they have succeeded at what they tried. Hence, happiness is not judged by the difficulty of the tasks attempted but, instead, by the extent to which the goals are attained and desires satisfied.

The vision of a happy life, and the way moral development relates to it, can differ from one theory to another. In some secular theories, the contribution of moral development to happiness is implied rather than asserted outright. Piaget's scheme assumes that as children mature and gradually learn the rules of amicable human relations, they will suffer fewer conflicts with other people and enjoy the rewards of social approval. Kohlberg's system suggests that advancing up his hierarchy of stages leads to an increasingly self-satisfying appreciation of human relations and enhances the general welfare of the populace. In effect, the higher a person's stage of moral development, the more authentic his or her happiness.

Implicit in psychoanalytic theory is the assumption that satisfactory progress through Freud's psychosexual stages enables people to avoid neuroses that generate emotional distress, mental confusion, and disturbed social relationships. Erikson's version of psychoanalysis implies happy outcomes that result from an individual's successfully resolving the crises encountered at each of Erikson's psycho social stages.

In Marxist theory, a state-socialist economy is depicted as ensuring that consumer goods and services are distributed evenly throughout the society, thus promoting the contentment of the many rather than of just the few.

Whereas the foregoing theories suggest connections between moral development and happiness, other secular theories do not. Such is the case with social-learning, information-integration, and delinquency models, as well as gender-role proposal.

Secular theories that suggest connections between moral development and happiness focus on the here and now. The desired contentment and success are to be enjoyed within the foreseeable future of one's life on earth. In like manner, several religious theories locate the consequences of moral behavior primarily, if not entirely, within a person's current lifetime. Such is true of the Confucian, Shinto, Navajo, Zulu, Vodou, and Okinawan belief systems.

In contrast to the here-and-now models are religious doctrines which promise that the bliss or misery people earn during their lifetime by their moral actions will be awarded following their physical death. Hence, most, if not all, of the consequences of moral behavior will occur during the soul's eternal life after the body's demise.

The holy books of the Judaic-Christian-Islamic tradition vividly portray the rapture to be enjoyed by the righteous and the torment to be suffered by the wicked in the hereafter. For example, the Islamic includes frequent passages depicting the delights to be found in the garden where the souls of the faithful will dwell:

> In it are rivers of water incorruptible,
> Rivers of milk of which the taste never changes,
> Rivers of wine, a joy to those who drink,
> And rivers of honey, pure and clear. . . .
> To [the righteous] will be passed round, dishes and goblets of gold.
> There will be there all that the soul could desire,
> All that the eyes could delight in. (Obeid, 1988, p. 165)

The conditions under which the wicked will spend eternity are also described:

> But those who deny [their Lord], for them will be cut out a garment of Fire.
> Over their heads will be poured out boiling water.
> With it will be scalded what is within their bodies as well as their skins.
> In addition, there will be maces of iron [to punish them].
> Every time they wish to get away there from anguish,
> They will be forced back herein,
> And [it will be said], "Taste ye the penalty of burning!" (Obeid, 1988, sp. 165)

By dint of *karma* and the transmigration of souls, Hinduism and its progeny—Buddhism, Jainism, Sikhism—also locate the consequences of moral actions in the hereafter rather than the here and now. Each of these belief systems portrays people's worldly existence as filled with pain and misery. Hence, the chief human desire—indeed, the main goal of life—is to end the pain. This is accomplished by a person's living an exceptionally pure moral life, a life that accords with the precepts of the gods so as to generate the *karma* that can transport one into a better future. The "better future" is of two sorts. The first comes immediately after death, when the soul is transported into a better body that will suffer less pain during its time on earth. The second is the condition ultimately desired, that of achieving nirvana, which consists of complete communion with the Cosmic Soul or Eternal Self-Existent. Unlike the Judaic-Christian-Islamic picture of happiness, the Hindu-Buddhist-Jain-Sikh aim is not to bask in an everlasting joyful condition but, rather, to eliminate all feeling—both pain and pleasure. The aim is to reach a state of nothingness, a state of equanimity devoid of all emotion and thought.

UNDERSTANDING THE MORAL DEVELOPMENT PROCESS

A key responsibility borne by parents, teachers, social workers, counselors, pastors, judges, and the like is to guide the moral development of others. I am assuming that the actions that such agents take in providing moral guidance will be determined principally by their conception of the development process. Among the components of this conception are convictions about (a) which moral values are desirable and which are not, (b) how people acquire their values, (c) what behavior options are available in different moral-decision situations, (d) how people acquire those behaviors, (e) under what circumstances particular behaviors are appropriate and under what circumstances they are not, and (f) what consequences can be expected from choosing particular behavior options rather than others in a given moral situation.

People can differ in the extent to which they believe the theory to which they subscribe is complete and true. Staunch, doctrinaire adherents of religious theories generally regard their chosen faith as the immutable, everlasting truth, because the doctrine is conceived to be the revealed word of such an authority as God, the Enlightened One, or the Cosmic Mind. Other people accept a secular theory as unquestionably sound because of the line of reasoning and the data on which it is founded. Such is the case with certain disciples of Sigmund Freud, Erik Erikson, Karl Marx, Carol Gilligan, or Jane Loevinger.

There are also individuals who are less than sure that the theory on which they depend is an accurate depiction of moral development. They consider the model to be no more than an estimate of the truth, an estimate likely requiring revision, refinement, or replacement. This tentative, qualified acceptance of a theory is found most often among people who base their convictions on empirical evidence and regard any finding or theoretical proposal as only an approximation of the truth that requires continual testing and verification.

The importance of the level of faith that individuals place in a model of development lies in how confidently they apply the model in interpreting and guiding their own and other people's moral beliefs and actions.

References

Adams, C. J. (Ed.). (1977). *A reader's guide to the great religions* (2nd ed.). New York: Free Press.

Adler, A. (1930). Individual psychology. In C. Murchinson (Ed.), *Psychologies of 1930.* Worcester, MA: Clark University Press.

Agency for Cultural Affairs. (1972). *Japanese religion.* Tokyo: Kodansha International.

Alberto, P., & Troutman, A. (1986). *Applied behavioral analysis for teachers* (2nd ed.). Columbus, OH: Merrill.

al-Faruqi, I. A. A. (1967). *Christian ethics.* Montreal: McGill University Press.

Allport, G. W. (1968). *The person in psychology: Selected essays.* Boston: Beacon Press.

Anderson, J. N. D. (1984). *Christianity and world religions.* Leicester, England: Inter-Varsity Press.

Anderson, N. H. (1991a). Preface. In N. H. Anderson (Ed.), *Contributions to information integration theory: Volume 3. Developmental.* Hillsdale, NJ: Erlbaum.

Anderson, N. H. (1991b). Moral-social development. In N. H. Anderson (Ed.), *Contributions to information integration theory: Volume 3. Developmental* (pp. 137-187). Hillsdale, NJ: Erlbaum.

Bach, M. (1961). *Strange sects and curious cults.* New York: Dodd, Mead.

Bahm, A. J. (1964). *The world's living religions.* New York: Dell.

Baldwin, A. L. (1968). *Theories of child development.* New York: Wiley.

Bancroft, A. (1974). *Religions of the East.* New York: St. Martin's.

Bandura, A. (1969). *Principles of behavior modification.* New York: Holt, Rinehart, & Winston.

Bandura, A. (1977). *Social learning theory.* Englewood Cliffs, NJ: Prentice-Hall.

Bandura, A. (1986). *Social foundations of thought and action: A social cognitive theory.* Englewood Cliffs, NJ: Prentice-Hall.

Bandura, A. (1990). Selective activation and disengagement of motor control, *Journal of Social Issues, 46* (1), pp. 27-46.

Bandura, A. (1991). Social cognitive theory of moral thought and action. In W. M. Kurtines & J. L. Gewirtz (Eds.), *Handbook of moral behavior and development: Volume 1: Theory.* Hillsdale, NJ: Erlbaum.

Barrett, D. B. (1995). World religious statistics. *Britannica book of the year.* Chicago: Encyclopaedia Britannica.

Beach, W., & Niebuhr, H. R. (1973). *Christian ethics.* New York: Ronald.

Besant, A. (1908). *Questions on Hinduism.* Benares: Theosophical Publishing Society.

Bloom, B. S. (1964). *Stability and change in human characteristics.* New York: Wiley.

Bloomfield, M. (1908). *The religion of the Veda.* New York: G. P. Putnam's Sons.

Brabeck, M. (1986). Moral orientation: Alternative perspectives of men and women. In R. T. Knowles & G. F. McLean (Eds.), *Psychological foundations of moral education and character development* (pp. 65-89). Lanham, MD: University Press of America.

Brandon, S. G. F. (1970). *A dictionary of comparative religion.* London: Weidenfeld & Nicolson.

Buhler, G. (1886). *The laws of Manu—Manu Smriti.* Vol. 25 of F. M. Muller (Ed.), *The sacred books of the East.* London: Oxford University Press.

Cahn, Z. (1962). *The philosophy of Judaism.* New York: Macmillan.

Carlson, J., & Lewis, J. (Eds.). (1988). *Counseling the adolescent.* Denver: Love.

Castro, J. (1992, October 5). Say three Hail Marys and watch it. *Time, 140* (14), 17.

Chai, C., & Chai, W. (1965). *The sacred books of Confucius, and other Confucian classics.* New Hyde Park, NY: University Books.

Chamberlain, B. H. (1932). *Translation of Ko-Ji-Ki.* Kobe, Japan: J. L. Thompson.

Chavel, C. B. (1967a). Criticisms of Maimonides' list of negative commandments. In M. Maimonides, *Sefer Ha-Mitzvoth of Maimonides* (Vol. 2, pp. 335-337). London: Soncino Press.

Chavel, C. B. (1967b). Criticisms of Maimonides' list of positive commandments. In M. Maimonides, *Sefer Ha-Mitzvoth of Maimonides* (Vol. 1., pp. 263-265). London: Soncino Press.

Chavel, C. B. (1967c). Foreword. In M. Maimonides, *Sefer Ha-Mitzvoth of Maimonides* (Vol. 1, pp. vii-xvi). London: Soncino Press.

Chavel, C. B. (1967d). Positive and negative commandments applicable today. In M. Maimonides, *Sefer Ha-Mitzvoth of Maimonides* (Vol. 2., pp. 347-356). London: Soncino Press.

Cheung, S. N. S. (1982). *Will China go capitalist?* London: Institute of Economic Affairs.

Chodorow, N. (1974). Family structure and feminine personality. In M. Z. Rosaldo & L. Lamphere (Eds.), *Woman, culture, and society.* Stanford: Stanford University Press.

Chodorow, N. (1978). *The reproduction of mothering.* Berkeley: University of California Press.

Colby, A., Kohlberg, L., Gibbs, J., & Lieberman, M. (1983). *A longitudinal study of moral judgment.* Monographs of the Society for Research in Child Development, Serial no. 200, vol. 48, nos. 1-2. Chicago: Society for Research in Child Development.

Cole, M. (Ed.). (1977). *Soviet developmental psychology.* White Plains, NY: Sharpe.

Combs, A. W., & Snygg, D. (1959). *Individual behavior.* New York: Harper & Row.

Conze, R. (1951). *Buddhism: Its essence and development.* Oxford: Bruno Cassirer.

Coomaraswamy, A. (1964). *Buddha and the gospel of Buddhism.* Hyde Park, NY: University Books.

Crim, K. (Ed.). (1981). *Abingdon dictionary of living religions.* Nashville, TN: Abingdon.

Darwin, C. (1859). *On the origin of species.* New York: Norton, 1975.

Davidov, V. V. (1985). Soviet theories of human development. In T. Husén & T. N. Postlethwaite (Eds.), *International encyclopedia of education* (Vol. 8, pp. 4721-4727). Oxford: Pergamon.

Davis, W. (1985). *The serpent and the rainbow.* New York: Warner.

Dawod, N. J. (Trans.). (1974). *The Koran.* New York: Viking Penguin.

Desmangles, L. G. (1992). *The faces of the god: Vodou and Catholicism in Haiti.* Chapel Hill: University of North Carolina Press.

Devaraja, N. K. (1969). *Hinduism and Christianity.* Bombay: Asia Publishing House.

Diver-Stamnes, A. C., & Thomas, R. M. (1995). *Prevent, repent, reform, revenge: A study in adolescent moral development.* Westport, CT: Greenwood.

Dunstan, J. L. (1961). *Protestantism.* New York: Braziller.

Eisenberg, N., & Fabes, R. A. (1988). The development of prosocial behavior from a life-span perspective. In P. B. Baltes, D. L. Featherman, & R. M. Lerner (Eds.), *Life-span development and behavior* (Vol. 9). Hillsdale, NJ: Erlbaum.

Eliot, C. E. (1921). *Hinduism and Buddhism* (Vol. 1). New York: Barnes & Noble.

Erikson, E. H. (1964). *Insight and responsibility.* New York: W. W. Norton.

Farah, C. E. (1968). *Islam: Beliefs and observances.* Woodbury, NY: Barron's Educational Services.

Farkas, A. J. (1991). Cognitive algebra of interpersonal unfairness. In N. H. Anderson (Ed.), *Contributions to information integration theory: Volume 3. Developmental* (pp. 43-99). Hillsdale, NJ: Erlbaum.

Feuer, L. S., & McLellen, D. T. (1994). Marx and Marxism. In *The new Encyclopaedia Britannica* (Vol. 23, pp. 531-535). Chicago: Encyclopaedia Britannica.

Freud, S. (1900). The interpretation of dreams. In J. Strachey (Ed.), *The standard edition of the complete psychological works of Sigmund Freud* (Vol. 4, pp. 1-338). London: Hogarth, 1953.

Freud, S. (1910). Five lectures on psychoanalysis. In J. Strachey (Ed.), *The standard edition of the complete psychological works of Sigmund Freud* (Vol. 11, pp. 141-185). London: Hogarth, 1957.

Freud, S. (1917). Introductory lectures on psychoanalysis, Part III. In J. Strachey (Ed.), *The standard edition of the complete psychological works of Sigmund Freud* (Vol. 16, pp. 243-482). London: Hogarth, 1957.

Freud, S. (1920). Beyond the pleasure principle. In J. Rickman (Ed.), *A general selection from the works of Sigmund Freud* (pp. 141-168). New York: Liveright, 1957.

Freud, S. (1923). *The ego and the id.* London: Hogarth, 1974.

Freud, S. (1938). *An outline of psychoanalysis.* London: Hogarth, 1973.

Freud, S. (1968). Sigmund Freud. In E. Fromm & R. Xirau (Eds.), *The nature of man* (pp. 239-249). New York: Macmillan.

Friedman, E. E. (1987). *Who wrote the Bible?* New York: Summit Books.

Fromm, E. (1968). Erich Fromm. In E. Fromm & R. Xirau (Eds.), *The nature of man* (pp. 307-312). New York: Macmillan.

Fromm, E. (1994). *On being human.* New York: Continuum.

Gard, R. M. (1961). *Buddhism.* New York: Braziller.

Garrod, A. (Ed.). *Approaches to moral development.* New York: Teachers College Press.

Gert, B. (1970). *The moral rules—A new rational foundation for morality.* New York: Harper & Row.

Gibson, J. Y. (1970). *The story of the Zulus.* New York: Negro Universities Press.

Gilligan, C. (1982). *In a different voice.* Cambridge, MA: Harvard University Press.

Gilligan, C., & Wiggins, G. (1988). The origins of morality in early childhood relationships. In C. Gilligan, J. V. Ward, & J. M. Taylor (Eds.), *Mapping the Moral Domain* (pp. 111-138). Cambridge, MA: Harvard University Press.

Glasenapp, H. V. (1942). *The doctrine of karman in Jain philosophy.* Bombay: Panalal Charity Fund.

Gopalan, S. (1973). *Outlines of Jainism.* New York: Wiley.

Goring, R. (Ed.). (1994). *Larousse dictionary of beliefs and religions.* New York: Larousse.

Grabowski, J., Stitzer, M. L., & Heninngfield, J. E. (Eds.). (1984). *Behavioral intervention techniques in drug abuse treatment.* Washington, DC: U.S. Government Printing Office.

Grusec, J. E., & Lytton, H. (1988). *Social development.* New York: Springer-Verlag.

Guenther, H. V., & Reynolds, F. E. (1994). Major systems and their literature. In *The new Encyclopaedia Britannica* (Vol. 15, pp. 280-284). Chicago: Encyclopaedia Britannica.

Haddad, Y. Y. (1980). *Contemporary Islam and the challenge of history.* Albany: State University of New York Press.

Hague, W. J. (1986). *New perspectives on moral development.* Edmonton: University of Alberta.

Haneef, S. (1993). *What everyone should know about Islam and Muslims* (11th ed.). Des Plains, IL: Library of Islam.

Hartman, D. (1990). Jewish theory of human development. In R. M. Thomas, (Ed.). *The encyclopedia of human development and education* (pp. 125-131). Oxford: Pergamon.

Hasan, S. N. (1979). Foreword to the first edition. In J. S. Grewal, *Guru Nanak in history.* Chandigarh, India: Punjab University.

Haste, H., & Baddeley, J. (1991). Moral theory and culture: The case of gender. In W. M. Kurtines & J. L. Gewirtz (Eds.), *Handbook of moral behavior and development: Vol. 1. Theory* (pp. 223-249). Hillsdale, NJ: Erlbaum.

Heider, F. (1958). *The psychology of human relations.* New York: Wiley.

Herbert, J. (1967). *Shinto: At the fountain-head of Japan.* New York: Stein & Day.

Hereford, R. T. (1971). *Talmud and Apocrypha.* New York: KTAV Publishing House.

Hersh, R. H., Miller, J. P, & Fielding, G. D. (1980). *Models of moral education.* New York: Longman.

Hippchen, L. J. (Ed.). (1978). *Ecological-biochemical approaches to the treatment of delinquents and criminals.* New York: Van Nostrand Reinhold.

Hoffman, M. L. (1984). Interaction of affect and cognition in empathy. In C. Izard, J. Kagan, & R. Zajonc (Eds.), *Emotions, cognition, and behavior* (pp. 103-131). New York: Cambridge University Press.

Hoffman, M. L. (1991). Empathy, social cognition, and moral actions. In W. M. Kurtines & J. L. Gewirtz (Eds.). *Handbook of moral behavior and development: Volume 1. Theory* (pp. 275-301). Hillsdale, NJ: Erlbaum.

Holtom, D. C. (1938). *The national faith of Japan: A study in modern Shinto.* London: Kegan Paul, Trench, & Trubner.

Holy Bible. (1611). (King James authorized version)

Hommers, W., & Anderson, N. H. (1991). Moral algebra of harm and recompense. In N. H. Anderson (Ed.), *Contributions to information integration theory: Volume 3. Developmental* (pp. 101-141). Hillsdale, NJ: Erlbaum.

Hook, S. (1959). Science and mythology in psychoanalysis. In S. Hook (Ed.), *Psychoanalysis, scientific method, and philosophy.* New York: New York University Press.

Husain, S. S., & Ashraf, S. A. (1979). *Crisis in Muslim education.* Jedda: Hodder-Stoughton & King Abdulaziz University.

Hutchison, J. A. (1977). *Living options in world philosophy.* Honolulu: University Press of Hawaii.

Iverson, P. (1981). *The Navajo nation.* Westport, CT: Greenwood.

Iyer, K. B. (1969). *Hindu ideals.* Bombay: Bharatiya Vidya Bhavan.

Jaini, P. S. (1979). *The Jaina path of purification.* Berkeley: University of California Press.

James, W. (1992). The moral philosopher and the moral life. In W. James, *William James: Writings 1878-1899.* New York: Library of America.

Johansson, R. E. A. (1969). *The dynamic psychology of early Buddhism.* London: Curzon Press.

Jones, E. E., & Davis, K. E. (1965). From acts to dispositions: The attribution process in person perception. In L. Berkowitz (Ed.), *Advances in experimental social psychology* (Vol. 2). New York: Academic.

Jung, C. (1953). *Collected works.* New York: Pantheon.

Juynboll, G. H. A. (1969). *The authenticity of the tradition literature.* Leiden: Brill.

Kato, G. (1973). *A historical study of the religious development of Shinto.* Westport, CT: Greenwood, 1988.

Kegan, R. (1982). *The evolving self: Problem and process in human development.* Cambridge, MA: Harvard University Press.

Keith, A. B. (1925). *The religion and philosophy of the Veda and Upanishads.* Cambridge, MA: Harvard University Press.

Kelley, H. H. (1971). *Attribution in social interaction.* Morristown, NJ: General Learning Press.

Kelley, H. H. (1972). *Causal schemata and the attribution process.* Morristown, NJ: General Learning Press.

Kelley, H. H. (1992). Commonsense psychology and scientific psychology. In M. R. Rosenzweig, & L. W. Porter (Eds.). *Annual review of psychology* (Vol. 43, pp. 1-23). Palo Alto, CA: Annual Reviews.

Ketterlinus, R. D., & Lamb, M. E. (Eds.). (1994). *Adolescent problem behaviors.* Hillsdale, NJ: Erlbaum.

Kidd, D. (1904). *The essential kafir.* London: Adam & Charles Black.

Kitagawa, J. M. (1987). *On understanding Japanese religion.* Princeton, NJ: Princeton University Press.

Knowles, R. T., & McLean, G. F. (Eds.). (1986). *Psychological foundations of moral education and character development.* Lanham, MD: University Press of America.

Kohlberg, L. (1967). Moral and religious education in the public schools: A developmental view. In T. R. Sizer (Ed.), *Religion and public education.* Boston: Houghton Mifflin.

Kohlberg, L. (1971). From is to ought. In T. Michel (Ed.), *Cognitive development and epistemology.* New York: Academic.

Kohlberg, L. (1984). *The psychology of moral development.* San Francisco: Harper & Row.

Kojiki. (1958). Tokyo: Iwanami Publishing Co.

Krige, E. J. (1950). *The social system of the Zulus.* Pietermaritzburg, South Africa: Shuter & Shooter.

Kuhn, D., Langer, J., Kohlberg, L., & Haan, N. S. (1977). The development of formal operations in logical and moral judgment. *Genetic Psychology Monographs, 95,* 97–188.

Kupfersmid, J. H., & Wonderly, D. M. (1980). Moral maturity and behavior: Failure to find a link. *Journal of Youth and Adolescence, 9,* 249-262.

Kurtines, W. M., & Gewirtz, J. L. (Eds.). (1991a). *Handbook of moral behavior and development: Volume 1. Theory.* Hillsdale, NJ: Erlbaum.

Kurtines, W. M., & Gewirtz, J. L. (Eds.). (1991b). *Handbook of moral behavior and development: Volume 2. Research.* Hillsdale, NJ: Erlbaum.

Ladd, J. (1957). *Structure of a moral code: A philosophical analysis of ethical discourse applied to the ethics of the Navaho Indians.* Cambridge, MA: Harvard University Press.

Laguerre, M. (1980). *Voodoo heritage.* Newbury Park, CA: Sage.

Langford, P. E. (1995). *Approaches to the development of moral reasoning.* Hillsdale, NJ: Erlbaum.

Lebra, W. P. (1966). *Okinawan religion.* Honolulu: University of Hawaii Press.

Legge, J. (1893). *Confucius: Confucian analects, the great learning, and the doctrine of the mean.* New York: Dover, 1971 reprint.

Leon, M. (1982). Rules in children's moral judgments: Integration of intent, damage, and rationale information. *Developmental Psychology, 18,* 835-842.

Lessa, W. A., & Vogt, E. Z. (Eds.). (1965). *Reader in comparative religion.* New York: Harper & Row.

Lever, J. (1976). Sex differences in the games children play. *Social Problems, 23,* 478-487.

Lin, H. Y. (1988). A Confucian theory of human development. In R. M. Thomas (Ed.), *Oriental theories of human development* (pp. 117-133). New York: Peter Lang.

Lin, H. Y. (1990). Confucian theory of human development. In R. M. Thomas (Ed.), *The encyclopedia of human development and education* (pp. 149-152). Oxford: Pergamon.

Little, D., & Twiss, S. B. (1978). *Comparative religious ethics.* New York: Harper & Row.

Loevinger, J. (1976). *Ego development: Conceptions and theories.* San Francisco: Jossey-Bass.

Loevinger, J. (1987). *Paradigms of personality.* New York: W. H. Freeman.

Maccoby, E. (1968). The development of moral values and behavior in childhood. In J. A. Clausen (Ed.), *Socialization and society.* Boston: Little, Brown.

Maimonides, M. (1967). *Sefer Ha-Mitzvoth of Maimonides* (Vols. 1 & 2). London: Soncino Press.

Mao, Z. (1973). Preface. In P. J. Seybolt, *Revolutionary education in China.* White Plains, NY: International Arts and Sciences Press.

Mao, Z. (1974). Remarks at the spring festival. In S. Schram (Ed.), *Chairman Mao talks to the people: Talks and letters, 1956-1971* (pp. 195-211). New York: Random House.

Marek, J. C. (1988). A Buddhist theory of human development. In R. M. Thomas (Ed.), *Oriental theories of human development* (pp. 76-115). New York: Peter Lang.

Marek, J. C., & Thomas, R. M. (1988). Hindus' replies to questions about development. In R. M. Thomas (Ed.), *Oriental theories of human development* (pp. 190-212). New York: Peter Lang.

Marx, K. (1859). Excerpt from A contribution to the critique of political economy. In L. S. Feuer (Ed.), *Marx & Engels: Basic writings on politics and philosophy.* New York: Doubleday, 1959.

Marx, K. (1898). Wages, price, and profit. In *Karl Marx and Friedrich Engels: Selected works* (Vol. 1). London: Lawrence & Wishart, 1950.

Marx, K., & Engels, F. (1848). The manifesto of the communist party. In L. S. Feuer (Ed.), *Marx & Engels: Basic writings on politics and philosophy*. New York: Doubleday (1959).

Maslow, A. H. (1968). *Toward a psychology of being*. Princeton, NJ: Van Nostrand.

McCarthy Brown, K. (1991). *Mama Lola: A Vodou priestess in Brooklyn*. Berkeley: University of California Press.

Mead, G. H. (1934). *Mind, self, and society*. Chicago: University of Chicago Press.

Michel, C. (1995). *Aspects educatifs et moraux du vodou haitien*. Port-au-Prince: Presses de l'Imprimerie Le Natal.

Michel, C. (1996). Of worlds seen and unseen: The educational character of Haitian Vodou. *Comparative Education Review, 40* (3), 280-294.

Miller, P. (1963). *The New England mind: The seventeenth century*. Cambridge, MA: Harvard University Press.

Morley, C. (Ed.). (1948). *Familiar quotations*. Boston: Little, Brown.

Morris, E. K., & Braukmann, C. J. (Eds.). (1987). *Behavioral approaches to crime and delinquency: A handbook of application, research, and concepts*. New York: Plenum.

M'Timkulu, D. (1977). Some aspects of Zulu religion. In N. S. Booth, Jr. (Ed.), *African religions: A symposium* (pp. 13-30). New York: NOK Publishers.

Musser, L. M., & Leone, C. (1986). Moral character: A social learning perspective. In R. T. Knowles & G. F. McLean (Eds.), *Psychological foundations of moral education and character development* (pp. 153-182). Lanham, MD: University Press of America.

Nagel, E. (1959). Methodological issues in psychoanalytic theory. In S. Hook (Ed.), *Psychoanalysis, scientific method, and philosophy*. New York: New York University Press.

Nasr, S. H. (1982). Islam and modern science. In Islamic Council of Europe, *Islam and contemporary society* (pp. 177-190). London: Longman.

A new catechism: Catholic faith for adults. (1969). New York: Herder & Herder.

Nihonshoki. (1958). Tokyo: Iwanami Publishing Co.

Nikhilananda, S. (1956). *The Upanishads: Aitareya and Brihadaranyaka* (Vol. 3). New York: Harper.

Noddings, N. (1984). *Caring: A feminine approach to ethics and moral education*. Berkeley: University of California Press.

Obeid, R. (1988). An Islamic theory of human development. In R. M. Thomas (Ed.), *Oriental theories of human development* (pp. 155-174). New York: Peter Lang.

Ono, S. (1962). *Shinto, the kami way*. Tokyo: Tuttle.

Osofsky, J. D. (Ed.). (1987). *Handbook of infant development* (2nd ed.). New York: Wiley.

Ott, L. (1974). *Fundamentals of Catholic dogma*. Rockford, IL: Tan Books.

Overton, W. F. (Ed.). (1983). *The relationship between social and cognitive development*. Hillsdale, NJ: Erlbaum.

Park, H. S. (1976). Changes in Chinese political ideology. In G. K. Bertsch & T. W. Ganschow (Eds.), *Comparative communism*. San Francisco: Freeman.

Peters, R. S. (1971). Moral development: A plea for pluralism. In T. Michel (Ed.), *Cognitive development and epistemology*. New York: Academic.

Piaget, J. (1963). *The origins of intelligence in children*, 2nd ed. New York: Norton.

Piaget, J. (1965). *The moral judgment of the child*. New York: Free Press.

Piaget, J. (1973). *The child and reality*. New York: Viking.

Piaget, J., & Inhelder, B. (1969). *The psychology of the child*. New York: Basic Books.

Piaget, J., Jonckheere, A. & Mandelbrot, B. (1958). *La lecture de l'expérience.* Paris: Presses Universitaires de France.

Pound, E. (Ed.). (1969). *Confucius.* New York: New Directions.

Pritchard, M. S. (1991). *On becoming responsible.* Lawrence: University Press of Kansas.

Rahula, W., & Reynolds, F. E. (1994). The life of the Buddha Gotama. In *The new Encyclopaedia Britannica* (Vol. 15, pp. 264-269). Chicago: Encyclopaedia Britannica.

Ramsey, P. (1950). *Basic Christian ethics.* New York: Charles Scribner's Sons.

Reeves, C. (1977). *The psychology of Rollo May.* San Francisco: Jossey-Bass.

Reichard, G. A. (1963). *Navaho religion: A study of symbolism* (2nd ed.). New York: Random House.

Renou, L. (1961). *Hinduism.* New York: Braziller.

Renou, L. (1968). *Religions of ancient India.* New York: Schocken.

Ross, F. H. (1965). *Shinto: The way of Japan.* Boston: Beacon Press.

Rotter, J. B. (1982). *The development and application of social learning theory.* New York: Praeger.

Rousseau, J. J. (1955). *Emile* (B. Foxley, Trans.). New York: Dutton, Everyman's Library.

Rubin, K. H., & Ross, H. S. (eds.). (1982). *Peer relationships and social skills in childhood.* New York: Springer-Verlag.

Sarma, D. S. (1953). The nature and history of Hinduism. In K. W. Morgan (Ed.), *The religion of the Hindus.* New York: Ronald.

Shakir, M. H. (Trans.). (1988). *The Qur'an.* Elmhurst, NY: Tahrike Tarsile Qur'an.

Shantz, C. U., & Hartup, W. W. (Eds.). (1992). *Conflict in child and adolescent development.* New York: Cambridge University Press.

Shastri, Y. S. (1994). *The salient features of Hinduism.* Ahmedabad: Yogeshwar Prakashan.

Shaver, K. G. (1975). *An introduction to attribution processes.* Cambridge, MA: Winthrop.

Shimabukuro, K. (1950). Okinawa no minzoku to shinko [Religion and folk customs in Okinawa]. *Minzokugaku Kenkyu* [Ethnological studies], *15,* 136-148.

Shinn, R. S., et al. (1970). *Area handbook for India.* Washington, DC: U.S. Government Printing Office.

Shinn, R. S. et al. (1969). *Area handbook for North Korea.* Washington, DC: U.S. Government Printing Office.

Shinto Committee. (1958). *An outline of Shinto teachings.* Tokyo: Jinja Honcho, Kokugakuin University, and Institute for Japanese Culture and Classics.

Shoemaker, D. J. (1990). *Theories of delinquency.* New York: Oxford University Press.

Siegel, M. (1982). *Fairness in children.* London: Academic.

Siegler, R. S. (1990). *Children's thinking* (2nd ed.). Englewood Cliffs, NJ: Prentice-Hall.

Sikh religion. (1990). Detroit: Sikh Missionary Center.

Singh, G. (1974). *The Sikhs and their religion.* Redwood City, CA: Sikh Foundation.

Singh, I. (1969). *The philosophy of Guru Nanak.* New Delhi: Ranjit.

Skinner, B. F. (1974). *About behaviorism.* New York: Knopf.

Smith, J. E. (1959). *The works of Jonathan Edwards: Volume 2. Religious affections.* New Haven: Yale University Press.

Smith, M. E. (1926). *An investigation of the development of the sentence and the extent of vocabulary in young children.* (University of Iowa Studies in Child Welfare, Vol. 3, No. 5). Iowa City: University of Iowa.

Smith, M. K. (1941). Measurements of the size of general English vocabulary through the elementary grades and high school. *Genetic Psychology Monographs, 24,* 313-345.

Spae, J. J. (1972). *Shinto man.* Tokyo: Oriens Institute for Religious Research.

Sprinthall, N. A., & Collins, W. A. (1984). *Adolescent psychology.* Reading, MA: Addison-Wesley.

Stevenson, M. S. (1915). *The heart of Jainism.* New Delhi: Munshiram Manoharlal, 1970.

Strong, A. H. (1907). *Systematic theology: A compendium and commonplace book designed for the use of theological students.* Valley Forge, PA: Judson.

Suhrawardy, A. A. al-M. (Ed.). (1941). *The sayings of Muhammad.* London: John Murray.

Sundkler, B. G. M. (1961). *Bantu prophets in South Africa.* London: Oxford University Press.

Sutherland, E. H., & Cressey, D. R. (1978). *Criminology* (10th ed.). New York: Lippincott.

Theses on socialist education. (1979-1980). *Vantage Point, 2* (11-12); *3* (1-2, 4, 6-8).

Thomas, R. M. (1983). The Democratic People's Republic of Korea (North Korea). In R. M. Thomas & T. N. Postlethwaite, *Schooling in East Asia.* Oxford: Pergamon.

Thomas, R. M. (1989). *The puzzle of learning difficulties: Applying a diagnosis and treatment model* (chapter 11). Springfield, IL: Charles C. Thomas.

Thomas, R. M. (1990). Christian theory of human development. In R. M. Thomas (Ed.), *The encyclopedia of human development and education* (pp. 131-137). Oxford: Pergamon.

Thomas, R. M., & Diver-Stamnes, A. C. (1993). *What wrongdoers deserve: The moral reasoning behind responses to misconduct.* Westport, CT: Greenwood.

Thomas, R. M., & Niikura, R. (1988). A Shinto theory of human development. In R. M. Thomas (Ed.), *Oriental theories of human development,* (pp. 135-253). New York: Peter Lang.

Trumbull, C. P. (Ed.). (1995). *Britannica book of the year.* Chicago: Encyclopaedia Britannica.

Tulving, E. (1972). Episodic and semantic memory. In E. Tulving & W. Donaldson (Eds.), *Organization and memory.* New York: Academic.

Ueda, K. (1972). Shinto. In *Japanese religion.* Tokyo: Kodansha International.

Vygotsky, L. S. (1978). Dust jacket. In M. Cole, V. John-Steiner, S. Scribner, & E. Souberman (Eds.), *Mind in society.* Cambridge, MA: Harvard University Press.

Waley, A. (1938). *The analects of Confucius.* New York: Knopf.

Ward, K. (1987). *Images of eternity: Concepts of god in five religions.* London: Darton, Longman, & Todd.

Ware, J. R. (1955). *The sayings of Confucius.* New York: Mentor.

Weiner, B. (1974). *Achievement motivation and attribution theory.* Morristown, NJ: General Learning Press.

Weiner, B. (1980). Dedication to Professor Heider. In D. Gorlitz (Ed.), *Perspectives on attribution research and theory.* Cambridge, MA: Ballinger.

Werblowsky, R. J., & Wigoder, G. (Eds.). (1966). *An encyclopedia of the Jewish religion.* New York: Holt, Rinehart, & Winston.

Winegar, L. R., & Valsiner, J. (1992). *Children's development within social context* (Vols. 1 & 2). Hillsdale, NJ: Erlbaum.

Woodward, K. L. (1995, September 11). Religion: God gets the he-ho. *Newsweek,* p. 76.

Yanagita, K. (1951). *Minzokugaku jiten* [A dictionary of folk culture]. Tokyo: n. p.

Yang, K. P., & Chee, C. B. (1963). North Korean educational system: 1945 to present. In R. A. Scalapino (Ed.), *North Korea today*. New York: Praeger.

Yi, Z. (1985). Fix eyes on money. *Chinese Education, 18* (1), 60-61.

Zhuang, J. (1986). *Conceptions of human development and of education in modern China: Mao Zedong compared to present-day leaders.* Unpublished manuscript, University of California, Santa Barbara.

Zhuang, J. (1989). *Education and social-class structure: The case of the People's Republic of China.* Unpublished doctoral dissertation, University of California, Santa Barbara.

Index

About the Author

R. MURRAY THOMAS is Professor Emeritus of Educational Psychology at the University of California, Santa Barbara. His other publications include *Education's Role in National Development Plans* (Praeger, 1992), *What Wrongdoers Deserve* (Greenwood, 1993), *A Study of Adolescent Moral Development* (Greenwood, 1995), and *Classifying Reactions to Wrongdoing* (Greenwood, 1995).

ISBN 0-313-30236-7

EAN

9 780313 302367

90000>

HARDCOVER BAR CODE